ITALIAN AUTO LEGENDS

Michel Zumbrunn
Text by Richard Heseltine

ITALIAN AUTO LEGENDS
Classics of Style and Design

First published 2006 by Merrell Publishers Limited

Head office
81 Southwark Street
London SE1 0HX

New York office
49 West 24th Street, 8th Floor
New York, NY 10010

merrellpublishers.com

Publisher Hugh Merrell
Editorial Director Julian Honer
US Director Joan Brookbank
Sales and Marketing Manager Kim Cope
Sales and Marketing Executive Amina Arab
Associate Manager, US Sales and Marketing
   Elizabeth Choi
Co-editions Manager Anne Le Moigne
Art Director Nicola Bailey
Designer Paul Shinn
Managing Editor Anthea Snow
Project Editors Claire Chandler, Rosanna Fairhead
Editor Helen Miles
Production Manager Michelle Draycott
Production Controller Sadie Butler

All illustrations copyright © 2006 Michel Zumbrunn, with the exception of the following:
   pp. 8–25 copyright © 2006 Giles Chapman Library
   p. 26 copyright © 2006 Richard Heseltine Archive
Text copyright © 2006 Richard Heseltine
Design and layout copyright © 2006 Merrell
   Publishers Limited

All rights reserved. No part of this publication may be reproduced, stored in a retrieval system or transmitted, in any form or by any means, electronic, mechanical, photocopying, recording or otherwise, without the prior permission in writing from the publisher.

British Library Cataloguing-in-Publication Data:
Michel Zumbrunn
Italian auto legends : classics of style and design
1. Automobiles – Italy 2. Automobiles – Italy – Pictorial works 3. Automobiles – Italy – Design and construction 4. Automobiles – Italy – Design and construction – Pictorial works
I. Title II. Heseltine, Richard
629.2'22'0945

ISBN-13: 978-1-8589-4336-7
ISBN-10: 1-8589-4336-1

Design concept by Matt Hervey
Layout by Jade Design
Copy-edited by Richard Dawes
Indexed by Hilary Bird
Printed and bound in China

Jacket front: 1963 Ferrari 250GTO
Jacket back: 1947 Cisitalia 202
Page 2: 1954 Alfa Romeo 2000 Sportiva
Page 5: 1960 Ferrari 250GT SWB
Pages 28–29: 1954 Maserati A6GCS/53
Pages 276–77: 1987 Lamborghini Countach QV

I should like to offer my sincere thanks to all the collectors of Italian cars, who, through their collections, are helping to preserve an important part of Italian culture and design. I must also extend particular thanks to Tito Anselmi, Lukas Hüni, Marcel Massini, René Wagner and Edi Wyss.

Michel Zumbrunn

Introduction 7

ITALIAN AUTO LEGENDS 29

Designer Profiles 278

Glossary of Motoring Terms and Styles 282

Directory of Museums and Collections 284

Index 286

INTRODUCTION

All fields of endeavour attract enthusiasts who revere excellence and pride themselves on their taste being more informed than the next person's. In this way the Italian motor industry has long had an adoring retinue, but one that is nevertheless educated to the whims and fancies, faults and frailties and general chaos that surround many of the greatest and most charismatic marques ever made. Whether the vehicle is a 'poverty-spec' hatchback or a testosterone-fuelled supercar, the Italian way of building cars engenders a sense of respect, romance and, most of all, a passion alien to the products of other countries. Think Ferrari, Lamborghini, Alfa Romeo, Lancia and Maserati: all copper-bottomed, blue-chip brand names that resonate the world over. An Italian car is not merely an appliance for getting you from A to B. It is made for *drivers*.

The history of Italian car manufacture is epic. That the nation has an automotive heritage in the first place is all the more remarkable when you consider that owning a car was way beyond the means of most Italians for decades after the birth of the 'horseless carriage'. Add two world wars, almost constant social and political upheaval, along with the occasional fuel crisis, and passion will only take you so far. Yet, faced by such seemingly insurmountable odds, Italian car manufacturers were – and remain – resilient.

Even so, Italy's ascent to motoring greatness was slow. Efforts to find an effective replacement for horses as a means of motive power stretch back to the seventeenth century. Over the following two hundred years the likes of Nicolas-Joseph Cugnot, Richard Trevithick, Léon Serpollet and the Count de Dion (or rather his engineers) all built steam-powered vehicles. But the first truly successful application of engine to vehicle came in 1885 when Germany's Karl Benz and then Gottlieb Daimler ushered in the internal-combustion-driven motor car.

It would be a further ten years before Italy caught up. In 1895 a professor of engineering at the University of Padua conceived a home-grown variation on the theme, and Enrico Bernardi's three-wheeler marked the nation's first, faltering steps into piston-powered legend.

An Italian auto legend. With the Miura, Lamborghini created a new species of automobile – the supercar. Other nations have tried to create similar cars but all true supercars are Italian.

From its first embryonic efforts in 1899, Fiat has grown to become a major force in the Italian automotive industry, with a portfolio encompassing Alfa Romeo, Lancia, Ferrari and Maserati.

Not that Italy was in a fit state to capitalize on Bernardi's efforts, for its attempts to establish itself as a colonial power were falling some way short. Riven by prolonged internal strife and losing many thousands of economic migrants, mainly to the United States, the country was too disorganized to establish its own automobile industry. Instead, would-be entrepreneurs merely copied existing designs or bought out foreign firms. In 1899 Edoardo Bianchi produced a car under his own name featuring the French De Dion single-cylinder engine. In the same year Cesare Isotta and Vincenzo Fraschini teamed up to import Renaults before producing their 'own' design, which owed much to the French manufacturer's inventiveness.

Adopted by the moneyed and the adventurous, the motor car was at first deemed anti-social and perilous by the majority. Some naysayers believed that speeds in excess of 30 kph, not quite 20 mph, would result in heads being severed by the sheer force of air against physiognomy. This fear was swiftly allayed, but, as the twentieth century dawned, motor cars genuinely *were* dangerous. There was no set pattern for what one should look like. Most models of the period resembled carriages, employing the same basic design and methods of construction that had existed for centuries. These days car designers think in terms of steel, aluminium or even carbon-fibre. A century ago it was wood and fabric, proven materials that did not fall apart at the first challenge from the topography.

And, without an outline to copy and paste, engineers and inventors engaged in all manner of ingenious – if occasionally bizarre – conceits: elliptical wheel patterns; passengers seated in *front* of the driver; giro-stabilizers. Nothing was too radical or too daring. Designers didn't so much think outside the box: they didn't know there was one.

Predictably, manufacturers in this nascent industry chose to publicize their wares to daring sportsmen by entering them in competitive events. Initially France led the way, the first 'reliability trial' being organized by the newspaper *Le Vélocipède* in 1887. The 'race', a short run from Paris to Versailles, was not a success: only one entrant turned up and the meeting was cancelled. Even so, with a head start in design and production techniques, the French were the principal force in embryonic motor sport. The first long-distance journey by an internal-combustion-driven vehicle was completed in 1891, by a Peugeot that travelled from the factory at Beaulieu-Valentigney to Paris, then on to Brest, in Brittany, and back. In the early 1900s, as motor sport in the accepted idiom came into being with the Gordon Bennett Cup and town-to-town road races, French marques generally triumphed. After several false starts the Italians gradually closed the gap and broke France's dominance in 1907 as Fiat triumphed in the French Grand Prix, Italy's Targa Florio road race and the first of Germany's Kaiserpreis contests. The template was drawn for a century of overwhelming Italian success in all forms of car-related competition.

The long-standing importance of Fiat to the national psyche, and to the country's economic and social development, cannot be overerestimated. For many, Fiat – or rather the Agnelli family, who control it – simply *is* Italy. The marque came into being in 1899 when Giovanni Agnelli invested in a scheme devised by the Turinese nobleman Emanuele Bricherasio di Cacherano to build motor cars, becoming a partner in Fabbrica Italiana di Automobili Torino in July of that year. The company's first car, a skimpy 679-cc model, proved a modest hit, with twenty-five made. Soon 150 employees were working in the factory in Turin's Corso Dante. Commercial success in building cars encouraged the firm to diversify into ball bearings, trucks, buses, trams, aeroplane engines and even ship-building.

According to the review *L'Auto d'Italia*, in 1907 fifty-eight companies had been set up to produce cars, of which forty-six were already operating. (Today only a tiny number survive.) At a time when cars were made in small runs as naked chassis requiring outside coachbuilders to clothe the bare bones, Fiat was the first, and for decades the only, Italian manufacturer to build them complete and in volume rather than plying its trade to elite customers. The first genuinely mass-produced Fiat, the Zero 12-15HP, was introduced in 1912. While the onset of the First World War destabilized the country as a whole, Fiat's involvement in the armaments and aeronautical sectors ensured that it came out of the conflict much stronger and more prosperous than when it entered.

Displaying considerable forethought, the company soon adopted aggressive export strategies while engaging in licensing agreements. As early as 1902 it had agents in France and the USA; by 1919 it had established Fiat France and Fiat Hispania and it went on to target the market in the rest of Europe and in South America. A policy of looking east began in 1912 with ventures in Russia and sales to Hungary followed four years later. By 1921 Fiat had completed a deal to build cars in Poland (as Polski-Fiat), before opening its vast Lingotto factory in Turin, complete with a 1-km (2/3 mile) test track on the roof, a year later. Using manufacturing techniques borrowed from Henry Ford, Fiat went beyond national success to become a major force in the international automotive arena.

Fiat was the first Italian marque to find glory in competition, winning the 1907 French Grand Prix with its 130HP. The Turin firm dropped out of front-line motor sport shortly afterwards and has made only fleeting appearances over the century since its early success.

Introduction 9

The result of this zealous programme of expansion was a massive growth in exports. Between the two world wars, Fiat was the motor manufacturer with the highest ratio of exports to production, averaging around 60%. With its introduction of cars such as the iconic Toppolino in 1936 to Italians hungering for cheap personal transport, Fiat had the domestic market sown up. By targeting the cheap seats rather than the dress circle, the automobile industry's most successful acronym managed to survive, although in time its portfolio would also embrace overtly patrician marques such as Lancia, Maserati and Ferrari. Without Fiat there would probably be no Italian motor industry left to celebrate.

During the earliest days of the motor car there was no such thing as styling. Automobiles were designed and built by engineers, with form strictly following function. Drivers sat perched atop their horseless carriages and what little bodywork there was served simply to protect the mechanical components from the elements, with driver and passengers alike bearing the brunt of whatever the weather threw at them. Wheels, generally constructed with wooden spokes, usually differed in size from front to rear. With typically little or no integration between the passenger compartment and the engine, scant artistry was demanded of the coachbuilder. However, this arrangement was soon to change beyond all recognition.

The art of coachbuilding may well have originated in fourteenth-century Hungary, where the first carriage is believed to have been constructed. Crafting horse-driven vehicles for the aristocracy and landed gentry soon became a respected and profitable business, so the skills of the trade were passed on from one generation to the next. By the advent of the automobile, most towns in Europe boasted at least one such concern.

The motor car continued this craft, with innumerable workshops bodying the new horseless carriages. Those that declared the car a passing fad were soon out of business. Yet as mass-production techniques took hold during the following decades, car manufacturers began to offer a choice of bodies conceived in-house. Nevertheless, at a time when ownership of a car was still a powerful social statement, there was always demand for individuality, for something nobody else had that was in tune with the fashions and whims of the day. During the inter-war years in particular, Italian *carrozzerie*, coachbuilders, produced some of the most dazzling examples of automotive art ever seen.

By the 1920s the car had become a major symbol of the industrialized society and each year the best coachbuilders would present their 'collections' in much the same way as a fashion designer does now. Over the next decade salons and concours d'élégance sprang up throughout the developed countries. There was a palpable sense of excitement among onlookers as each motorized means of artistic and personal expression was presented to an expectant crowd. For high-volume car manufacturers, these automotive catwalks came to act as barometers of taste, as they realized that 'styling' attracted customers and provided a degree of valuable brand recognition. Far from distancing themselves from *carrozzerie*, car makers began working hand in glove with some of the more respected practitioners. As well as borrowing their ideas, they occasionally offered the coachbuilders' creations as factory-sanctioned models in order to generate 'showroom traffic'.

Yet, as mechanical innovation gathered speed, traditional coachbuilding was in danger of being left behind: new methods of construction had to be learned and perfected. Car bodies were no longer crafted from fabric and wood, or hand-painted by brush, as these materials and methods were no longer efficient for volume production. Steel and aluminium had long since taken over as materials of choice, spawning panel-beating workshops all over Europe. Italy was at the forefront of this movement, for relevant skills perfected by Turin armourers in the previous century had already been passed on to other cities. Bodies became more integrated with chassis by means of 'bushing' between the wooden inner frame and the chassis – a method borrowed from the aeroplane industry – thus eliminating the use of 90-degree angles demanded by timber construction to ensure torsional rigidity.

Whereas British coachbuilders were renowned for the strength and quality of their output, and their French counterparts for the rakish sophistication of their designs, the Italian *carrozzerie* soon came to be prized for the sheer elegance of their work. Firms such as Boneschi, Pinin Farina, Viotti, Bertone and Zagato clothed proprietary chassis from Isotta-Fraschini, Alfa Romeo and OM, among others, with breathtaking outlines that appeared pared down and well proportioned compared with the audacious but frequently overblown offerings of their Parisian contemporaries such as Figoni et Falaschi.

With this great revolution in the domestic industry, the car began to take a hold on Italy's collective consciousness. Once the former journalist Benito Mussolini became dictator in 1925, he bought some stability to the nation, for all his odious traits. Industry benefited in this still heavily agricultural economy, and an urban middle class began to emerge. New methods of financing meant cars were now within reach of many young men and women, while Italy's success in motor racing fuelled a demand for more sporting

Small Italian firms were at the forefront of coachbuilding between the wars. Most luxury cars in this period were supplied as bare chassis requiring the bodywork to be crafted by a *carrozzeria* to the customer's tastes.

Introduction   11

cars and convertibles. *Carrozzerie* began to tailor chassis to meet this demand. Bodies became lower and sleeker, bonnets longer and grilles shorter.

But it could not last. In the years after the Wall Street Crash of 1929, car sales went into freefall, driving a number of manufacturers out of the market. Many *carrozzerie* followed in their wake, but through hardiness and persistence some of the bigger names survived to secure the nation's reputation as the car-styling capital of the world.

ALFA ROMEO, ENZO FERRARI AND ITALY'S RISE TO MOTOR-SPORT DOMINANCE
With the possible exception of Ferrari, no Italian marque has inspired greater national pride than Alfa Romeo. Between the wars the Milan company weathered economic and infrastructural instability to produce some of the most beguiling road cars offered anywhere in the world, while asserting Italy's dominance in motor sport in the face of French and German rivalry. Although the marque is now more celebrated for its mass-produced sporting saloons, for the first half of its existence Alfa Romeo derived its prominence entirely from building small runs of exotic cars that married engineering excellence and technological advancement with dizzying beauty. As Henry Ford once put it, "Every time I see an Alfa Romeo, I raise my hat".

Like many other Italian marques, Alfa Romeo was humble in origin. The firm grew out of a scheme hatched by a group of Milanese businessmen to produce Darracq cars under licence. Alexandre Darracq had earlier attempted to build bicycles in volume but realized that there was more money to be made producing electric cars. Or so he thought. In 1898 the Bordeaux-born would-be motor mogul turned his attention to internal combustion and bought the patents to a 5-bhp engine from his rival Léon Bollée. This was soon rendered obsolete when Renault revolutionized the industry with shaft drive to the rear axle: much more efficient than Bollée's belt system. Resolute in the face of financial ruination, Darracq pressed on with a new single-cylinder car that was a success on its launch. This in turn led to both more ambitious models and triumphs in motor sport.

Flushed with success, Darracq expanded into Great Britain, producing a range of vehicles for the high end of the market. However, realizing that the real money was to made from cheaper cars, he launched a range of small, one- and two-cylinder models in 1907, and it was with these that he targeted Italy. With finance in place, a new factory was built in Portello, on the outskirts of Milan, but the Frenchman ran into problems almost immediately. Not only did a slump in the European motor industry slow his progress, but the cars soon proved underpowered for the intended market: they were simply incapable of coping with the hilly terrain of northern Italy. By early 1909 the Italian offshoot was facing bankruptcy and ties with Darracq were severed.

The reconfigured company came into being in June 1910 as Anonima Lombarda Fabbrica Automobili, or Alfa (which translates as the Lombardy Car Manufacturing Company), its directors determined to build worthy competitors to the likes of Isotta-Fraschini and Itala. Two definitive Alfas were soon in production, offering a choice between 2413-cc or 4084-cc four-cylinder engines. The company having poached chief designer Giuseppe Merosi from Bianchi, these models bore a certain technological pedigree, thanks to mechanically operated intake valves and updraught carburettors.

Alfa displayed its sporting intent the following April when factory test driver Nino Franchini won his class in the 1500-km (2400 miles) Criterium di Regolarità at Modena with the 24HP Tipo Corsa. Although the company was principally concerned with building large, stately machines and aeroplane engines, it soon recognized motor sport as an effective means of promoting the brand. However, the fledgling marque suffered from a lack of funds to progress, a situation made worse by repeated strikes at its factory and problems with outside suppliers: difficulties faced by its competitors alike.

In December 1915 Italian industrialist Nicola Romeo came to the rescue, becoming the firm's main shareholder. The thirty-nine-year-old was a self-made man, having risen from humble origins to become a successful producer of mining equipment and portable air compressors. The timing of his buy-in was impeccable. With Italy plunged into the First World War, manufacturing space at Romeo's factory in Arese, near Milan, was given over to supporting the military campaign. Production of munitions under a fat new operating budget called for the workforce to leap from 300 to 2500.

After a change of name to Alfa Romeo in 1918, it was not long before the company began car production in earnest. The marque recorded its first racing victory when Giuseppe Campari won the 1920 Circuit of Mugello in a pre-war 40/60 model, a feat he would repeat the following year. In 1921 Alfa Romeo introduced its RL series, which achieved further motor-sport success, yet within twelve months the old problem of labour disputes had brought the company to the verge of collapse.

Founded in 1910 as Alfa, Alfa Romeo became the great Italian sporting marque of the interwar era, achieving repeated success in grands prix and endurance events such as the Le Mans 24 Hours and the Mille Miglia.

Introduction 13

Intervention by the state and financiers saved the manufacturer, ushering in a period of great success on the race track if not commercial progress. Vittorio Jano, one of the greatest engineers in automotive history, joined the firm in 1923 from Fiat and made an instant impression. He put together a staff of ten and their first design was a 2-litre straight-eight engine that powered the P2 single-seater to victory in the 1925 World Manufacturers' Championship. Such was the secrecy in which the P2 was conceived that only those directly involved in the project knew of its existence. That year Jano was appointed chief designer after Merosi gave up his position to work for the French company Mathis. Within two years Alfa Romeo was heading towards nationalization under the fascist regime, with Nicola Romeo remaining a shareholder but lacking any control over the running of the company.

Jano's other great feat was to improve the design of the company's touring and sports cars, which did much to heighten Alfa Romeo's profile internationally. He replaced Merosi's ageing pushrod OHV engines with a beautiful 1487-cc, six-cylinder unit that, when used in the 6C model bodied by Carrozzeria Zagato, yielded one of the world's most dazzling and advanced sports cars. In supercharged Gran Sport trim, the car proved equally impressive on the racetrack, winning four major events in 1928 before being overshadowed by the even lovelier 1752-cc, 85-bhp 1750 Super Sport. Blessed with lightweight Zagato coachwork, the supercharged works racers won the Mille Miglia, Spa Francochamps 24 Hours and Irish Grand Prix in 1929 and the Mille Miglia and Tourist Trophy the following season.

Alfa Romeo was on a roll, the proceeding 8C model bearing an unparalleled competition pedigree and winning the Le Mans 24 Hour race every year from 1931 to 1934 and the Mille Miglia from 1932 to 1938; for the first three years with the SC and from 1935 to 1938 with the sensational 8C 2900. Along with its success in grands prix, Alfa Romeo dominated international motor sport until the arrival of Germany's Mercedes-Benz and Auto-Union cars.

By this time it was no longer a viable commercial concern. In 1933 control of Alfa Romeo passed to the Istituto Ricostruzione Industriale, a governmental organization that allowed directors relative independence even though the company was now state-owned. The government would retain control of the marque until November 1986, when custodianship passed to Fiat.

Key to Alfa Romeo's sustained involvement in motor sport after the government buyout was a man who would in time be deified by Italian – by the world's – car enthusiasts: Enzo Ferrari. Without him the Milan firm would never have risen to the German challenge. Without Alfa Romeo there probably would not have been the Ferrari marque. Enzo was born in 1898 to the owner of a small metalworking shop, next to the family home, that supplied axles to Italy's railways. Moderately wealthy, Ferrari senior was one of the first men in Modena to possess a car, something that fired his son's imagination. So did motor racing, although Enzo originally dreamed of becoming an opera singer. This notion was thwarted by a lack of talent, as were his hopes of a career in journalism, even though his by-line appeared in *La Gazzetta dello Sport* when he was sixteen.

Ferrari then resolved to become a racing driver. After being turned down by Fiat, he gained employment with a firm that converted Lancia trucks into road cars. His job as a test driver brought him into close contact with some of the more successful racers of the day, and friendship with Ugo Sivocci led to him taking a role alongside the former cycling ace at Costruzioni Meccaniche Nazionale. It was with CMN that Ferrari got his first taste of competition. Although prone to self-mythologizing, 'Il Commendatore' later claimed that he made his racing debut in the 1919 Parma–Poggio di Bercetto hillclimb meeting, in which he finished fourth overall. CMN then dispatched Ferrari and Sivocci to the Targa Florio, where an apoplectic Enzo endured an eventful race. Reportedly held up by a presidential procession, he was credited with ninth place, but only after much shouting, threats and gesticulation; but then young Ferrari always did carry a gun.

A year later Ferrari arrived at Alfa Romeo, repaying Sivocci's faith by getting him hired, like himself, as an addition to an already formidable line-up of drivers. A return to the Targa Florio saw Ferrari placed second overall. But it was an event in 1923 that proved a watershed. Entered into the Circuit de Savio at Ravenna, Ferrari put on a bravura performance to win overall and set the lap record against more powerful opposition. His efforts did not go unnoticed, the crowd holding him aloft at the end of the race. It was also the occasion on which the father of the great First World War fighter pilot Francesco Baracca presented Ferrari with his dead son's Cavallino Rampante (prancing horse) symbol for his bravery. This would later become the iconic emblem added to all Ferrari road and race cars.

But not before it appeared on Alfa Romeos. Throughout the rest of the 1920s Ferrari enjoyed intermittent competition success as a driver but astutely arrived at the conclusion that his talents lay behind the scenes. Over dinner in a Bologna restaurant, Ferrari, along with the brothers Alfredo and Augusto Caniato and Mario Tadini, decided to form a *scuderia*, a motor-racing team. Scuderia Ferrari was born on 1 December 1929.

Although Ferrari left Alfa Romeo's employ, links with the firm remained close. He became a marque distributor for the Emilia and Marche provinces while occasionally competing himself, at least for a few more years. In 1930 the team entered thirty races, winning eight. Thus began a transfer of authority, with Alfa's technicians and equipment leaving for Modena and the manufacturer pulling out of single-seater

racing altogether in early 1933. But the name would live on under Ferrari, who persuaded the management to let him continue campaigning its successful P3 model. Results were instantaneous, the équipe's star driver, Tazio Nuvolari, winning the Circuit of Alessandria and the Pescara Grand Prix, among other events. Add a sports-car victory in the Le Mans 24-hour endurance classic and it was a dominant year for Scuderia Ferrari, with only Maserati and Bugatti providing any real competition.

There would be many other wins, but the team was facing new challenges: the might of Germany's engineering excellence and the Nazis' propaganda machine. More advanced Alfa Romeo single-seaters were still no match for the infinitely better-funded competition from Mercedes-Benz and Auto-Union. In 1937 the parent company bought 80% of the team from existing shareholders, and so the *scuderia* that bore his name was now out of Ferrari's direct control. He was enraged that having kept Alfa Romeo's name in the limelight for all those years, his team had effectively been sold behind his back. However, he continued to run the squad, amid much rancour with Alfa Romeo's directors, until 1939, when Scuderia Ferrari was officially disbanded.

Ferrari was now a wealthy man but a clause in his contract precluded his building a car under his own name for a further four years. Undeterred, he started a new firm, Auto Avio Costruzioni. But as war threatened Europe, car factories were being turned over to production of armaments and shortages of materials allowed little progress with the project, although two cars were made. Soon after Germany invaded Poland in September 1939, interest in motor racing and sports cars dwindled away in Italy as the stark realities of conflict gripped the country. Alfa Romeo would be reborn after the war, but the days of producing hugely expensive exotica were all but over. Enzo Ferrari, however, was only just getting started.

REBIRTH AND RENAISSANCE: ITALY SPREADS ITS INFLUENCE
Unlike some other European nations, Italy did not lose its entire motor industry during the war, although production was reduced to almost nil once manufacturing space was given over to military needs. As a result of Allied bombing, however, many of the country's factories were razed and post-war reconstruction was protracted, partly because of shortages of raw materials. Nevertheless, under the Marshall Plan, American know-how was passed on to defeated nations, Chrysler in particular assisting Fiat and Alfa Romeo with production techniques. By the 1950s Alfa would become a mass producer, leaving behind the exclusivity of its earlier years.

Small-scale independent car firms began to emerge, with the likes of Ermini, Stanguellini, Giaur and Moretti building short runs of sports and racing machines. The number of *ecceterini*, as they were

Although outgunned and outflanked by better-equipped opposition, Tazio Nuvolari upheld Italian honour when he won the 1935 German Grand Prix for Alfa Romeo in Adolf Hitler's presence.

The tiny Ghia concern was saved from extinction by joining forces with America's Chrysler Corporation. The result throughout the 1950s was a stream of sensational show cars, some entering limited production.

later dubbed, was bolstered by the Ferrari marque, which built its first car, the 125, in 1947 at Maranello, near Modena. This marked the concern's first hesitant leap towards legendary status while other similar firms disappeared as quickly as they appeared.

It was also a time at which Italy's *carrozzerie* and styling houses began their gradual march to virtual hegemony over global car design. With creativity given free rein, designers and metal-shaping artisans began to emerge from the doldrums, often with radical new forms that sent the automobile industry into a spin. Firms such as Allemano, Bertone, Frua, Touring and Vignale all clothed proprietary chassis with dramatic and influential coachwork but the two *carrozzerie* that were to make the biggest initial impact were Pinin Farina and Ghia, although only one of them would last the distance.

By the early 1950s the Italian car industry was flourishing, with demand for sports cars at an all-time high. Overseas sales were crucial for the communist politicians, who encouraged a sense of duty, more concerned that workers should be gainfully employed than that they should build opulent machines for the rich. As Italy's aviation industry died, a pool of talented metal workers was ready for service. *Carrozzerie* soaked up the excess and the USA in particular became a key export market. But traffic was moving in both directions as foreign manufacturers began courting coachbuilders and stylists who could inject life into their wares.

Whereas Pinin Farina was wooed for its styling pedigree, Ghia, like so many coachbuilders, was attractive to overseas firms because of its ability to build one-offs or small runs in double-quick time. And, compared with the USA, its labour rates were cheap. Founded in 1915 by Giacinto Ghia as Carrozzeria Ghia & Gariglio, the company initially clothed chassis for some of Italy's most prestigious marques, gaining an enviable reputation for its innovative, lightweight aluminium sports-car bodies. Ghia began an association with Chrysler in the early 1950s: a timely union as in the immediate post-war years the bombed-out firm had been reduced to making bicycles.

The Detroit giant had approached Pinin Farina in 1951 to build show cars but the deal fell through and shortly afterwards an agreement was reached with Ghia instead. The Turinese concern was to create a series of cars to the outlines of Chrysler's chief stylist, Virgil Exner. During a fifteen-year partnership, the tiny workshop crafted a number of highly distinctive and beautifully made concept cars, some of which entered limited production.

The collaboration began with the Chrysler-Ghia GS-1 coupés, which were sold exclusively in Europe by Société France Motors. Ghia also built a small run of copies of 1954's Dodge Firebomb dream car, the Chrysler-powered Dual-Ghias marketed by Dual Motors Corporation of Detroit from 1955 to

1958 and the Chrysler Crown Imperial limousines built from 1957 to 1965. The US-Italian association blossomed through the 1950s, with ideas of design and construction flowing in both directions.

Then, in 1963, the majority share in Ghia was bought by Leonidas Ramadas Trujillo, son of the recently deposed dictator of Dominica. Trujillo was not remotely interested in cars or running a *carrozzeria*: the only use he found for the firm was to design labels for his wine bottles. Ghia soon passed to Argentinian émigré Alejandro de Tomaso, by which time all links with Chrysler had ended.

Pinin Farina emerged from the Second World War as it meant to continue. Among the most significant car designs of the twentieth century, the Cisitalia 202 coupé married scientific thinking with breathtaking beauty. Ultimately a commercial flop, this Fiat-based sports car nevertheless sparked massive interest on its release in 1947. Although attributed to Pinin Farina, the basic design was the work of aerodynamicist Giovanni Savonuzzi. Taking his racing-car outline and narrowing the rear section of the roof and re-profiling the rear wings, Pinin Farina achieved a purity of form that was undoubtedly an influence on General Motors' products, including the Oldsmobile Delta 88 and Bentley's Continental fastback.

Over the following decade Pinin Farina formed alliances with several major international players, including the biggest, General Motors, bodying a range of Cadillacs on its behalf. With Peugeot it began a relationship that continues to this day, producing a number of saloons, convertibles and attractive coupés. But, in a development that was perhaps of greater significance, the firm began to dictate what mainstream British cars should look like.

It was the British Motor Corporation's managing director, George Harriman, who first commissioned Pinin Farina to develop styling themes for a range of new products. This decision caused consternation among the UK company's in-house designers, but the switch to the Italian *carrozzeria* was made as much for reasons of internal politics as for commercial ones. Having absorbed various

The Cisitalia 202 coupé was the first truly landmark car design of the early post-war years. A commercial flop when introduced in 1947, it nevertheless enjoyed lasting kudos as an exhibit in the New York Museum of Modern Art.

marques, BMC's management neatly sidestepped any accusations of favouritism among offshoots. The first result of the union was the Austin A40 Farina, which appeared startlingly modern when launched in 1958. The design was distinguished by signature flat panels, crisp lines and minimal overhangs, but it also foreshadowed the demand for hatchbacks with its horizontally split tailgate and folding rear seats.

Met with rapturous praise on its debut, the A40 led to the next generation of Austin Cambridge and Westminster saloons and the 1100/1300, which was the most successful (in sales terms) British model range of the 1960s. Further proposals included the great might-have-been Aerodinamica saloons, passed over by BMC; their bold outlines, designed by Leonardo Fioravanti, were later cribbed wholesale by Citroën for its GS and CX models. With further mergers creating British Leyland in 1968, the Anglo-Italian relationship drew to a close, although Pininfarina (by now the name had become one word) did rework the Jaguar XJ6 in the late 1970s.

Others followed Pininfarina's lead. Giovanni Michelotti – perhaps the forgotten man of post-war car design – was responsible for styling all of Standard-Triumph's output during the 1960s while also adding a dose of contemporary chic to the emerging Japanese motor industry. Perhaps bearing more prestige, Carrozzeria Touring created the landmark Aston Martin DB4/5 range as well as perfecting its *Superleggera* method of construction: ironically, the DB5 in particular is held up as a peerless example of *British* design excellence. This situation was a likely factor in Touring's going to the wall in 1966. Aston Martin continued using its patented manufacturing techniques with the proceeding DB6 but without mention of the firm that gave birth to them; nor did it have to pay any longer for the privilege.

Touring's plight was shared by many similar concerns as the 1960s drew to a close. A socialist mindset had swept across Italy, bringing with it the utopian dream of equality. The rich, and all their symbols of conspicuous consumption, were now frowned upon. Incessant labour disputes exacerbated the car industry's problems and a number of smaller coachbuilders were swept aside.

Perhaps of greater impact was the now near-wholesale use of unitary construction, which made tailoring of cars more difficult. In addition, mainstream manufacturers now sold a wide range of models, some of which would hitherto have been the preserve of the coachbuilder. There was now a divergence between Italian styling houses and the traditional *carrozzerie*. Many long-established firms, such as Boneschi, turned to building ambulances and truck cabs or armouring saloon cars for the government and less savoury types. Bigger companies, such as Pininfarina and Bertone, weathered the storm, constructing cars in volume – sometimes as mere subcontractors – while also acting as stylists for hire with great success. The likes of Giorgetto Giugiaro, the magic marker-wielding colossus behind Ital Design, stuck

In the 1960s Pinin Farina tried to tempt the British Motor Corporation into manufacturing its series of Leonardo Fioravanti-styled Aerodinamica concept cars. BMC was too short of vision and funds to adopt such radical ideas, but many of the styling features were later appropriated by Citroën.

Opposite: Pinin Farina's styling of the Austin A40 was as striking as it was modern, ushering in the hatchback style of small car. It proved a huge success for BMC in the 1960s.

Introduction   21

The Touring-styled Aston Martin DB5 remains one of the most easily identified sports cars of all time thanks to its exposure in the James Bond films. For all its Italian styling, it has more recently been heralded as a milestone in British industrial design.

only to consultancy work (apart from the BMW M1 supercar, which his firm made with the aid of many outside suppliers), with impressive results. While coachbuilding in the accepted sense is all but dead, Italy's influence on car styling continues to be far-reaching.

THE CULT OF THE SUPERCAR

If Italy can lay claim to originating an entire sub-genre of automobile, it is the supercar. When Lamborghini unveiled the Miura at the 1966 Turin Motor Show, it ushered in a new breed of performance vehicle, one that conceded little in practicality, economy or general ease of use. Supercars had only two real functions: to look good and go fast. *Very* fast.

That it would be Lamborghini, a marque then barely three years old, that would bring about such a seismic shift in packaging and styling superiority sent the world's specialist sports-car manufacturers reeling. Understandably, for with the Miura, the Sant' Agata minnow had uprooted the goalposts and run away with them.

Yet the idea of a mid-engined supercar was not entirely new. Although the Miura is routinely held up as the earliest of the breed, it was in fact the second: just the first to find anything like recognition.

The origins of the supercar mirror concurrent progress in motor-racing technology. During the 1950s Italy had enjoyed considerable success in Formula One with Alfa Romeo (if only briefly), Ferrari and, to a lesser extent, Maserati. Then, towards the end of the decade, small British constructor Cooper changed everything: it began entering cars with engines placed behind the driver for better tractability and handling. The result was a brace of World Championships for Australian driver Jack Brabham in 1959–60. By this time Ferrari was the only major Italian player left on the grand-prix scene and team principal Enzo was adamant that he would not yield on engine position. So he lost more ground before reluctantly conceding that the *garagistes* had a point after all: the mid/rear-engined 'Sharknose' 156 Ferrari proceeded to win the 1961 World Championship for American ace Phil Hill.

It was at this point that the seeds were sown for what would become known as the supercar. At the end of the season an unexpected palace coup occurred after a group of eight senior team members, including Hill and engineers Carlo Chiti and Giotto Bizzarrini, walked out in response to being shown the door by *Il Commendatore*. Ferrari's action followed disagreements over the future direction of the squad, working conditions and, above all, the role of his reputedly less than diplomatic wife in overall decision making.

Expecting a contrite Ferrari to beg them to come back, the departees were to be disappointed. Within a few weeks, however, a new marque came into being: ATS (Automobili Turismo Sport). Its existence would prove a brief one. From its two-pronged attack on Ferrari in Formula One and the sports-car market, great things were expected. At grand prix level, ATS's 1963 season proved utterly woeful, with lead driver Phil Hill failing to finish all but one race and without recording a solitary championship point. Its 2500GT road car, however, electrified everyone who witnessed its unveiling at the Geneva Salon that same year.

Among the first mid-engined Italian sports cars – and one of the few offered anywhere in this configuration – this brave 2.5-litre V12 machine could exceed 240 kph (150 mph) and members of the press lucky enough to get behind the wheel raved about the experience. Unfortunately, financiers had overstretched themselves and ATS folded in 1964.

Enzo Ferrari naturally remained unmoved; just as he did when Lamborghini first showed its bare chassis for the Miura in 1965. It was all smoke and mirrors and would never catch on. A year later the press was eulogizing the new strain of Italian exotica and Ferrari's GT cars were now viewed as anachronistic. The same went for Maserati's front-engined coupés. It did not matter that the Miura was shamefully underdeveloped: to the wider world Lamborghini was now the standard-bearer for performance cars. Enthusiasts expected an immediate response from Ferrari, a mid-engined retort to the impudent tractor-manufacturing upstart from just over the hill. Their hopes were to be dashed.

In much the same way as the Maranello-based marque was slow to react to the arrival of British ascendancy in Formula One, Ferrari's response to the Miura was another range-topping, front-engined GT: the 365GTB/4, or Daytona. On the car's maiden outing at the 1968 Paris Motor

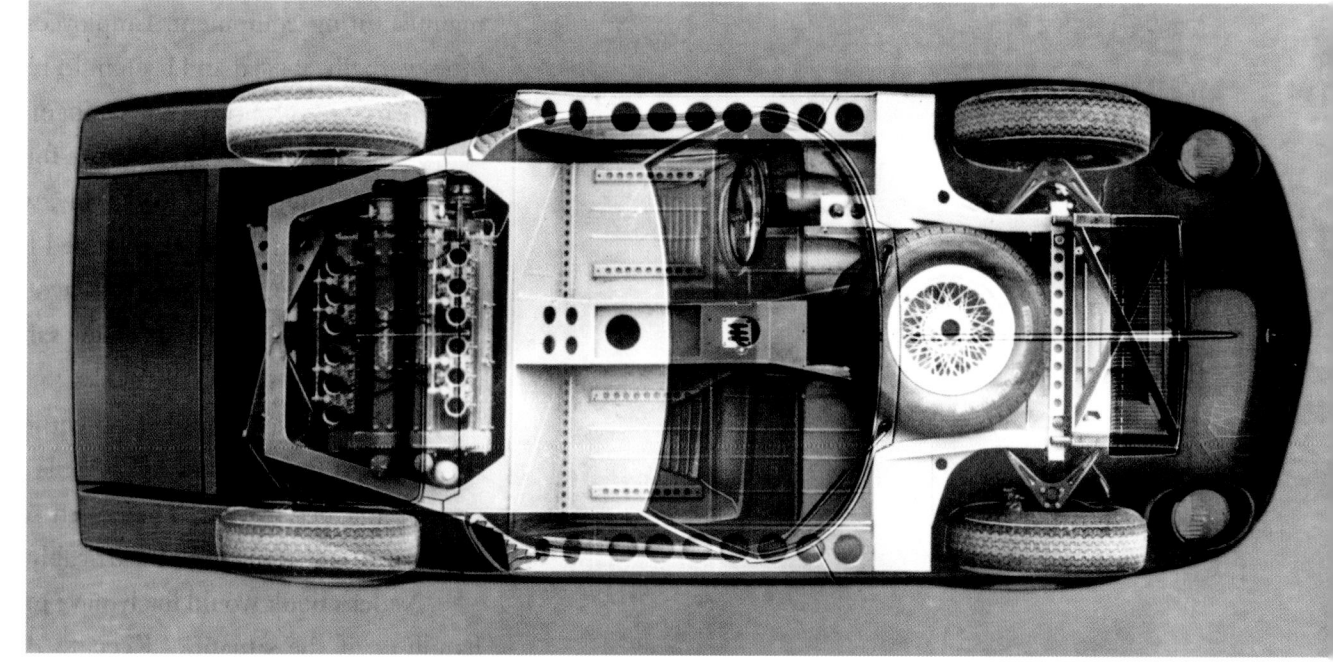

Introduced in 1966, the Lamborghini Miura possessed a beauty that was not merely skin deep. The transverse positioning of its V12 engine behind the occupants was a remarkable feat of engineering. At a stroke, the first true supercar was born.

Show, the dramatic coupé was admired for its Leonardo Fioravanti-penned beauty but there was lingering disappointment that the marque had not followed Lamborghini's lead and 'placed the horse behind the cart'. This soon ebbed once the press reported that it was in fact (marginally) faster and a better all-round car. But even though it outsold the Miura roughly two to one, the Daytona outwardly appeared to be a dinosaur and the divergence between GTs and real supercars was about to get wider. A supercar war was in the offing.

SUPERCARS TAKE CENTRE STAGE BUT TROUBLE LOOMS
By the end of the 1960s the market for high-end Italian road cars was the healthiest it had ever been. Exports were booming, as was the number of manufacturers ready to take on the established élite. But there was trouble ahead, the euphoria felt by designers, engineers and marque principals proving short-lived. And many of these problems were endemic in Italy.

The aspirations of the average working man and woman had changed and there would be repercussions. Unions rose to power as inflation soared. While there were reasonable grounds for discontent in some instances (health care and education in particular), 'legitimate' strikers and flying pickets began targeting all businesses, big or small. Factory sit-ins became frequent, as did vandalism to manufacturing equipment. Employees who refused to strike or participate in 'affirmative action' were often verbally abused and beaten. In response some companies resorted to hiring 'muscle' to sort out the agitators. Communism was rampant in universities and the emergence of the Red Brigades saw capitalism become a crime: a cause for concern if your business was making expensive cars. The effects were far-reaching. The Orsi family, which controlled Maserati, sold out to French automotive giant Citroën in 1968. Having earlier jilted Ford at the altar at the very last moment, Ferrari became a division of Fiat a year later, along with the favoured body-builder, Scaglietti.

Even more pressing were new safety regulations that would govern the design and construction of cars on a global scale. All thanks to a crusading American lawyer: Ralph Nader. While hitchhiking around the United States he had witnessed the aftermath of automobile accidents and deemed many of the resultant deaths avoidable. While still in his early twenties he wrote a book entitled *Unsafe at Any Speed*, published in 1965. The targets of his wrath were a number of humdrum production cars, although one that would come to be inextricably linked with his cause was the Chevrolet Corvair.

Nader's book would likely have passed with little publicity were it not for General Motors' bungled handling of the situation. Keen to discredit his findings, Chevrolet's parent company hired private investigators to dig up dirt on the safety campaigner: when they couldn't find any, attention switched to personality assassination and smear tactics. Prostitutes were dispatched to solicit Nader at his home but he wouldn't bite. All this skulduggery provoked Nader to fight back and in doing so he gained a platform from which to preach his safety mantra. A man who didn't (and still doesn't) own a car or hold a driving licence became a national figure, giving testimony to Congress that led to the 1968 National Safety and Motor Vehicle Act.

Nader has probably had greater effect on the direction of post-war car design than any engineer, stylist or manager. The consequences of these new laws caught all the major domestic manufacturers on the hop, with crash testing, bumper and headlight positioning and emission control all giving cause for great change. For small-fry purveyors of exotic cars thousands of miles away, the fallout was potentially catastrophic.

Those specialist manufacturers that remained in business were being attacked on all sides, whether by the unions at home or by pressure to reconfigure their products to meet still uncertain foreign regulations. To make matters worse, a new local tax was levied on high-displacement vehicles that made them less attractive to those wealthy Italians still brave enough to be seen driving expensive cars. Then, in October 1973, came the biggest hit of all: a fuel crisis. Every country was affected; even the USA and Canada. In those that were entirely dependent on imported oil, such as Italy, the consequences were felt by everyone.

While Maserati and Ferrari sought refuge under the umbrella of large organizations, Lamborghini suffered more than most. In 1972, after a business deal with the Bolivian government for the supply of several thousand tractors turned sour, Ferruccio Lamborghini was forced to sell the majority shareholding in the company. This in turn led to serial ownership, and by the end of decade the company's production of cars was in double figures and bankruptcy loomed. It is only since the late 1990s, under the protection of Audi, that the firm has really prospered.

Yet throughout all the turmoil, another marque rose to prominence: De Tomaso. Having made a series of unsuccessful racing cars in the early 1960s, Alejandro de Tomaso had changed tack and built a mid-engined sports car dubbed the Vallelunga before introducing the fabulous Mangusta in 1966. Unlike many of his more exalted contemporaries, de Tomaso favoured using proprietary running gear rather than developing his own from scratch. Powered by a 4.7-litre Ford V8 engine and clothed in a dramatic Giorgetto Giugiaro-styled skin, the 'Mongoose' was reputedly a handful to drive but it signalled the beginning of a fruitful, if brief, relationship with Ford.

Always a canny operator, de Tomaso thrashed out a deal with Ford president Lee Iacocca for a new supercar, one that would be sponsored by the Detroit giant and sold in the United States through its Lincoln-Mercury dealerships. The resultant Pantera debuted in March 1970. Derived, if only in part, from a stillborn design proposal for Isuzu, the dramatic Tom Tjaarda-styled silhouette was beautifully proportioned and great things were expected of the 5766-cc V8-powered challenger. And it did sell. With a price tag below $10,000, the Pantera was a sensation: a supercar within everyone's reach. Unfortunately, quality control was almost non-existent and Ford was forced to set up facilities on the east and west coasts to rectify the car's many inherent flaws. It cost the company a fortune and by 1974 the relationship was over, although the model lived on in Europe until the 1990s.

Ford's experience of Italian quality control mirrored that of many customers in the 1970s, a decade when the reputation of Italian car making in general suffered massively. The industry's use of porous Russian steel resulted in problems with rust and once-respected names suffered financial meltdown dealing with warranty claims.

Sponsored by Ford and styled by Tom Tjaarda, the De Tomaso Pantera was intended as a supercar for everyman. Unfortunately, poor build quality gave it a brief lifespan in its target market of North America.

RESURGENCE OF THE LEGENDARY MARQUES

Yet by the dawn of the 1980s the ugly violence and general chaos damaging Italian industry was diminishing as union power weakened and the country returned to normality. Italy's supercar constructors had lost ground to German competition but their recovery was swift. Ferrari had lost out the least of all the small-scale manufacturers and charged ahead with the Testarossa and lesser models. Lamborghini retained the Countach's relevance with ever more outlandish variations until its replacement, the Diablo, arrived in 1990.

There would be further bumps in the road, not least the worldwide economic slump of the early 1990s, which once again depressed demand for supercars, Bugatti being among the casualties. But this time many firms came out of the slowdown relatively unscathed. Ferrari in particular has since introduced a range of truly brilliant machines that marry technological superiority with commendable build quality. Its success with road cars mirrors that on the circuits: at the time of writing, the team has won six straight constructors' titles in this decade. With Maserati once again flourishing under the Fiat umbrella (its tenure with De Tomaso from 1975 to the late 1990s saw it move further away from its roots) and Lamborghini prospering under German ownership, there are more Italian auto legends in prospect. For this we can all be truly thankful.

ITALIAN AUTO LEGENDS

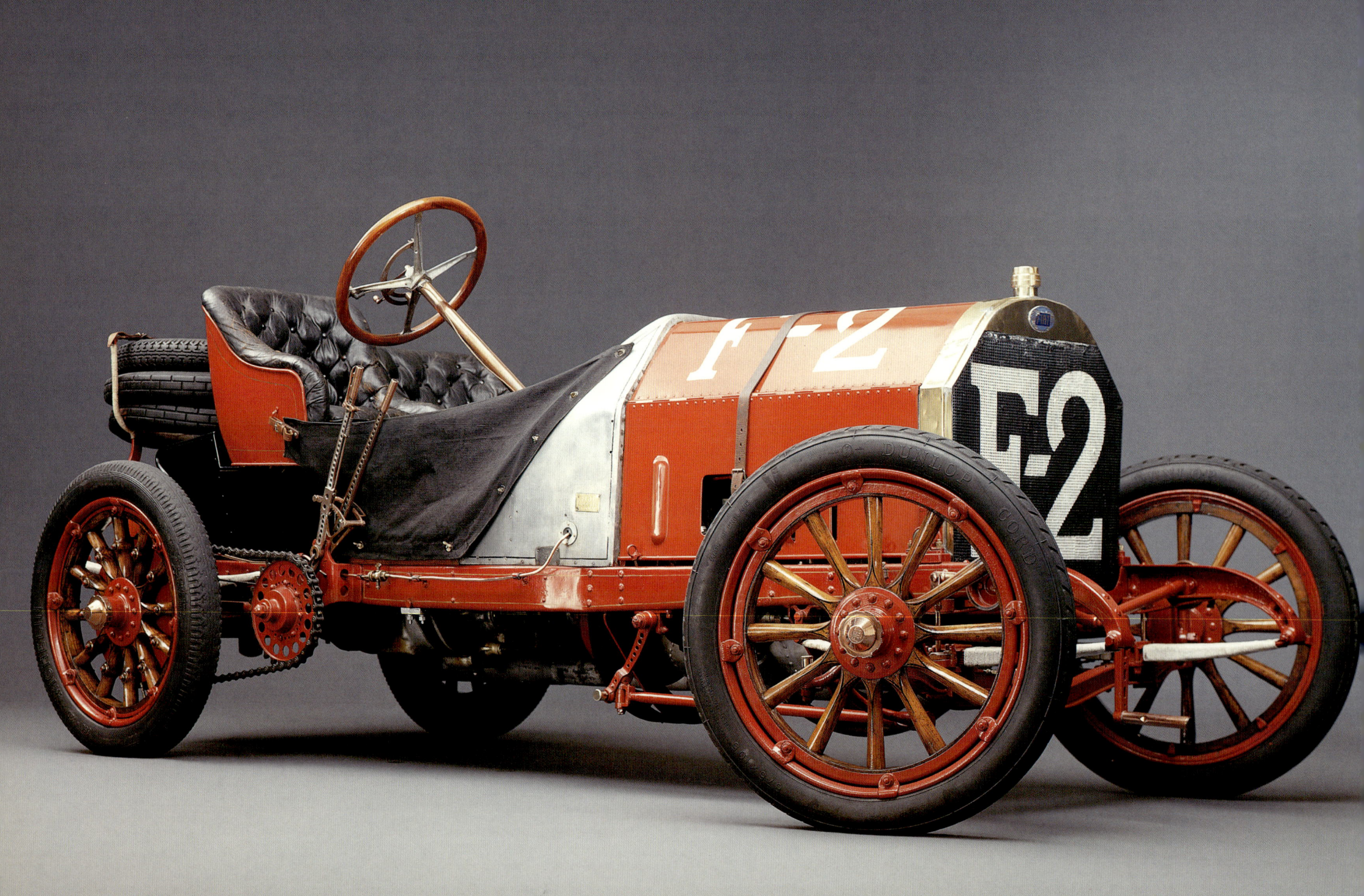

1907 FIAT 130HP

For much of its existence Fiat has generally shunned front-line motor sport, yet with the 130HP it set a precedent for Italian success in grand-prix racing. In 1907 the Automobile Club de France devised a competition formula based on a minimum fuel consumption figure – 30 litres per 100 km (9.4 mpg) – but without any corresponding weight or engine-capacity limits. Desperate to end French dominance in the sport, Fiat's technical director, Carlo Cavalli, laid out a new car, borrowing heavily from the earlier 110-bhp Gordon Bennett Cup racer, not least its engine.

Producing 130 bhp at just 1600 rpm, this 16,256-cc, overhead valve, four-cylinder monster abused the scales at more than 907 kg (2000 lb); each piston weighed nearly 4.5 kg (10 lb). Mounted into a ladderframe chassis with rigid axles and semi-elliptical springs at either end, the bodywork was minimalistic in an effort to offset the engine's heft. In a further effort to save weight, holes were drilled into the external hand brake, gearshift and steering drop arm. The result was a car capable of around 161 kph (100 mph) – all the more terrifying given the narrow tyres and lack of front brakes.

Scoring first time out in the 1907 Targa Florio road race in Sicily, works Fiat driver Felice Nazzaro steered his 130HP home ahead of team mate Vincenzo Lancia. Three cars were then entered into the most important race in the calendar, the French Grand Prix. Against the might of the factory Renaults, Nazzaro stormed to victory at Dieppe and, for good measure, achieved fastest lap.

Fiat kick-started Italy's dominance in grand-prix racing with the 130HP. As was commonplace in early racing models, the car had a small second seat for a riding mechanic.

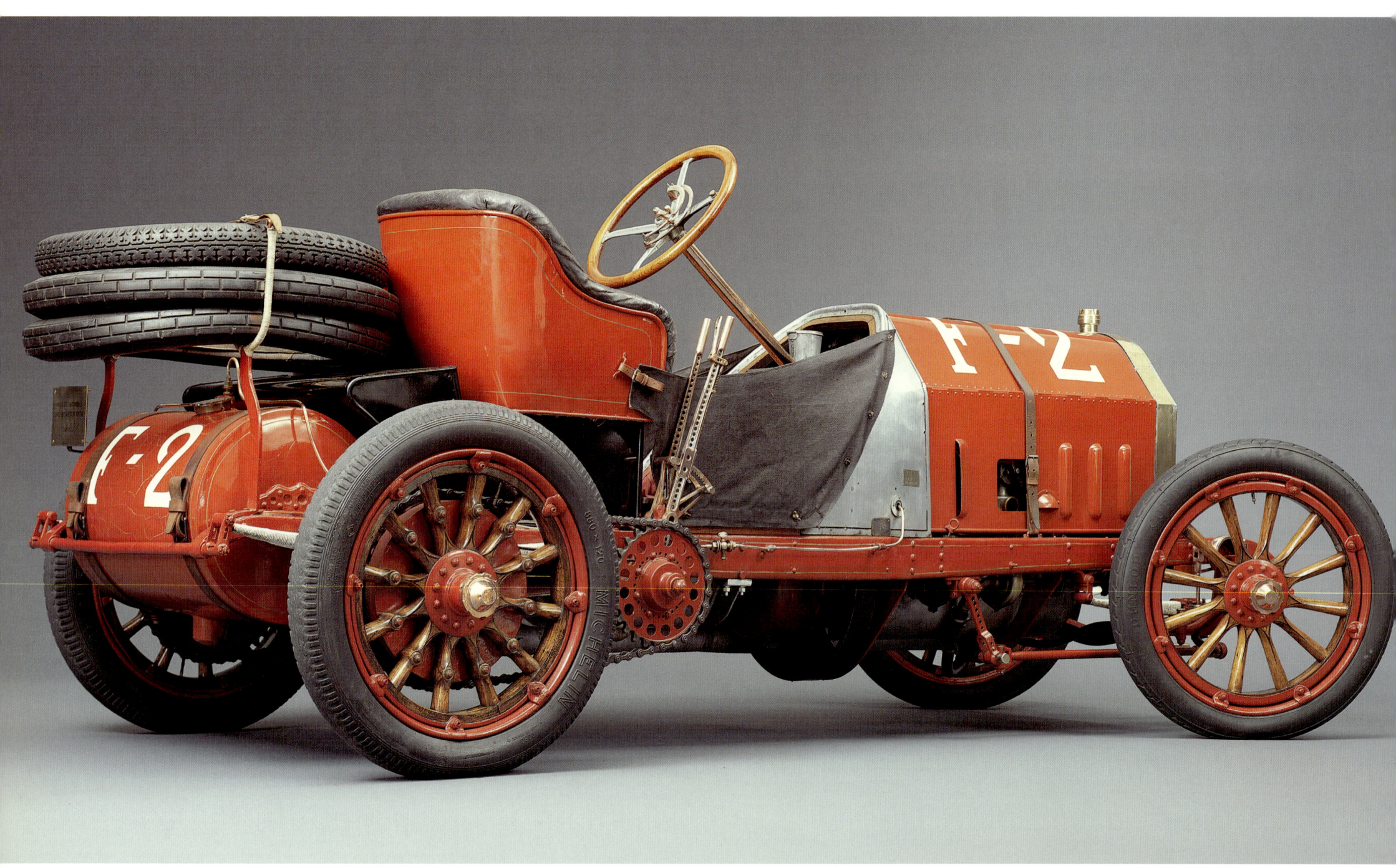

The rest of the car may have been pared back, but the Fiat 130HP's four-cylinder engine weighed an astonishing 907 kg (2000 lb). Producing 130 bhp, the 16,256-cc unit borrowed heavily from an earlier racing engine designed by the firm's technical director, Carlo Cavalli. What it lacked in artistry, it made up for in huge power and brutal efficiency.

Opposite: Fiat's monstrous racer won the 1907 Targa Florio road race and the French Grand Prix in the same year.

1907 ITALA

It was an extraordinary challenge. In March 1907 the French newspaper *Le Matin* ran an editorial by Luigi Barzini that asked: "Will anyone agree to go, this summer, from Peking to Paris by motor car?" The bait was soon taken by Prince Scipione Borghese, who entered the race against four other teams in his 7.4-litre Itala with chauffeur Ettore Guizzardi as designated co-driver and mechanic. Barzini joined them to cover the event for his paper.

Itala was formed in 1904 by Matteo Ceirano and Guido Bigio, and the Turin-based marque enjoyed some success in motor sport with its powerful and hugely expensive designs. Borghese's car was typical of the breed, consisting of a steel perimeter frame that housed the huge four-cylinder engine, four-speed transmission and rigid axles suspended by semi-elliptical springs. To this was added rudimentary bodywork with two front seats and one in the rear flanked by 150-litre (33 gallons) fuel tanks. The back seat was often used to carry luggage, in which case the third man would sit on the front floor with his feet on the running boards. At first the Itala had iron mudguards but, in what became a systematic process of weight reduction, these were discarded en route and it completed most of the trip as an open-wheeler.

The competing cars left Peking on 10 June, travelling into Russia over railways bridges and along the southern edge of Lake Baikal. A road bridge collapsed under the Itala's weight, but the greatest obstacle was the mud of eastern Russia, to which one of the wheels succumbed in the Urals. This repaired, the trio headed for a lavish reception in St Petersburg before being escorted into Germany. With the Prince at the wheel, the Itala reached Paris on 10 August, exactly two months after the start of a remarkable adventure.

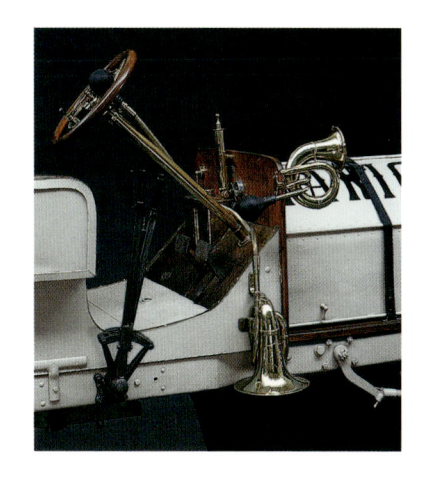

Prince Scipione Borghese sat perched atop his Itala on the drive from Peking to Paris. What passed for a cabin was at best rudimentary, although the brass horn provided a decorative flourish.

Nominally a three-seater, the Itala had stark bodywork that left the occupants open to the elements. During the epic journey the car's iron mudguards were jettisoned to save weight.

Itala 37

1924 FIAT MEPHISTOPHELES

Stocky, bespectacled Englishman Ernest Eldridge appeared an unlikely land-speed record breaker yet this fearless money lender drove his Mephistopheles, with its 21,706-cc aeroplane engine, as though chased by the devil himself. One Sunday morning in July 1924 he aimed the flame-belching beast between the trees along a narrow, bumpy road near Arpajon, just north of Paris and, accompanied by his intrepid passenger John Ames, recorded a mighty 236 kph (146.8 mph). After his French rival René Thomas, who had achieved 143.31 mph (232 kph), protested that his car lacked a reverse gear, Eldridge returned a week later, having somehow contrived a modification, and set the world two-way kilometre record at 235 kph (146.01 mph).

Unlike Thomas's state-of-the-art Delage, Eldridge's Fiat-based machine was a hybrid brute built in a backstreet garage. Already a successful racing driver, he came upon the six-cylinder engine in London before snapping up a 1908 Fiat grand-prix car with which to mate it. However, the ageing chassis was far too short, so it had to be cut in half and lengthened by 400 mm (16 in.) – apparently using side members from the frame of a London bus – to accommodate the ex-fighter bomber unit. With further engine modifications, the reborn Mephistopheles developed 320 bhp at just 1800 rpm, around tick-over, and made its debut at Brooklands, Surrey, in June 1925. By Easter of the following year it was lapping the banked track at 196 kph (122 mph).

Mephistopheles remained a spectacular sight at Brooklands throughout the 1920s before Eldridge tired of the car. After surviving the bombing raids of the Second World War tucked away in a garage in Preston, it was restored by the Naylor family and raced in historic events until 1961, when it was purchased by Fiat. Eldridge had retired from competitive driving before the Second World War, after losing an eye in a colossal accident. He later assisted his close friend George Eyston's attempt at the world land-speed record but died in 1937 after contracting pneumonia, just days before Eyston's successful 555-kph (345 mph) run at Utah.

It is hard to believe that Ernest Eldridge and a passenger were able to squeeze into the confines of this land-speed record car. Note the close proximity of rear wheel to cabin.

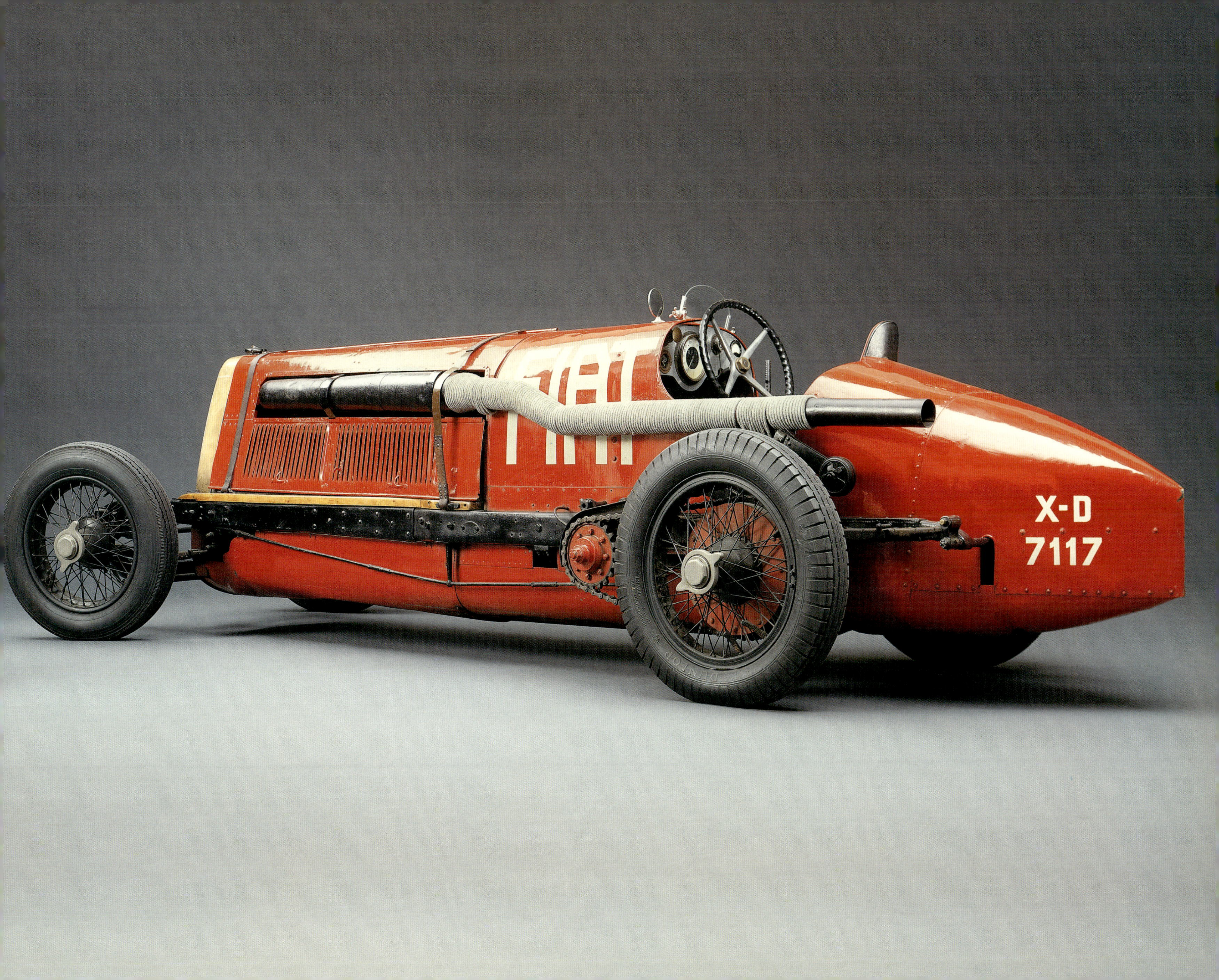
FIAT
X-D
7117

1925 ALFA ROMEO RL

Given its latter-day practice of reviving past designations, it is unlikely that Alfa Romeo will rekindle 'Normale'. This tragically dreary appellation was worn by the first of the Milan firm's RL series from 1922 before it was wisely dropped in favour of 'Turismo' three years later. Introduced with a 2916-cc, overhead-valve, straight-six designed by Giuseppe Merosi, the car bore the English classification '21/70', a combination of horsepower, as defined by Britain's Royal Automobile Club, and nominal top speed.

Almost concurrently, a shortened variation, the RLS, was announced, with engine capacity enlarged to 2994 cc, giving 71 bhp and a top speed of around 129 kph (80 mph). The ultimate production iteration was the RLSS, which appeared in 1925: with little changed internally, this sportier edition produced 83 bhp.

Five cars, all based on the RLS but with even more abbreviated frames, were entered in the 1923 Targa Florio road race. Ugo Sivocci was victorious with an overbored 3.1-litre engine, while Antonio Ascari was runner-up and first in class with his 3-litre car. Later that season he won at Cremona, while future Alfa Corse team boss Enzo Ferrari took the spoils at Savio.

Suitably bolstered, Alfa returned to Sicily for the Targa Florio a year later with two of its entries featuring slightly squatter bodywork and seven-bearing, 3620-cc engines that produced 125 bhp. Ascari was all set to win, only for his engine to seize within sight of the finish, causing the car to spin. By the time he had pushed the stricken machine across the line, Christian Werner had got there first for Mercedes-Benz.

In total, 2631 RL series cars of all types were made until 1927. The model enjoyed considerable success in overseas markets, several examples wearing bespoke bodywork by the likes of Zagato, Montescani, Cesare Sala and Castagna.

Among the most charismatic of Italian marques, Alfa Romeo has weathered repeated upheaval to produce landmark road and racing cars. The RL was bodied by some of the finest coachbuilders of the day and also served as a platform for competition success.

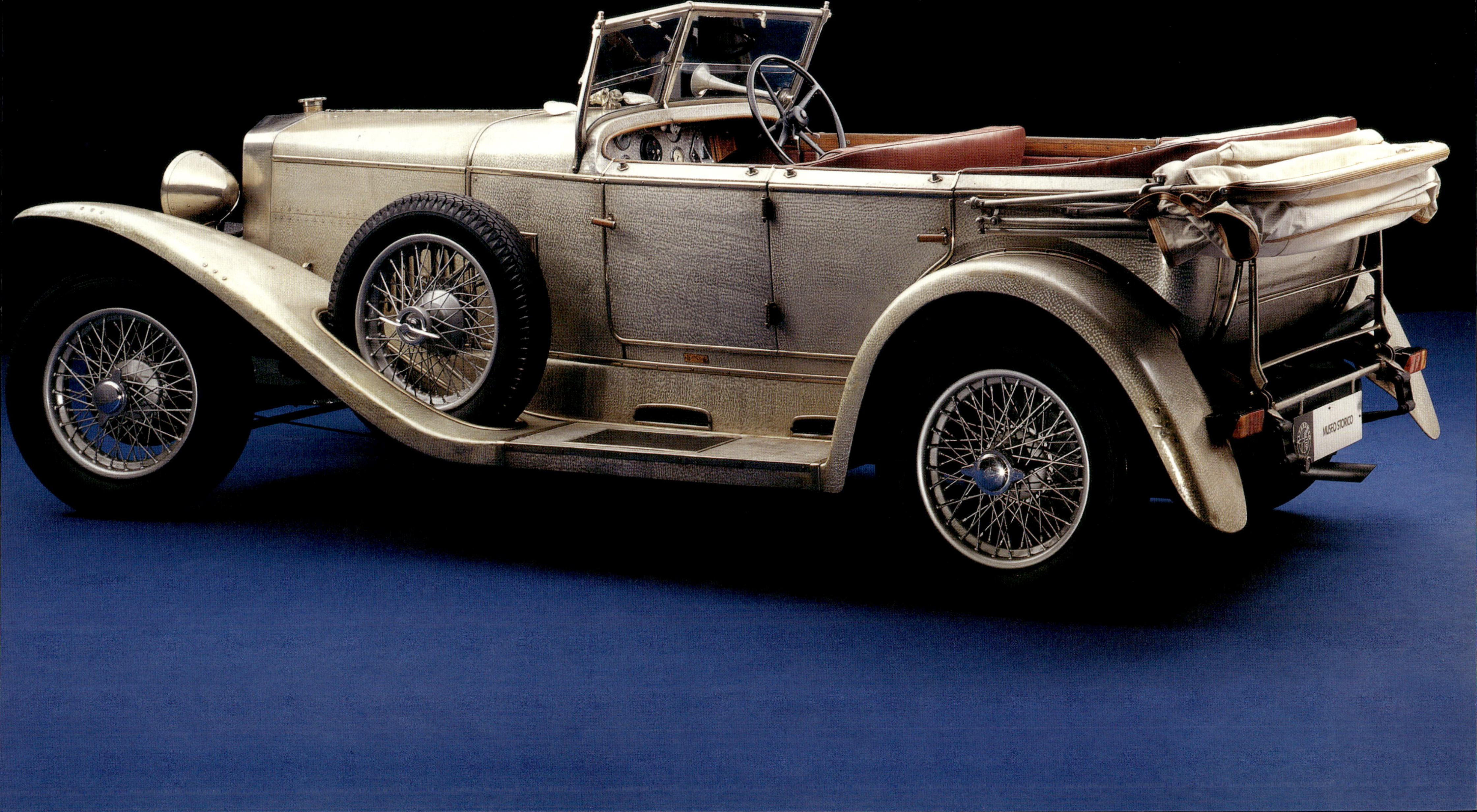
MUSEO STORICO

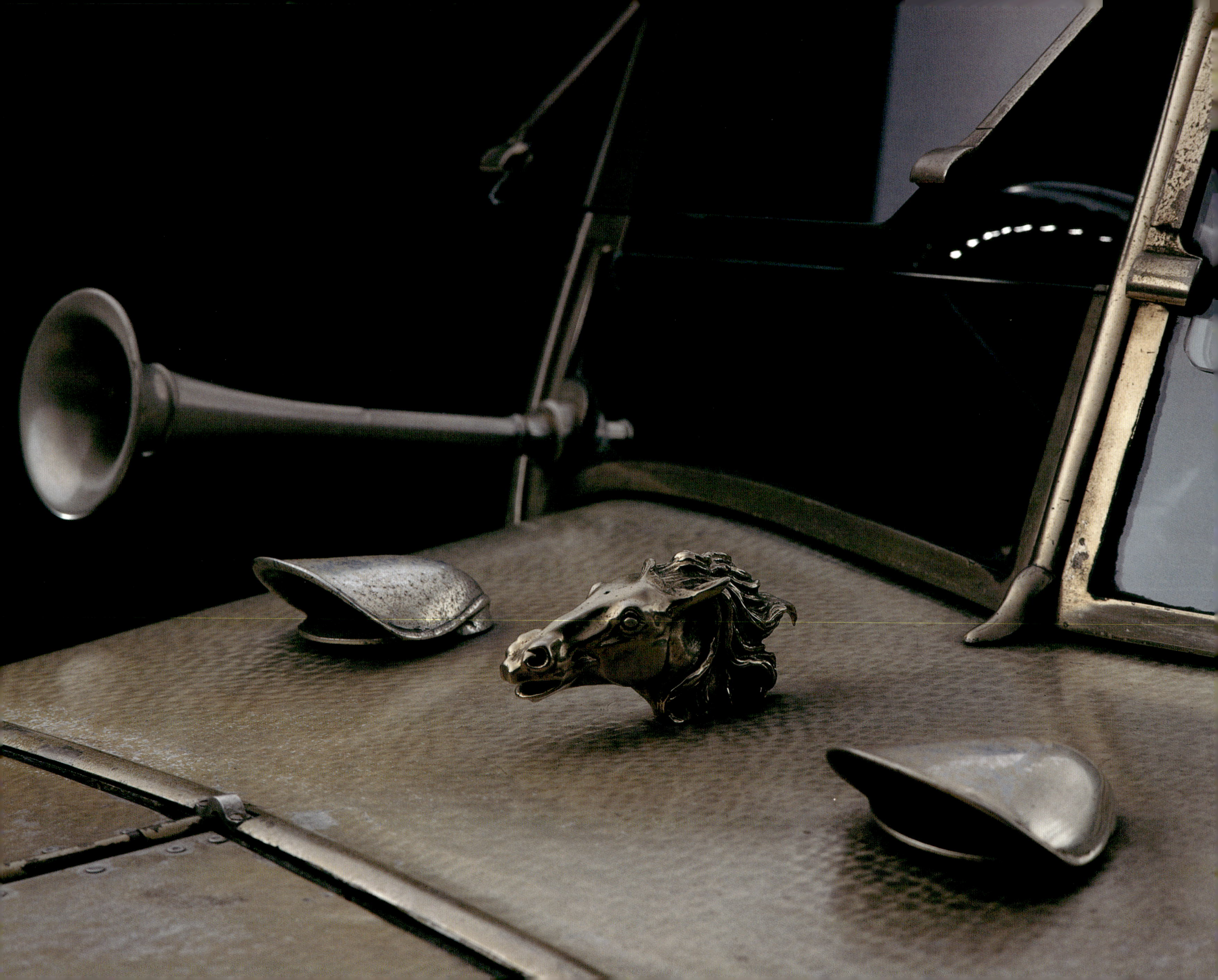

Opposite: The RL's split V-shaped windscreen was a carry-over from boat design and was a popular styling trait of the era.

Right: A perpendicular grille and full wings lend this RL a dignified air – a far cry from the look of the RLS racer that it spawned.

Alfa Romeo RL   43

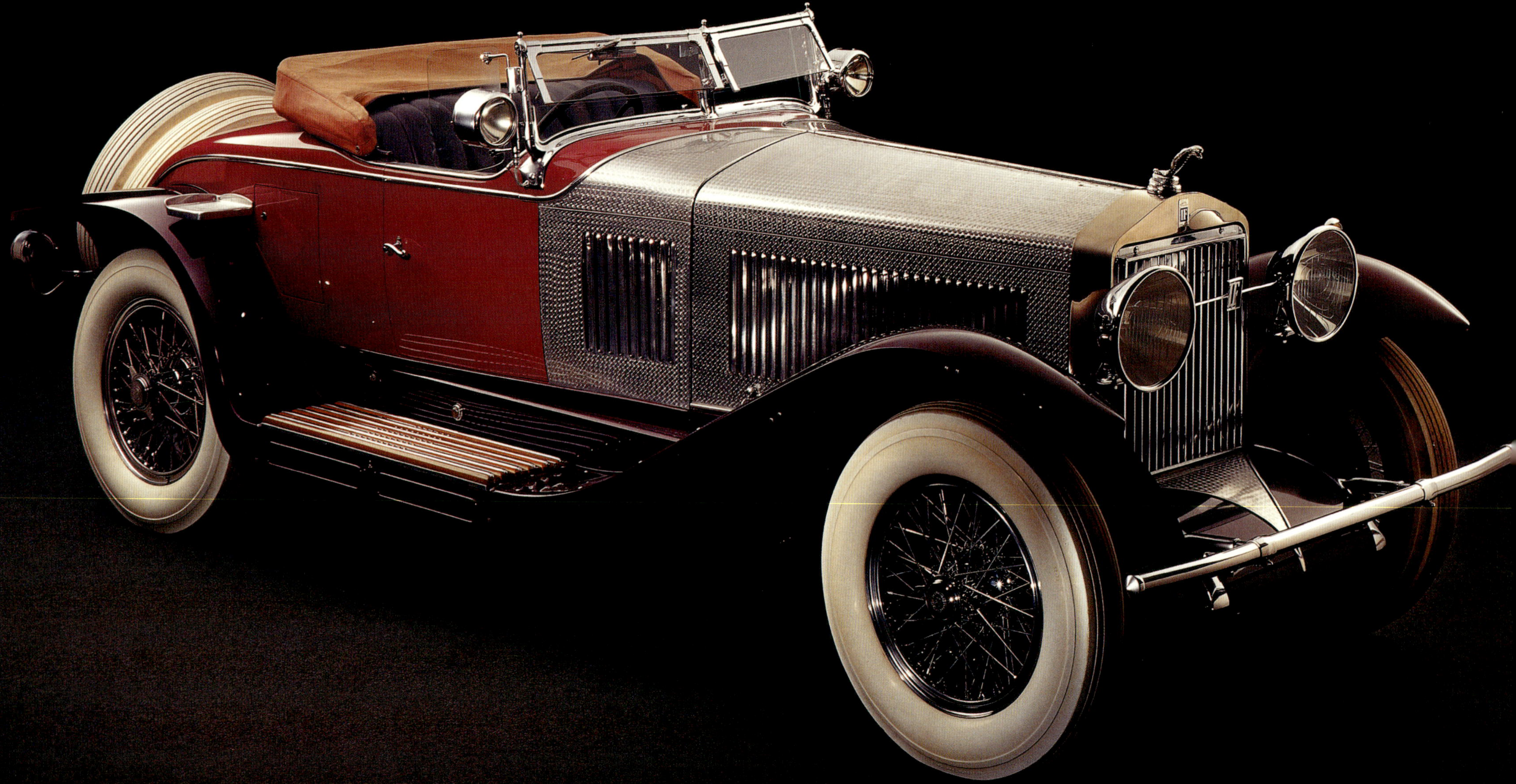

1926 ISOTTA-FRASCHINI TIPO 8A

From its foundation in 1901, Isotta-Fraschini was renowned for its excellence of design and engineering. Cesare Isotta and Vincenzo Fraschini, whose firm was one of the most progressive of the early manufacturers of luxury cars, enjoyed numerous competition successes before turning their attention to building aeroplane engines during the First World War. Emerging from the conflict a much more prosperous and diversified concern, Isotta-Fraschini put its advanced technology to good use with just one production model: the Tipo 8.

The man responsible for designing this remarkable machine was Giustino Cattaneo, whose CV listed thirty-six individual car designs, nineteen industrial and military vehicles – including tanks – and eighteen aero engines. For the Tipo 8, he conceived the first straight-eight powerplant to be offered in a motor car; it was also the first car to feature brakes on all four wheels.

Typically, the firm made only the chassis and running gear. It was left to outside *carrozzerie* to do the rest, with the likes of Castagna, Farina and Touring producing breathtaking coachwork, tailored in each case to suit the customer's whim. This particular example – a Tipo 8A with an enlarged 7370-cc engine – was commissioned by the Hollywood silent-screen star Rudolf Valentino. Unusually, it wore bodywork by Fleetwood Metal Body Company of Pennsylvania, better known for its output on Packard chassis. This exceptionally well-made creation came complete with the actor's trademark Cobra mascot atop the radiator cowling.

Despite Isotta-Fraschinis being the vehicles of choice for royalty, a Pope and a dictator – Mussolini had one – the firm's reliance on the North American market cost it dear. When Wall Street crashed in 1929, car production followed suit shortly afterwards. Attempts to revive the marque, the most recent being in the late 1990s with a Tom Tjaarda-styled, Audi-powered coupé, all foundered.

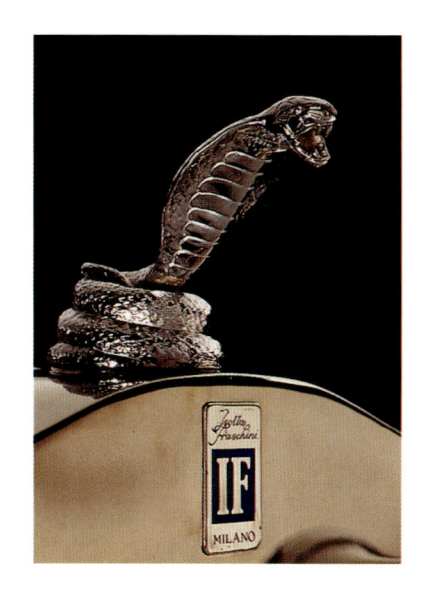

Rudolf Valentino's Cobra mascot adorns the radiator cowling.

Opposite: Fleetwood hand-crafted this superb machine's bodywork, the engine-turned bonnet and cowl reflecting the laborious nature of the build.

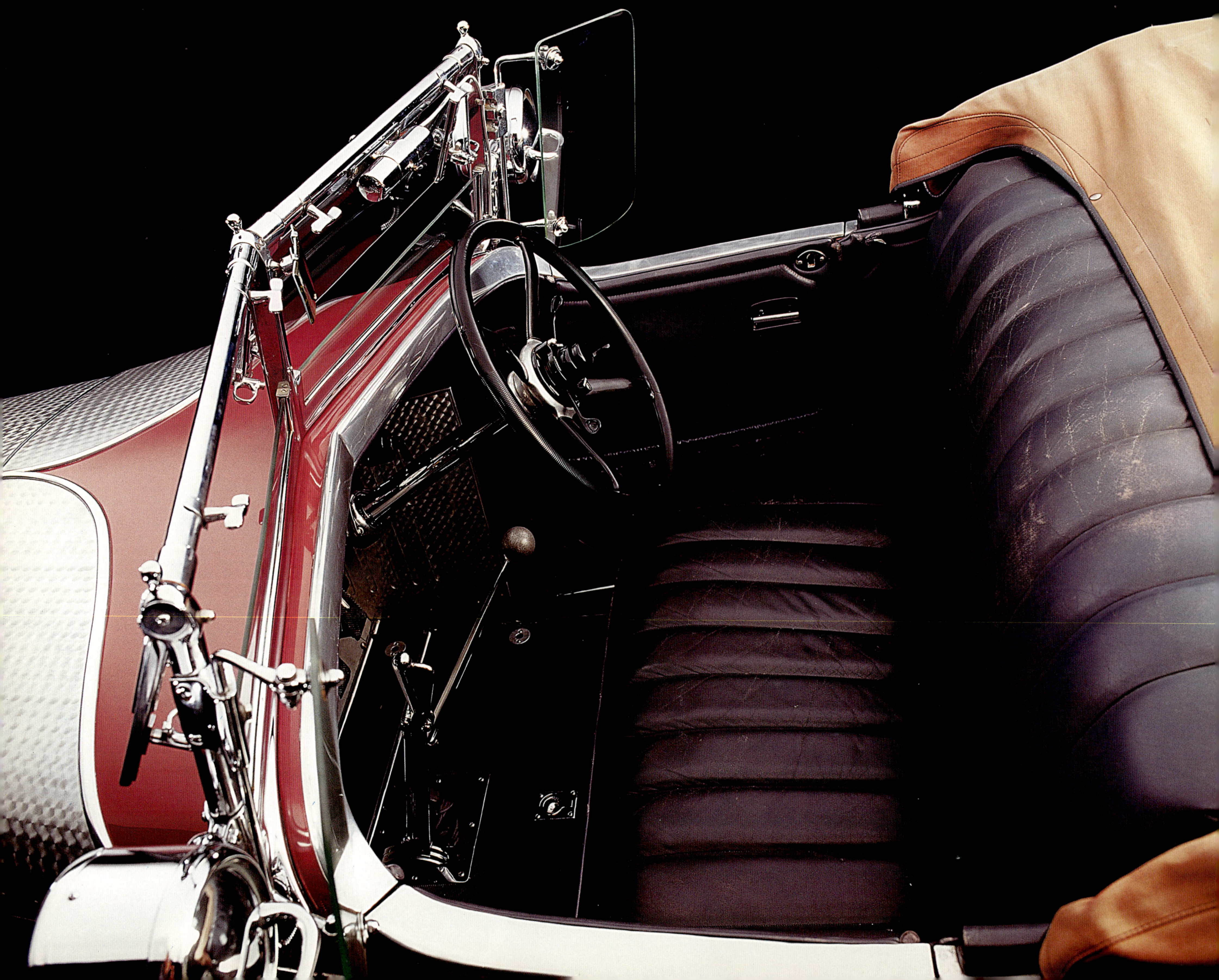

Opposite: Opulent by the standards of the day, the cockpit features engine-turned panelling, a leather-clad bench seat and a split-V duVal windscreen.

Right: With the radiator in-line with the front axle, the lithe Tipo 8A was among the more elegant coachbuilt classics of the period.

The car's dashboard was generously equipped with instrumentation and each component beautifully made.

Opposite: Every item of brightwork was elaborately fashioned for this remarkable Italian-American confection.

48

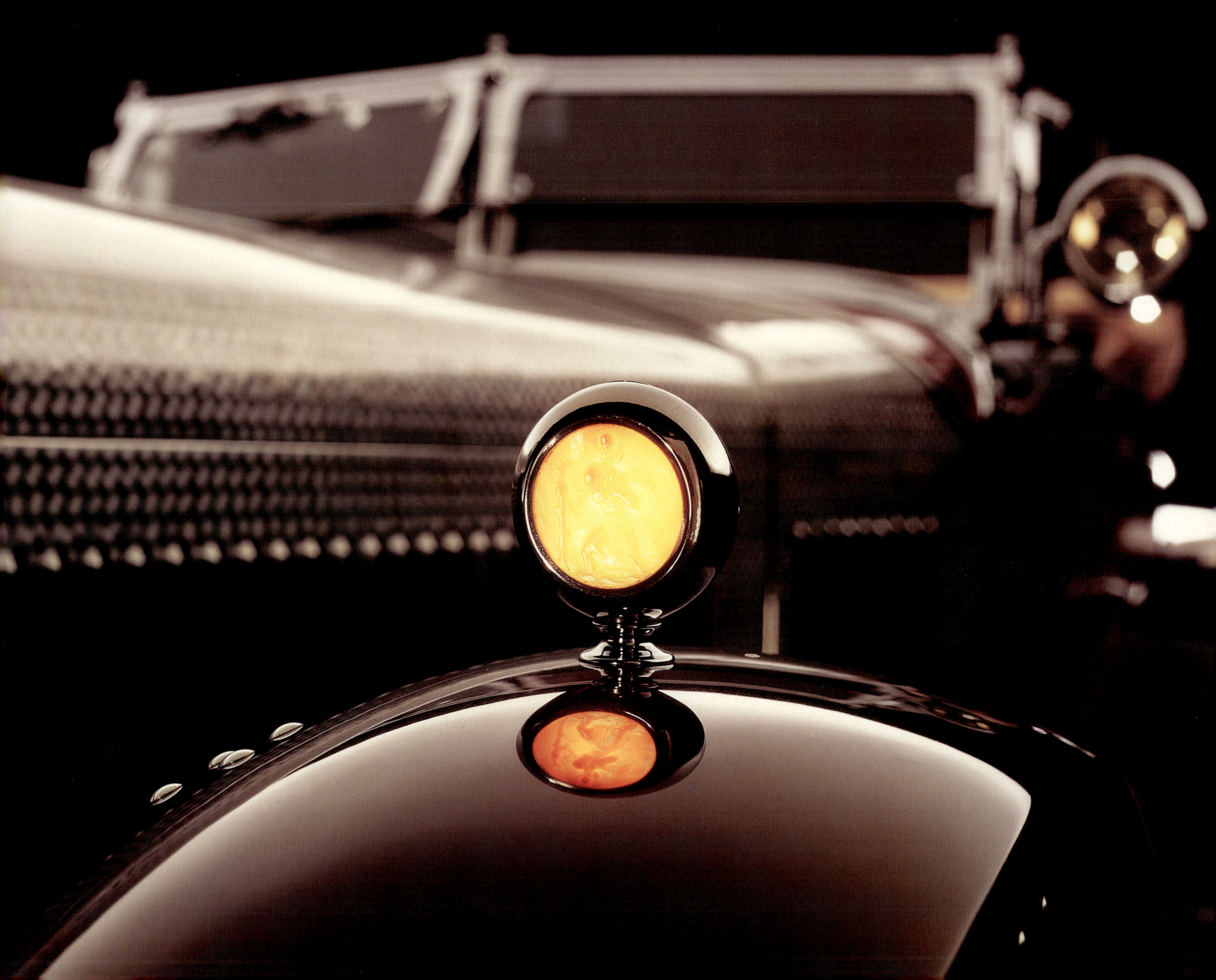

1928 LANCIA LAMBDA

To appreciate the Lambda fully you have to know what came before. Until its launch in 1922, Italian manufacturers had mainly produced upmarket machines with ladderframe-type chassis, lazy side-valve engines, solid beam axles and a choice of bodywork as long as you engaged an outside *carrozzeria*. The Lambda, by comparison, was as radical as radical gets, rendering its competition almost obsolete at a stroke.

Impeccably well made, the Lambda was of unitary construction, bore a highly sophisticated and compact overhead-cam V4 engine, independent front suspension and four wheel brakes rather than the usual rears only. None of these features was unique to the car but the combination of them all in one package was a first: it was, in short, a major technical milestone in the history of automotive design.

If the Lambda had a flaw it was a by-product of its monocoque-style structure. This did not appeal to coachbuilders because there was no separate frame; it also made building a closed version difficult. Nonetheless, the Lambda was steadily developed, the most important changes being an increase in displacement from 2120 cc to 2.4 litres in 1926 and to 2.6 litres two years later, along with a change from a three- to a four-speed transmission in 1925. The final series, produced until the model's demise in 1931, had a platform chassis to appease the coachbuilders. Around 13,000 of all types were made during the car's eight-year lifespan.

Although marque founder Vincenzo Lancia had been a hugely successful racing driver before forming his own company in 1906, he viewed the Lambda as a tourer, yet the car's fine handling soon attracted the attention of privateers: one example held second place in the 1928 Mille Miglia for much of the race. A remarkable performance on just 49 bhp.

The Lambda helped establish Lancia's reputation for quality and innovation. For its day, the compact V4 engine was highly sophisticated, as indeed was the rest of the car.

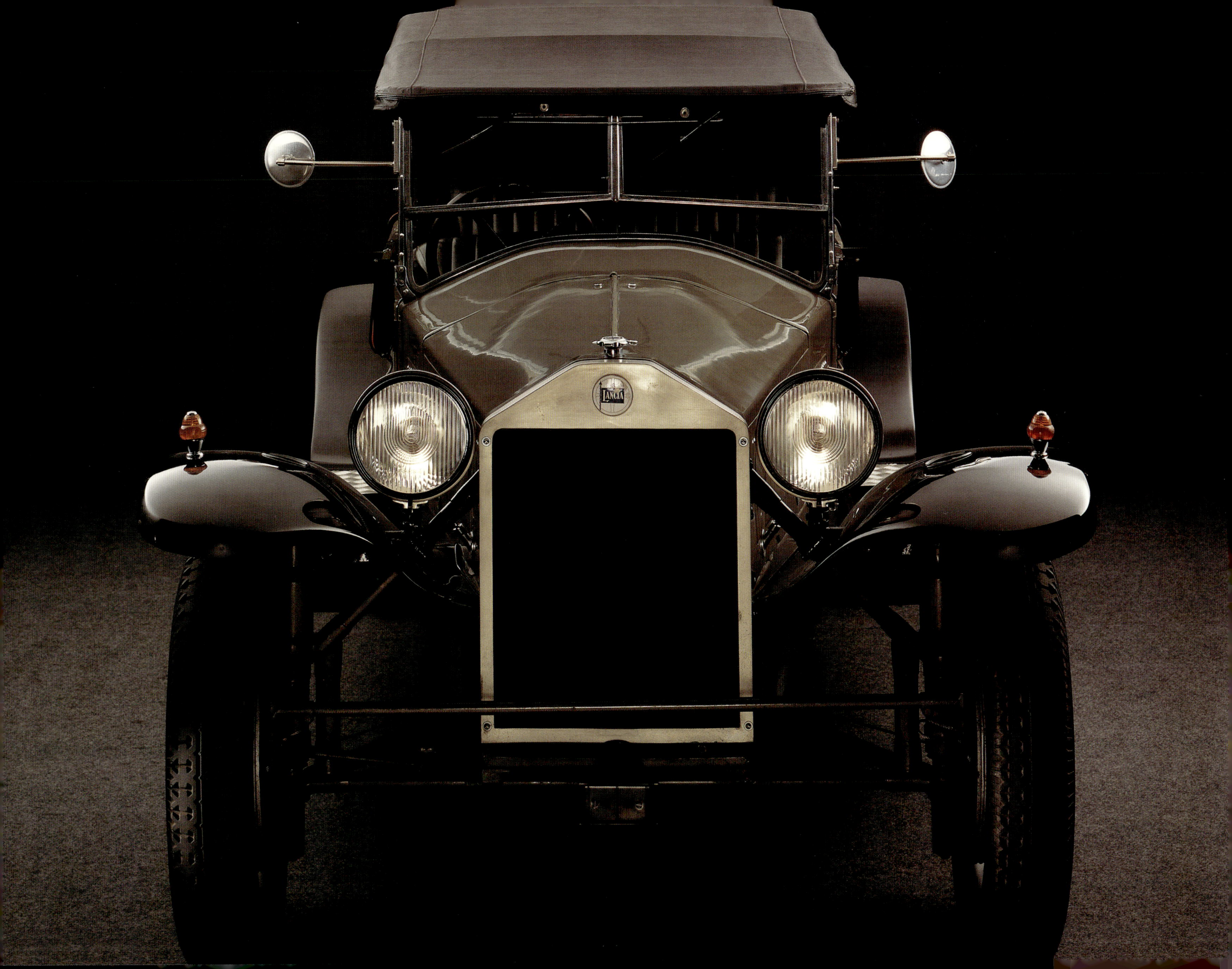
LANCIA

Above: Despite its square-rigged looks, the Lambda concealed a wealth of originality, although its unitary construction made it less appealing to coachbuilders because there was no separate frame.

Opposite: With the Lambda, form followed function. Marque instigator Vincenzo Lancia wanted it that way, conceiving this highly advanced machine to be a tourer as opposed to an outright performance car.

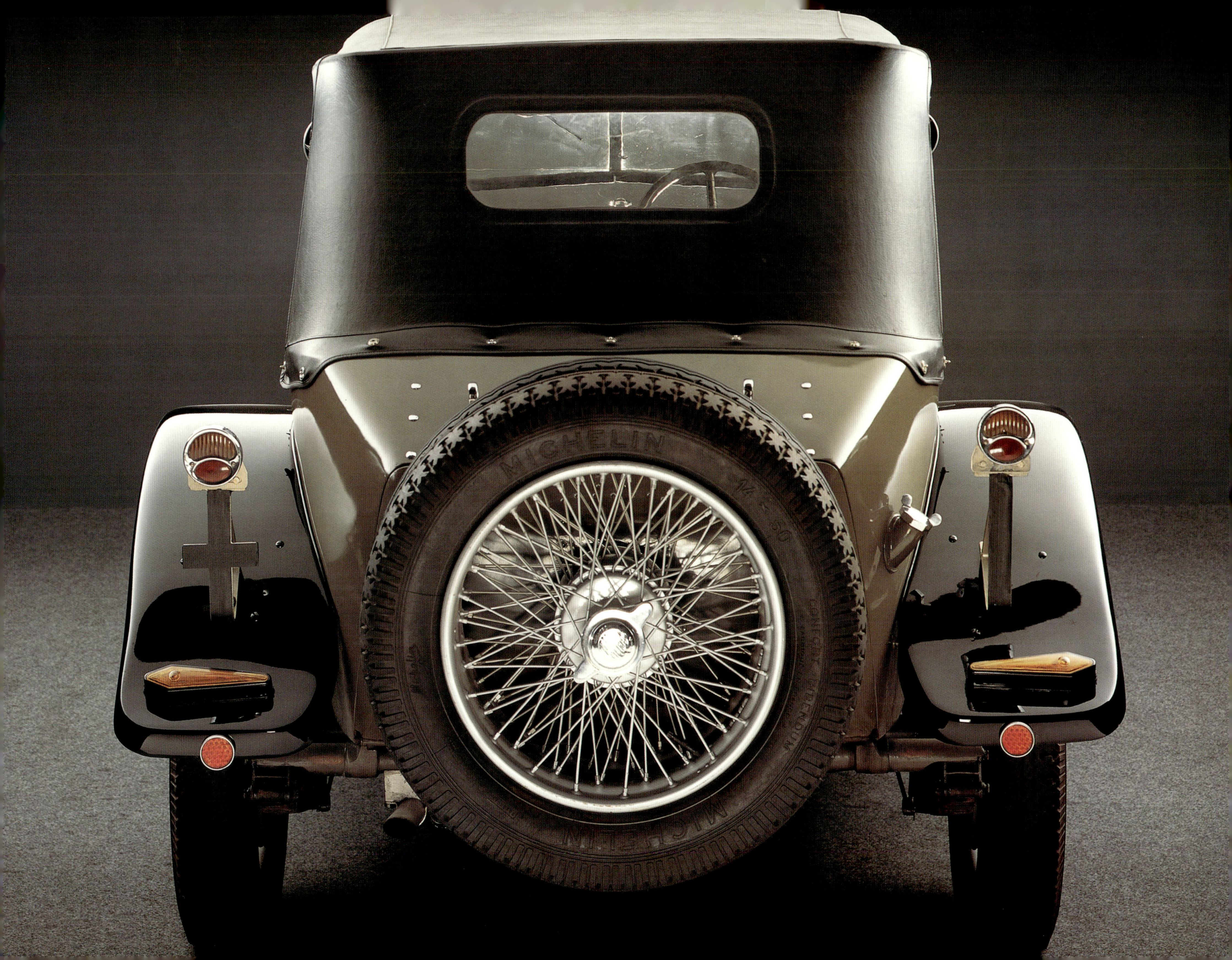
MICHELIN

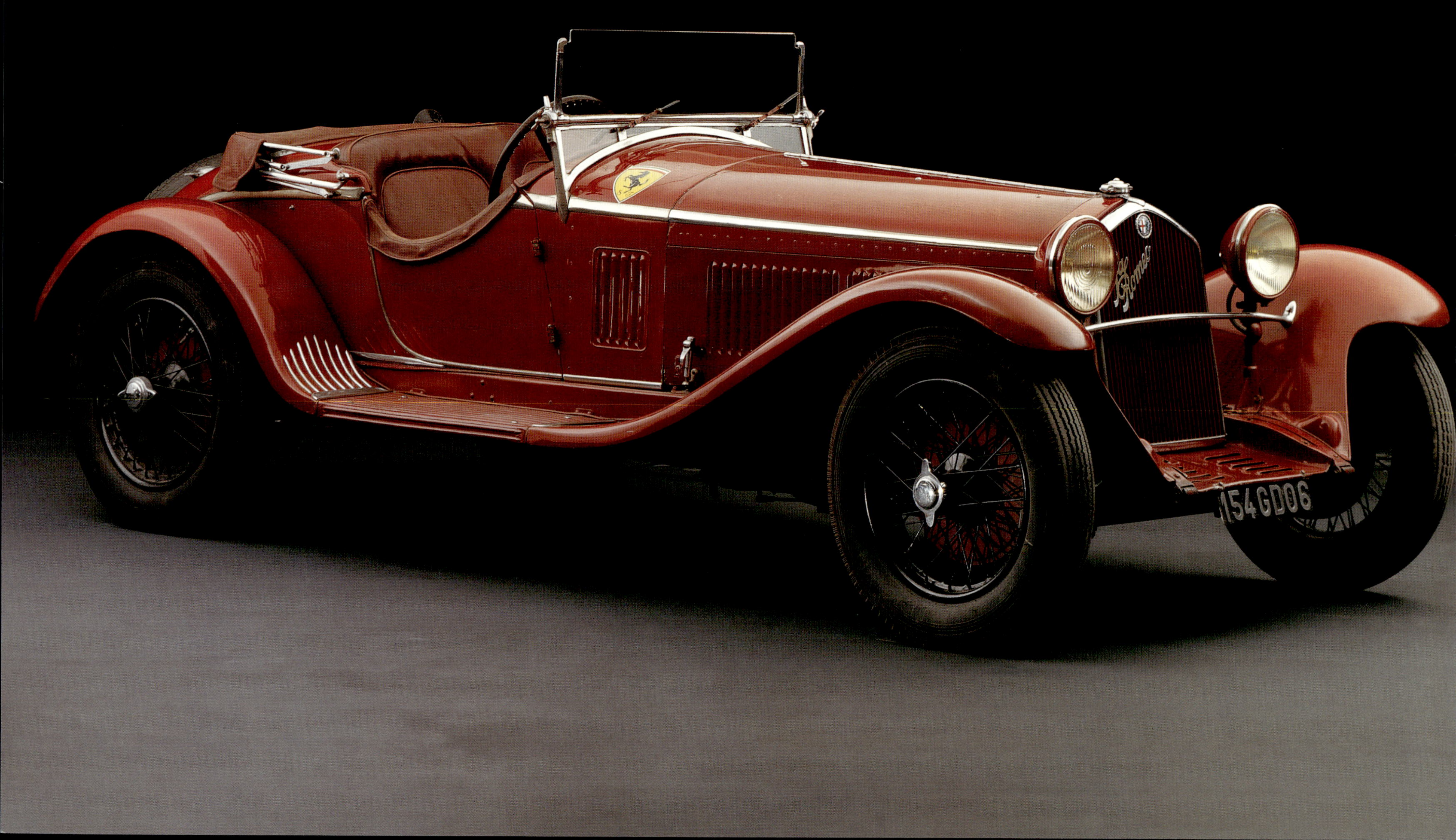
154GD06

1930 ALFA ROMEO 6C 1750

For a marque that has enjoyed many more hits than misses, Alfa Romeo's 6C 1750 is widely considered to be one of the Milan firm's landmark designs. And with good reason. Adept on road or circuit, the car relied on a 1752-cc, twin-cam straight-six that proved remarkably durable yet offered a very impressive output for its meagre capacity. Further benefiting from excellent handling, by the standards of the day, and a pliant ride quality despite its then customary solid axles and cart springs, it remains among the most compelling and desired of all Alfas.

The casting on the Vittorio Jano-conceived engine is jewel-like, not least areas such as the finned intake manifold. Yet it is the outer beauty that remains the major draw. The 6C 1750 is significant for introducing in-house manufactured saloon bodies but these are of minor note compared with those versions produced by external coachbuilders. Firms such as Touring, Castagna and Garavani, along with English company James Young, all clothed chassis, but it was Carrozzeria Zagato that produced the most elegantly proportioned and unfussy offerings.

With a lightweight Zagato body and a supercharged engine, the 6C 1750 could comfortably exceed 161 kph (100 mph). Therefore it was no great surprise that Alfa Romeo conquered the 1929 Mille Miglia, repeating the feat twelve months later, in addition to taking the Targa Florio. These and scores of other wins provided a platform for Mussolini's jingoistic bravado: Il Duce used motor-racing success as nationalistic propaganda.

By 1933, the final year of 6C 1750 production, Alfa Romeo was almost pauperized by the Depression, and staring death in the face. Mussolini nationalized the firm and used it as a springboard to greater competition success, not least victory in the 1935 German Grand Prix against the might of Mercedes-Benz and Auto-Union – under the nose of his ally Adolf Hitler.

With the 6C 1750, Alfa Romeo achieved the rare feat of creating a car that proved itself on both road and track while also showcasing dizzying beauty. It is still lauded as a motoring milestone.

Designed by the brilliant Vittorio Jano, the 6C 1750 was offered with in-house manufactured saloon-car bodies, but it was Zagato's skimpy sports-car outlines that caught the imagination.

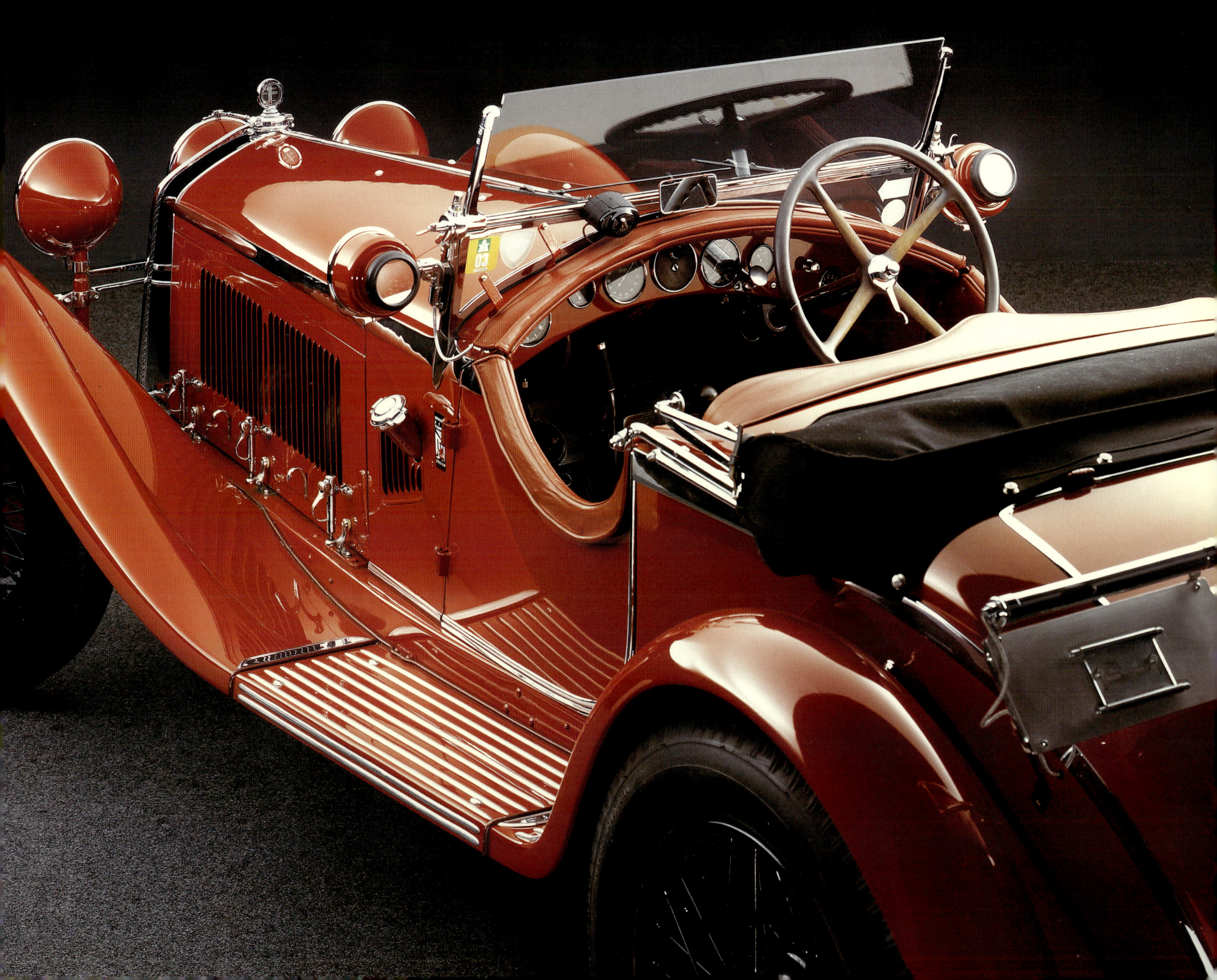

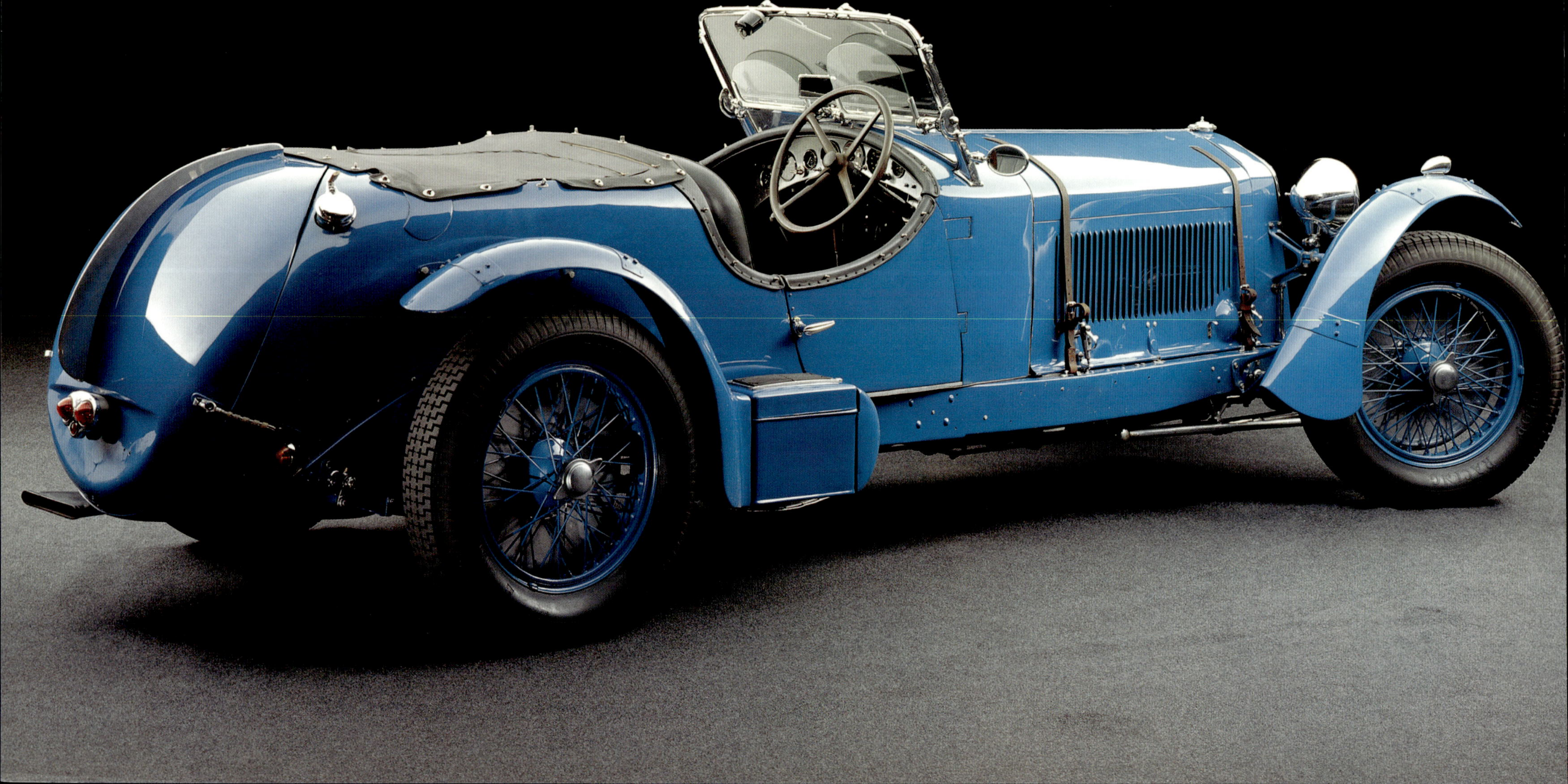

1931 ALFA ROMEO 8C 2300

By the dawn of the 1930s Alfa Romeo had lost its status as the dominant force in motor racing. If the financially straitened firm was to regain its standing, it needed to produce a single design flexible enough to power both sports and outright competition machines. With the success of his six-cylinder sports car behind him, chief designer Vittorio Jano was well up to the task. His 8C engine design borrowed heavily from the 6C but had two extra cylinders, engine blocks being cast in two pairs, separated by a central train of gears that drove a supercharger and twin overhead camshafts.

For grands prix the 8C bore a stumpy 2600-mm (8 ft 8 in.) wheelbase with the sports-car variants built along two wheelbases: the Corto (short) at 2700 mm (9 ft) and the Lungo (long) at 3050 mm (10 ft 2 in.). Aside from its sheer mechanical beauty, the car possessed a slender build enhanced by some of Italy's best *carrozzerie*. Coachwork by Castagna, Touring and Zagato adorned these remarkable machines, the finest example perhaps the last's Spider two-seater on the Corto chassis. With its abbreviated, curved tail embellished with a central spine, angled spare wheel recessed into it, and glorious sweeping wings, this was among the most elegant of all pre-war sports cars.

Jano's design achieved huge success in competition, with triumphs in 1931 in Sicily's Targa Florio road race and the ten-hour Italian Grand Prix at Monza. Britons Tim Birkin and Earl Howe took their long-chassis car to victory in the 1932 Le Mans 24 Hours, setting up the first of four consecutive wins in the endurance classic, while 8Cs also won the Mille Miglia and Spa 24 Hours in 1932 and 1933.

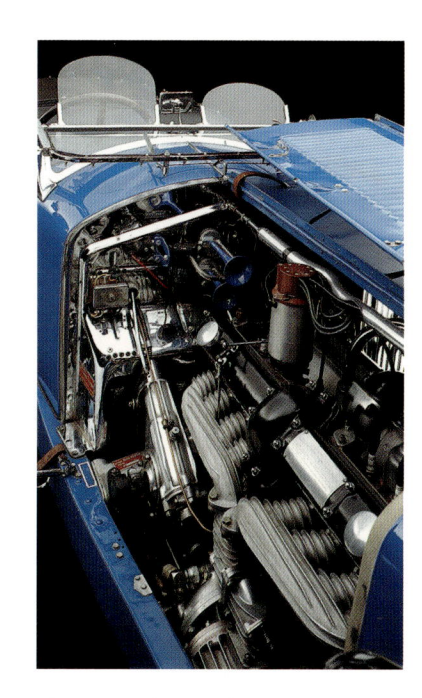

The 8C 2300's supercharged straight-eight engine was a work of art that mirrored the car's outer beauty. This model helped re-establish Alfa Romeo as the dominant force in European motor sport.

60

Functional elegance typifies the 8C 2300. This model vanquished rivals at Le Mans, Spa and in the Mille Miglia thanks to a combination of power, light weight and good handling.

Alfa Romeo 8C 2300   61

1933 MASERATI 8CM

With Alfa Romeo refusing to release its team cars for 'non works' drivers, there was only one choice for patriotic Italian single-seater privateers in the early 1930s: Maserati's 8CM. Conceived as a production racer, it was based on a powerful 245 bhp, 3-litre engine and a strong, four-speed gearbox (including Fiat parts), together contained in a narrow, ladderframe chassis with beam axles front and rear.

This particular car was the first true Maserati *monoposto*, or single-seater. The subsequent run of fourteen further 8CMs became wider and fatter, with a stepped, heavily louvred body and higher cockpit sides. This machine bore a cleaner, more functional elegance, its body being just 525 mm (21 in.) wide. The car's supercharged, twin-cam straight-eight matched the exterior aesthetics, being a legacy of company co-founder Alfieri Maserati, who died in 1932 after an operation to cure five-year-old racing wounds. In principle, this unit dates back to the first Maserati, after ambitious plans involving front-wheel drive and V4 units were dropped.

In theory, 1933 should have been Maserati's year, with Alfa withdrawing its dominant Tipo Bs and new cars from Bugatti and Mercedes-Benz still unfinished. The first two completed 8CMs were sold to Raymond Sommer, the newly appointed Maserati agent for France: this car, 3005, and a second, wider version for Freddie Zehender. Finding the slender car to be beyond even his proven talent, Sommer returned it to the factory, which in turn sold it to the great Tazio Nuvolari, along with a new, sister 8CM. The 'Flying Mantuan' paid 160,000 lire for the pair in July of that year. After finding success with the wider-bodied car, including victory in the Belgian Grand Prix, 3005 was surplus to requirements and sold to Piero Taruffi, the following owner reclothing it as a sports car. This outstanding machine would have to wait until 1988 to be restored to its former glory.

This, the first 8CM racer, differed in detail from its fourteen brothers, being narrower and more elegant. For a time it was owned by Tazio Nuvolari, widely considered to be the greatest racing driver of the immediate pre-war era.

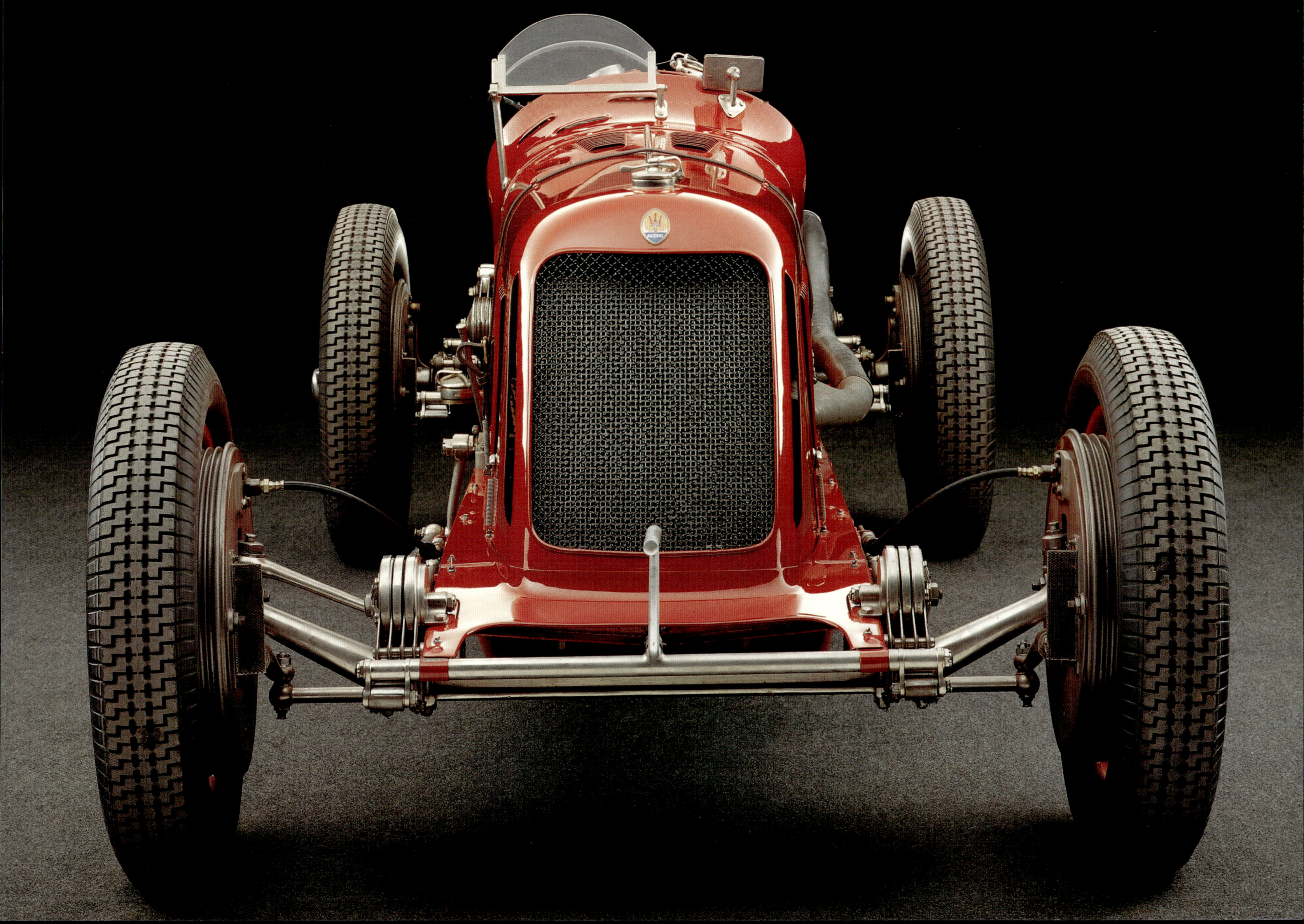

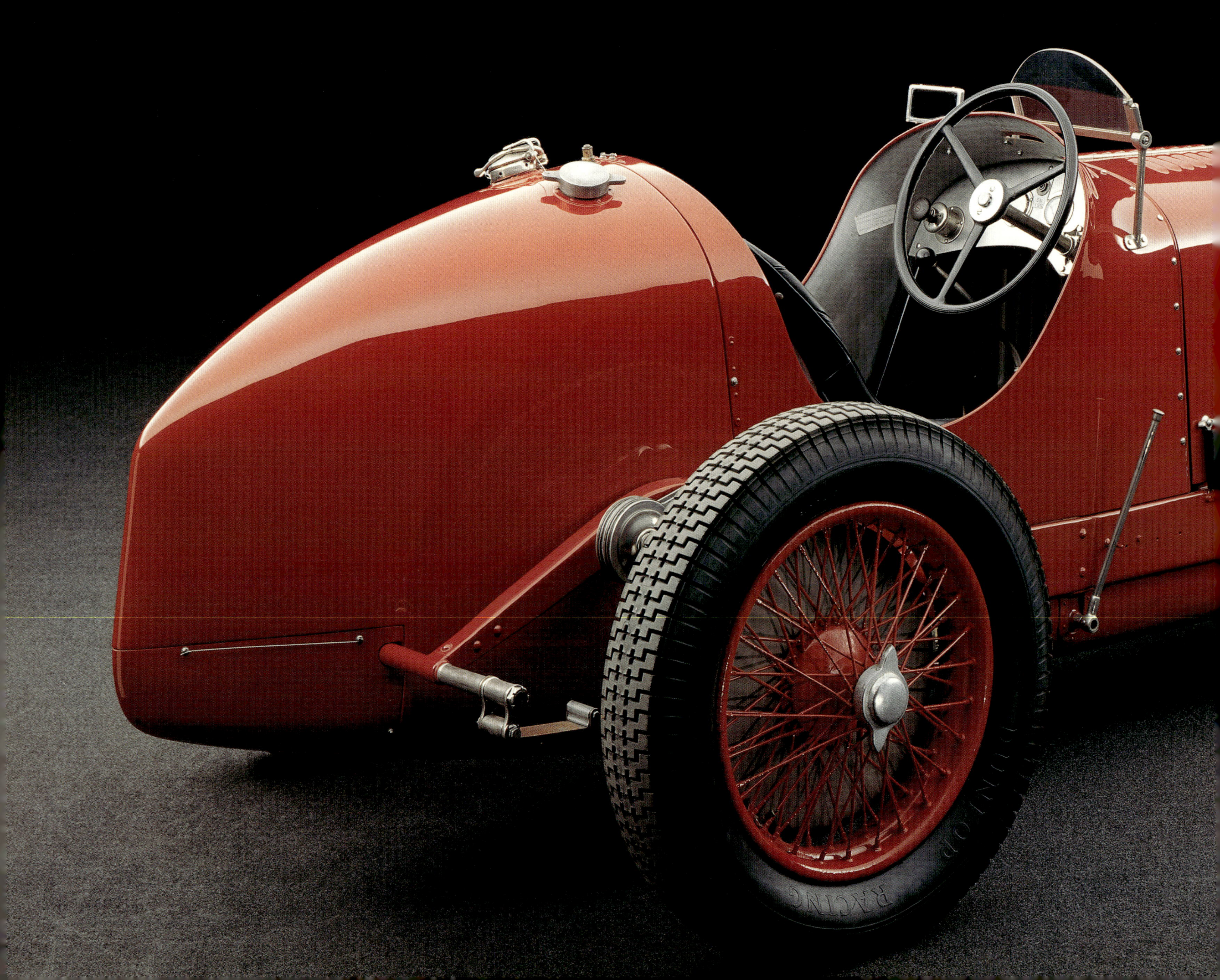
RACING

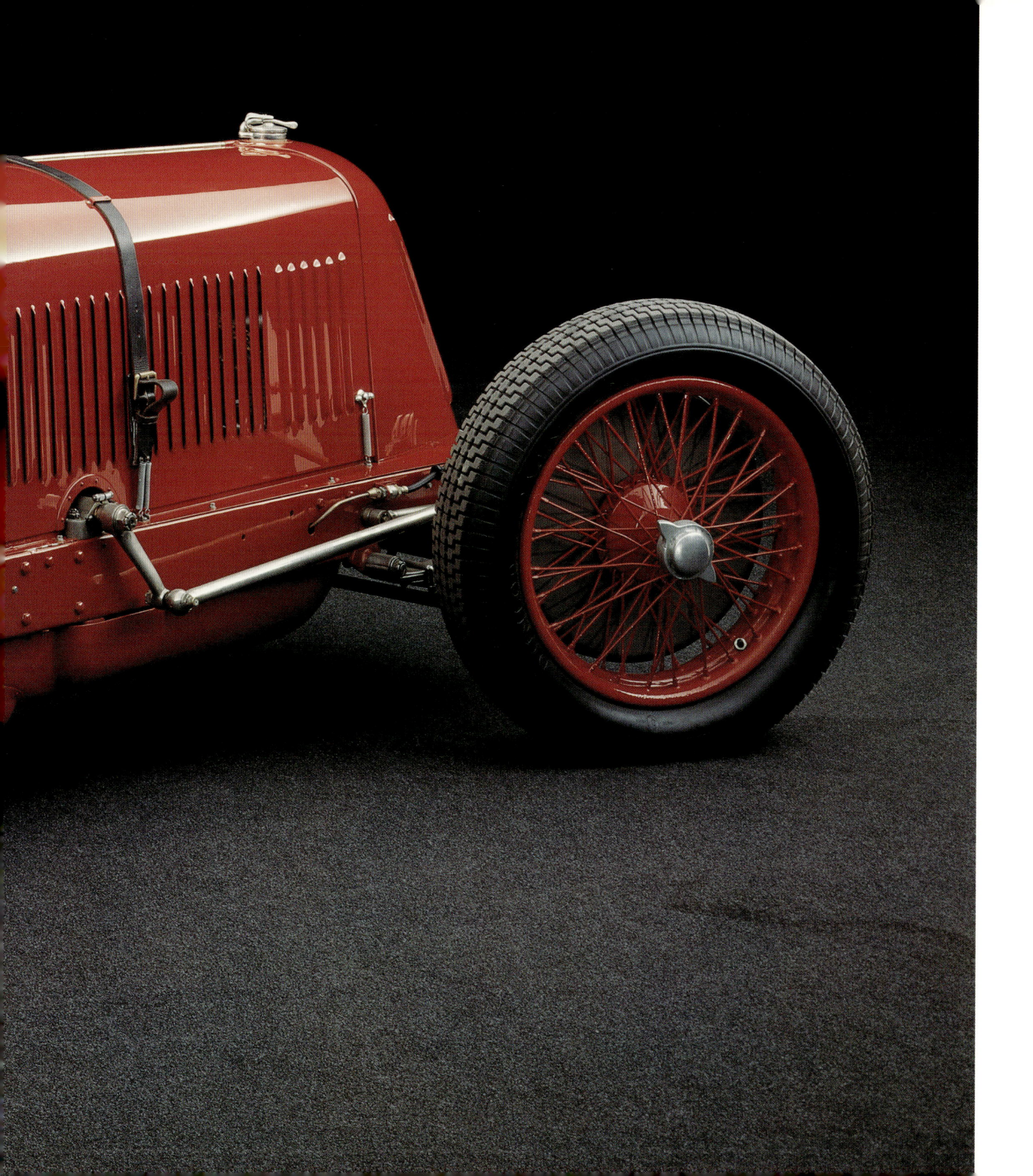

Conceived as a production racing car, the 8CM found success in grands prix but was generally outclassed by better-funded rivals. This example proved tricky to drive and was later reworked as a sports car.

Left: This, the first 8CM, was narrower than its sister cars and better-looking because of it. Sadly, it did not prove particularly competitive despite the efforts of many of the greatest drivers of the era.

Opposite: This 8CM featured a lower, more sculptured cabin aperture than other Maseratis of the day as well as fewer bonnet louvres.

Maserati 8CM 67

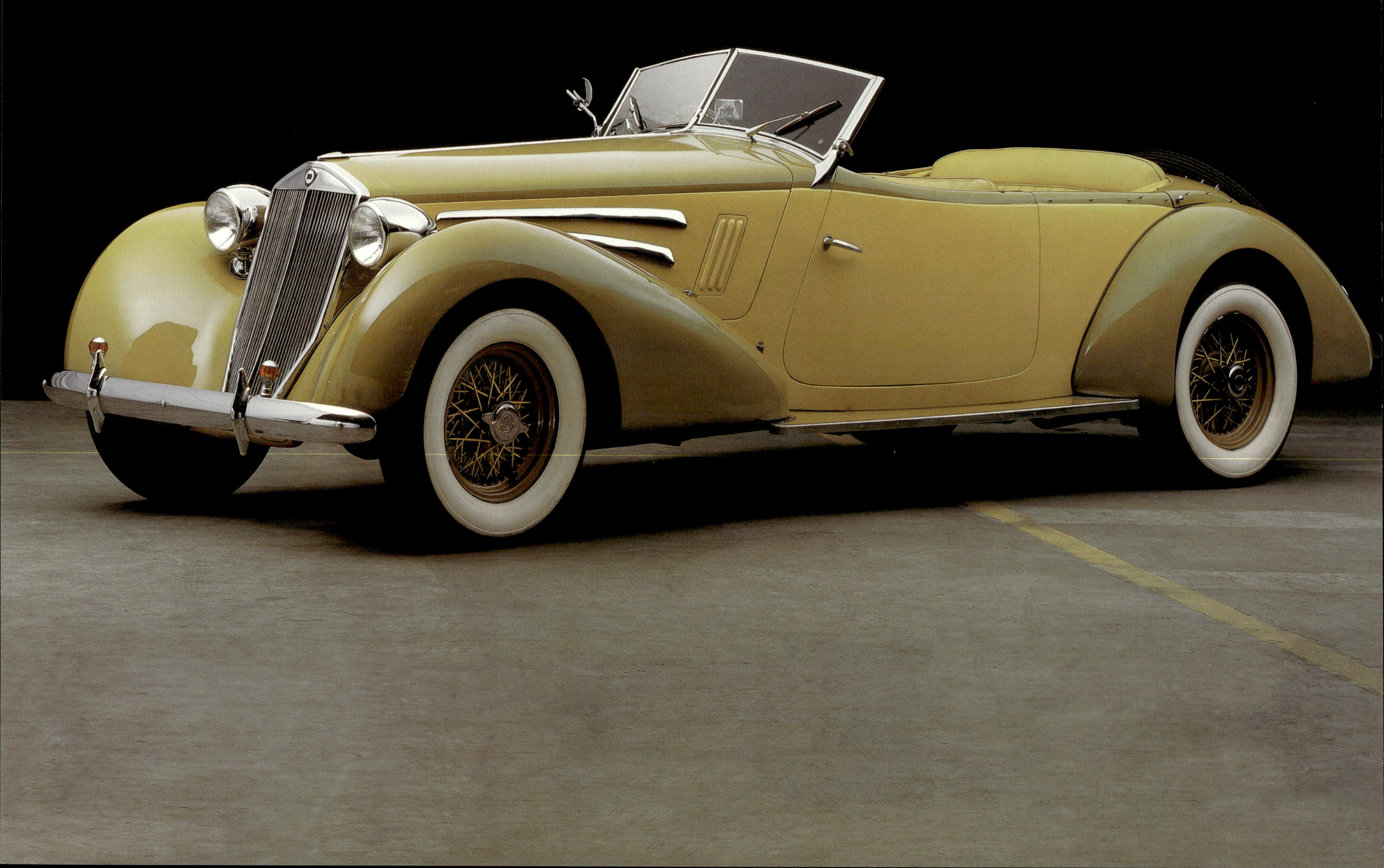

1935 LANCIA ASTURA

Replacing the Lambda was always going to be a tough challenge, so Lancia succeeded it with two cars: the Artena and the Astura, named after an Italian town and castle, respectively. The first was conceived as a relatively cheap production car, the second as a more luxurious variation. But, although they shared the same basic architecture, the Astura had eight cylinders, four more than its sibling.

Underpinning the Astura was a neat and simple box-section chassis, ease and affordability of construction being paramount in the austere early 1930s. Front suspension was provided by Lancia's patented sliding-pillar arrangement; at the rear a live axle was suspended by semi-elliptical springs and friction dampers. The remarkably compact 2604-cc engine developed 73 bhp, which ensured the relatively lightweight Astura's lively performance: the bare chassis weighed 960 kg (2116 lb) and, with a factory-fitted body, just 1250 kg (2756 lb).

The highlight of the coachbuilt Astura era would be the arrival of the third-series edition in 1933, two years after the first model was introduced. A choice of wheelbases was offered – 3140 mm (10 ft 4 in.) Lungo (long) or 2950 mm (9 ft 4 in.) Corto (short) – and engine capacity was boosted to 2972 cc, giving an additional 10 bhp. In addition, local *carrozzerie* produced some of the most attractive outlines that old-style body-building had yet seen. Pinin Farina, the firm founded by Battista 'Pinin' Farina, enjoyed a particularly close relationship with the marque that resulted in some exceptionally elegant coupés and cabriolets. Yet the Astura's allure spread outside Italy's borders, with Weinberger and Bühne bodying cars in Germany and John Charles, Abbott and Kevill-Davies & March doing likewise in Great Britain.

By 1937 the Astura had morphed into a virtually new car, although the engine, transmission and axles remained unchanged. It now had a still longer wheelbase, prompting most local coachbuilders to look to America for inspiration. The result was some fabulously overblown creations that contrasted greatly with the clean-cut elegance of only a few years before.

With the Astura, Lancia created a lightweight and compact car that was a favourite with European coachbuilders, whose output became increasingly overblown as the 1930s grew to a close.

A bulbous wing design and narrow grille lend this Astura a rakish air. This much-loved Lancia was a favourite with European coachbuilders.

Moderate use of chrome only served to highlight the perfect proportions of the four-seater tourer. As was typical at the time, the front doors were hinged at the rear.

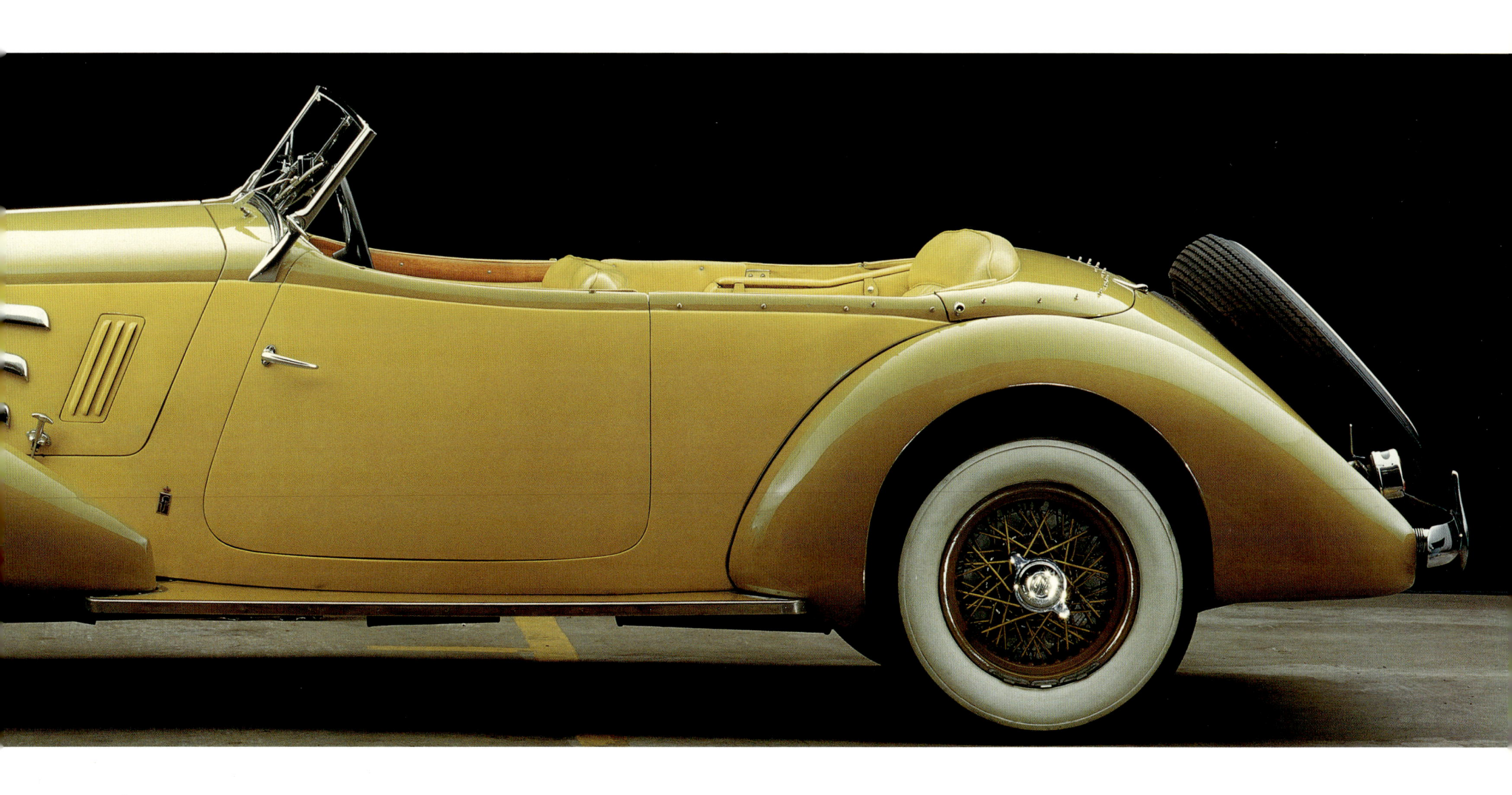

Lancia Astura

1936 FIAT 500 TOPOLINO

Conceived to bring motoring to the Italian masses, the Fiat 500, or Topolino, was the smallest mass-produced car on sale when launched in 1936. Derived from a concept by Antonio Fessia, and fashioned by engineering genius Dante Giacosa, it was an instant success, the formula consisting of two seats and a 13-bhp, 596-cc, air-cooled, two-cylinder engine within a pretty eggshell-style body. There were few concessions to luxury: just a functional elegance that set the template for subsequent baby Fiats.

The first iteration remained in production until 1948, by which time around 122,000 had been made. Outwardly, its 500B replacement appeared largely unchanged, but there were minor alterations beneath the skin. The engine received an increase in power of 3.5 bhp, while the suspension, brakes and electrical equipment were uprated to counter earlier criticisms. That same year a four-seater estate version – marketed as the Giardiniera or Belvedere, according mainly to the degree of trim – was introduced with a longer steel and wood hull.

A year later the 500C was unveiled at the Geneva Salon, the engine having received a new aluminium cylinder head, although power output remained as before, while outer changes were mainly cosmetic: a new, boxier front end replaced the curvy original, to the car's detriment. Some 376,370 were made to 1955.

More than anything, the 500 helped mobilize Italy like no other vehicle, save perhaps the Vespa scooter. It also provided a welcome boost for local small-scale car manufacturers such as Siata, Ermini and Stanguellini, all of which used its running gear with varying degrees of success. Unwittingly, the 500 also helped end Italian dominance in 1950s grand-prix racing. *Garagistes* John and Charles Cooper, based in Surbiton, Surrey, used Fiat suspension on their Formula Three cars in the late 1940s. By the end of the following decade they had broken Ferrari's and Maserati's stranglehold on Formula One.

With the Topolino, Fiat succeeded in mobilizing Italy. At last there was a cheap, small car for the masses, and it set the template for future baby Fiats.

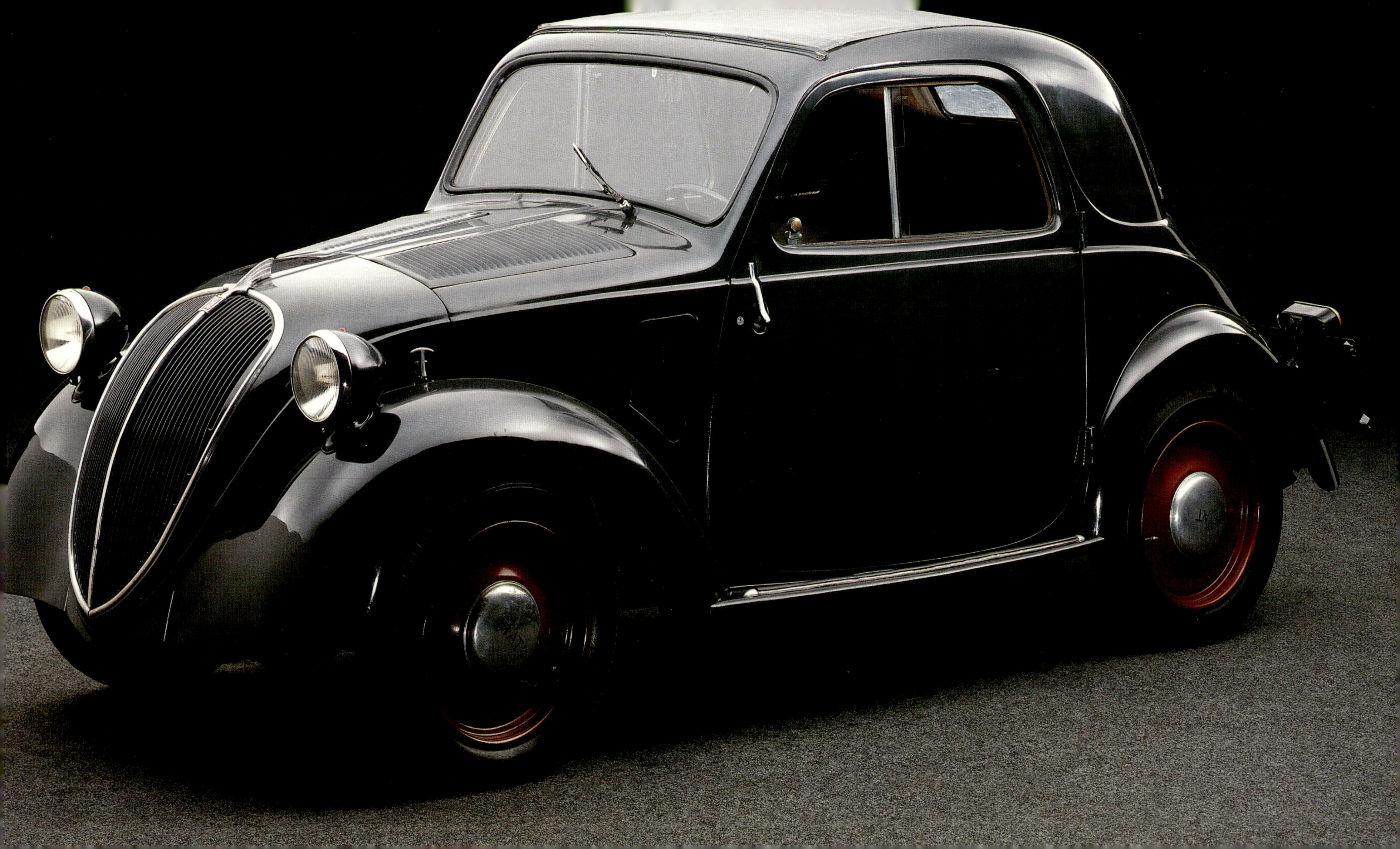

Nicknamed 'Mickey Mouse' by locals, the baby 500 was cute but tough. It had to be to cope with some areas of Italy where roads were a stranger to asphalt.

When the roof was folded down for *al fresco* fun, the steel side members maintained structural rigidity. The 500 was also available as an estate car.

Fiat 500 Topolino

Left: The Topolino's tiny 596-cc, air-cooled, two-cylinder engine produced a meagre 13 bhp. This was the smallest mass-produced car on sale in 1936.

Opposite: No concessions to luxury here. Inside, the cabin was stark to the point of austerity.

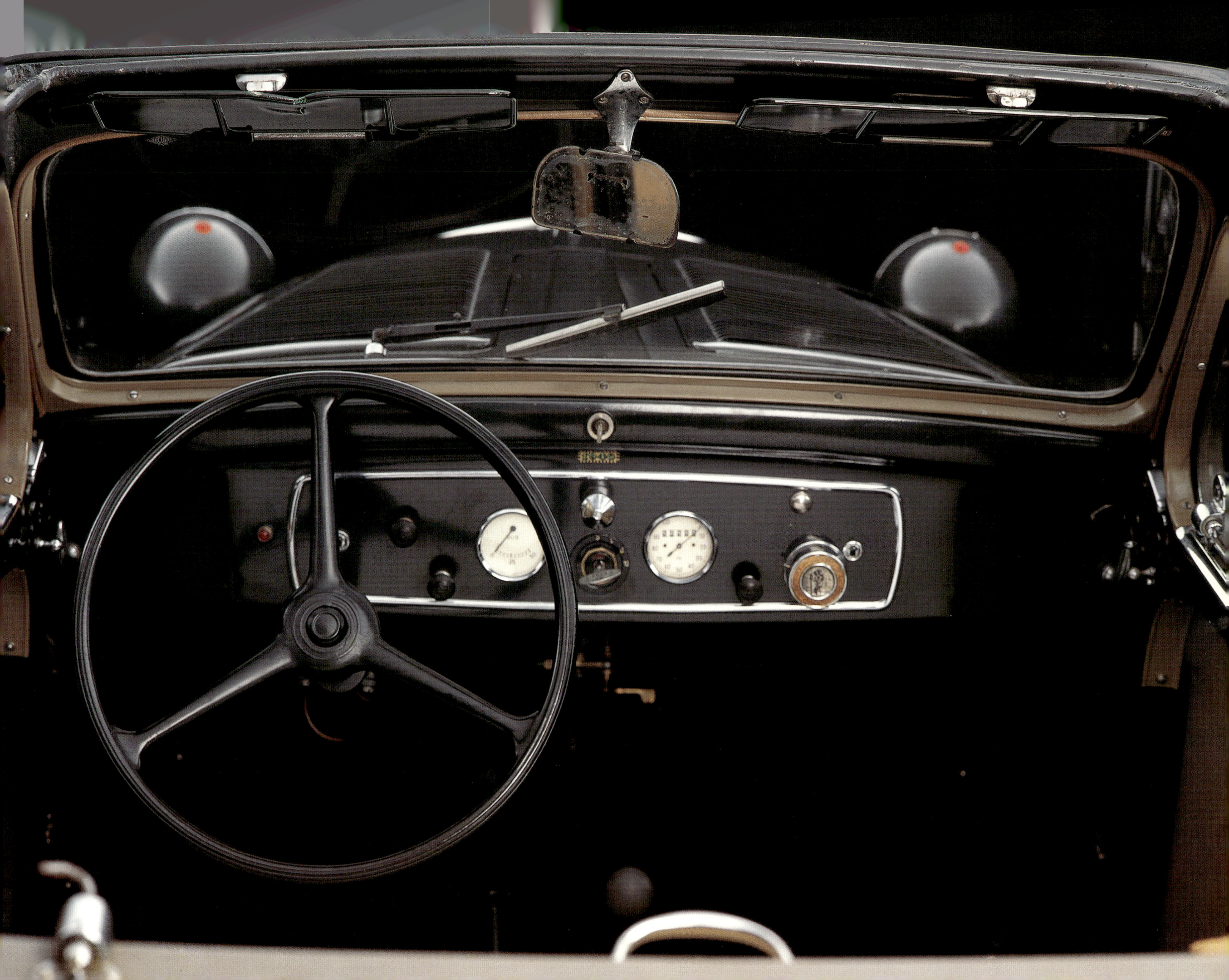

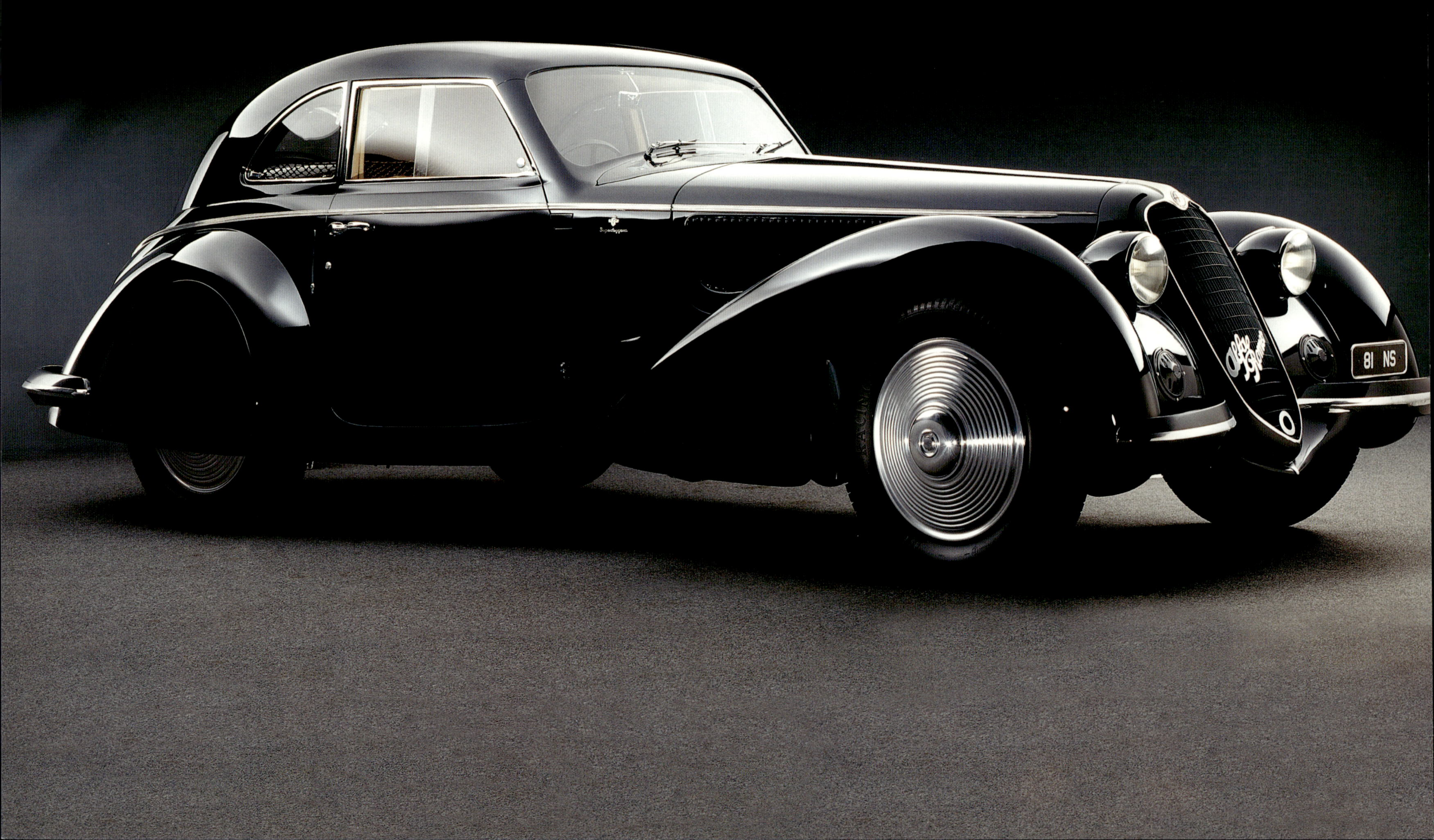
81 NS

1938 ALFA ROMEO 8C 2900

Given that it won the Mille Miglia four times, Alfa Romeo's 8C 2900 deserves veneration, yet this still sells short the dream car of the 1930s and early 1940s. The model's matchless competition pedigree is only part of the package. Marrying giddying beauty with technological advancement, this was the fastest production car built before the Second World War, with a top speed of at least 209 kph (130 mph) and sometimes, depending on the configuration of engine tuning and bodywork, considerably more.

Providing this mighty performance was a 2905-cc, straight-eight conceived by Vittorio Jano and sharing a direct lineage with Alfa's grand-prix cars. Of all-aluminium construction with twin overhead camshafts, this advanced unit was effectively two four-cylinder blocks on a common crankcase with twin Rootes-type superchargers primed to produce 75 bhp per litre: a respectable figure for cars sixty years its junior.

Sophisticated running gear lay behind the 2900's reputation as one of the best-handling cars of its period. At a time when independent front suspension was still considered unusual, to have it at the rear was truly remarkable. A rear-mounted four-speed transaxle gave near-perfect weight distribution, while aluminium brake drums aided the causes of unsprung weight and brake cooling.

Priced at £2000 – before a coachbuilder clothed the chassis – the car, unsurprisingly, attracted royalty, Prince Bernhard of The Netherlands and King Carol of Romania being among owners. Just forty-three were built, including seven Touring-bodied Berlinetta coupés, one of which was driven to victory in the first post-war Mille Miglia in 1947 by Emilio Romano and Clemente Biondetti, nine years after their car was built. The model was still competitive in the following decade, with future Formula One World Champion Phil Hill establishing his credentials with successes on America's west coast in 1951.

Regarded by many as the greatest pre-war sports car, Alfa Romeo's sublime 8C 2900 bore grand-prix levels of technology and performance. Of the forty-three cars built, just seven wore Touring coupé bodies, as here.

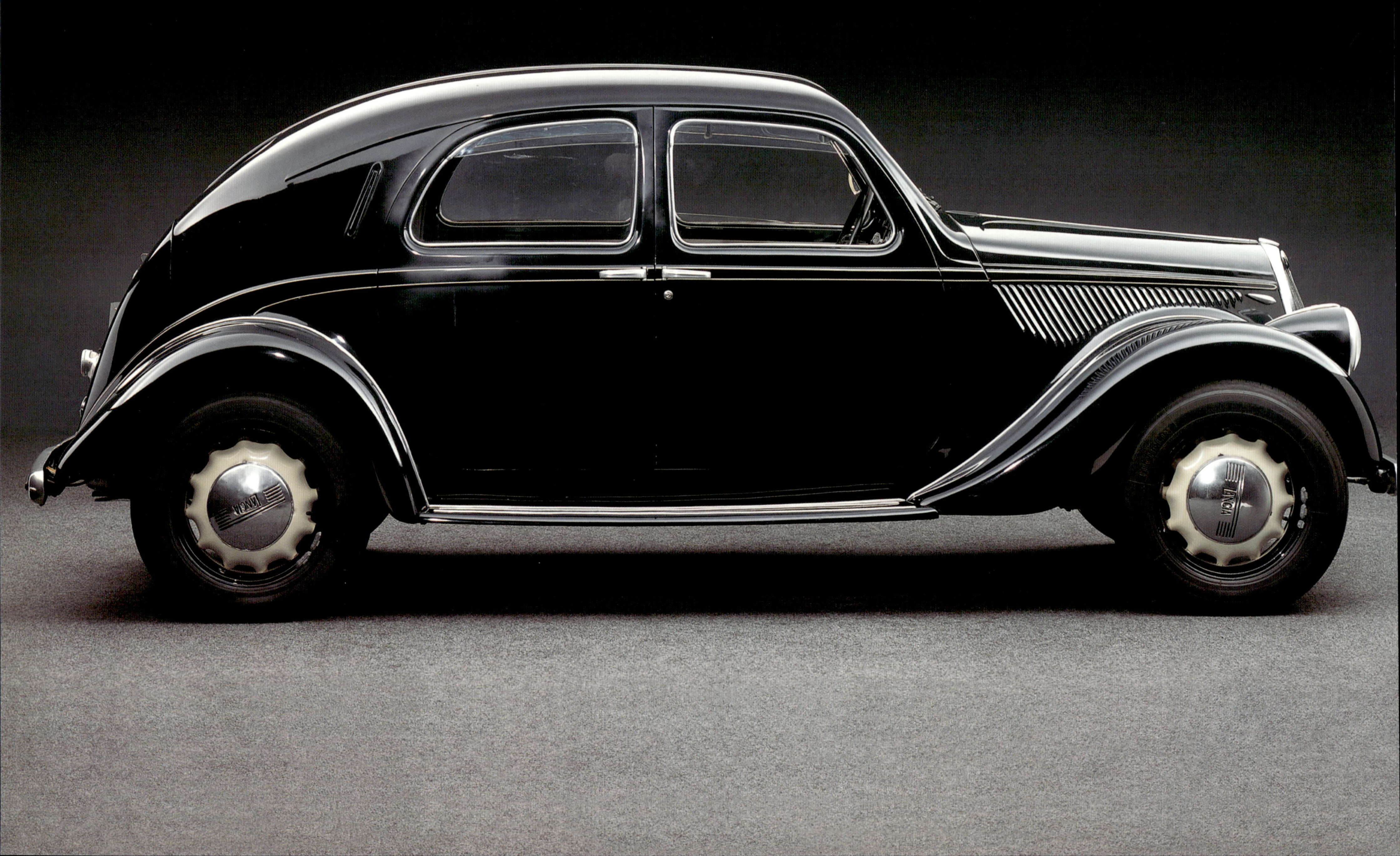

1938 LANCIA APRILIA

With a specification that would humble most sports cars of the day, Lancia's inspiring Aprilia sustained the company's reputation for innovation and class superiority. Arguably the ultimate representation of pre-war small-car engineering, the original concept was even more radical: a teardrop outline with the driver placed in the middle with one passenger either side and a third housed in the tapered rear. Although the design was patented in 1934, Vincenzo Lancia dismissed the idea, concerned about customer resistance. Instead, he placed emphasis on seating for five, compact dimensions, unitary construction and efficient aerodynamics.

In a close collaboration between the firm and the Polytechnic of Turin, the car's pillarless body was honed in a wind tunnel, recording a drag coefficient of 0.47: a remarkably low figure in the 1930s. Nothing was allowed to interrupt the airflow: Lancia went as far as demanding the door hinges be concealed, causing much consternation within his engineering department. Refinement was key, and even the ever-critical Vincenzo was moved to exclaim, "What a fantastic car!" during the first test in 1936, from Turin to Bologna, having sat in silence for much of the trip.

Others thought the same when the Aprilia was shown at the Paris and London Motor Shows later that year. In its category, nothing came close in packaging or quality to this car, with its 1352-cc (later 1486-cc) V4 engine, four-speed gearbox and all-independent suspension. At £330 it was not cheap, but it swiftly built a loyal clientele in the UK and at home.

More than 27,600 Aprilias were made before production ceased in 1949. Sadly, Vincenzo Lancia was not around to witness his masterwork enter production. A workaholic, he refused to listen to his doctor's advice to slow down and suffered a fatal heart attack in 1937, aged fifty-six.

The pared-back functionality of the Aprilia's dashboard is in keeping with this fabulous car's rational design ethos. The baby Lancia was better made and more innovative than most cars of the day, regardless of class or cost.

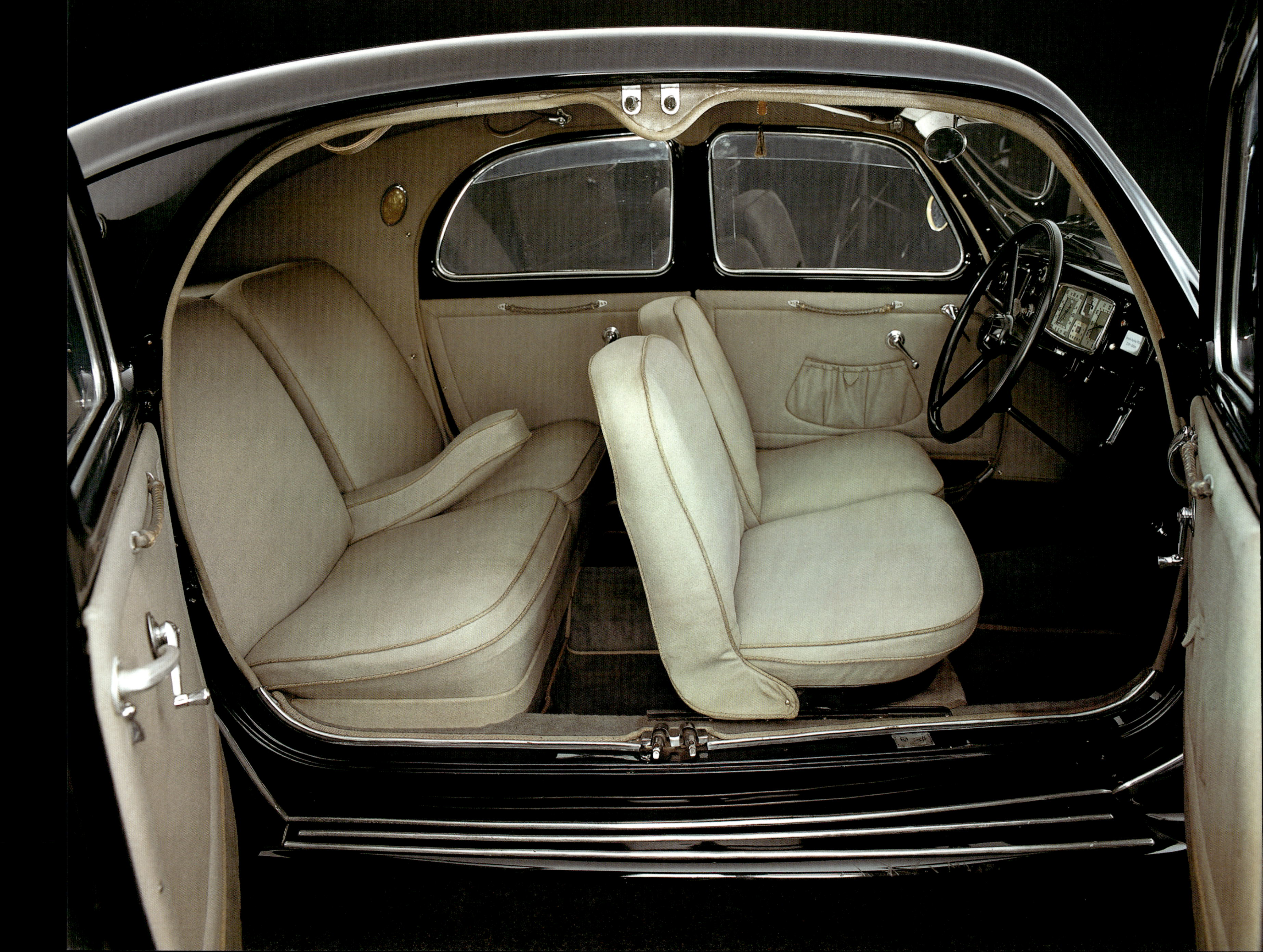

Opposite: Despite its small dimensions, the Aprilia's airy cabin could seat four in complete comfort. The lack of central door pillars made for easy access.

Right: As was once atypical for Lancia, the Aprilia featured a V4 engine that, despite its meagre output, punched above its weight in its category.

Lancia Aprilia   83

The Aprilia's narrow, tapering tail restricted its luggage capacity – a situation not helped by the fact that the spare wheel took up so much room.

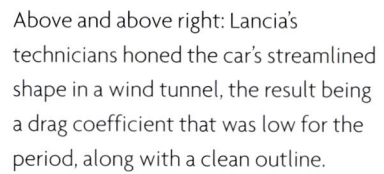

Above and above right: Lancia's technicians honed the car's streamlined shape in a wind tunnel, the result being a drag coefficient that was low for the period, along with a clean outline.

Lancia Aprilia

1939 ALFA ROMEO 6C 2500

Mussolini was a customer, as was half the Italian elite. When bodied by Carrozzeria Touring, Alfa Romeo's striking 6C 2500 was a masterpiece of the coachbuilder's art. This trendsetter's clean lines provided inspiration for generations of automotive designers even if the model's arrival in 1939 meant that its best years were lost to the Second World War.

With its lightweight, twin-cam, straight-six – the ultimate evolution of Vittorio Jano's masterwork that dated back to the 6C 1750 – and fully independent suspension, the 6C 2500 had a modern character that highlighted the disparity between high-end exotica and more mainstream offerings. Initially two versions were offered: one had soberly attractive bodywork produced in-house under the Turismo banner, but Alfa wisely produced a shorter-wheelbase (by 250 mm/10 in.) Sport variation that swiftly proved attractive to the smaller body shops.

Milan-based *carrozzeria* Touring was closely linked with the 6C 2500 from its inception and produced a four-seater berlinetta with plump rear wings that practically enshrouded the rear wheels and a cabriolet version that featured in Alfa Romeo's factory-model line-up. Both editions were hallmarked by streamlined frontal treatments, with headlights incorporated into the bodywork between the wings and radiator grille.

During the war years Alfa Romeo was not entirely dormant, although much of its tooling was melted down to make aeroplane engines and military jeeps. Enough spare parts survived to build further cars once hostilities ended but Italy was more in need of domestic gas stoves than expensive road cars. What remained of Alfa Romeo's Portello factory in Milan after Allied bombing was largely turned over to civilian needs. Touring bodied its last Sport chassis in 1948, although Turin-based rival Pinin Farina persisted with the 6C 2500 until the model was dropped in 1953.

Touring's understanding of streamlining ensured that its take on the 6C 2500 bore few extraneous styling trinkets that would interrupt airflow. The same basic design was reworked on other proprietary chassis.

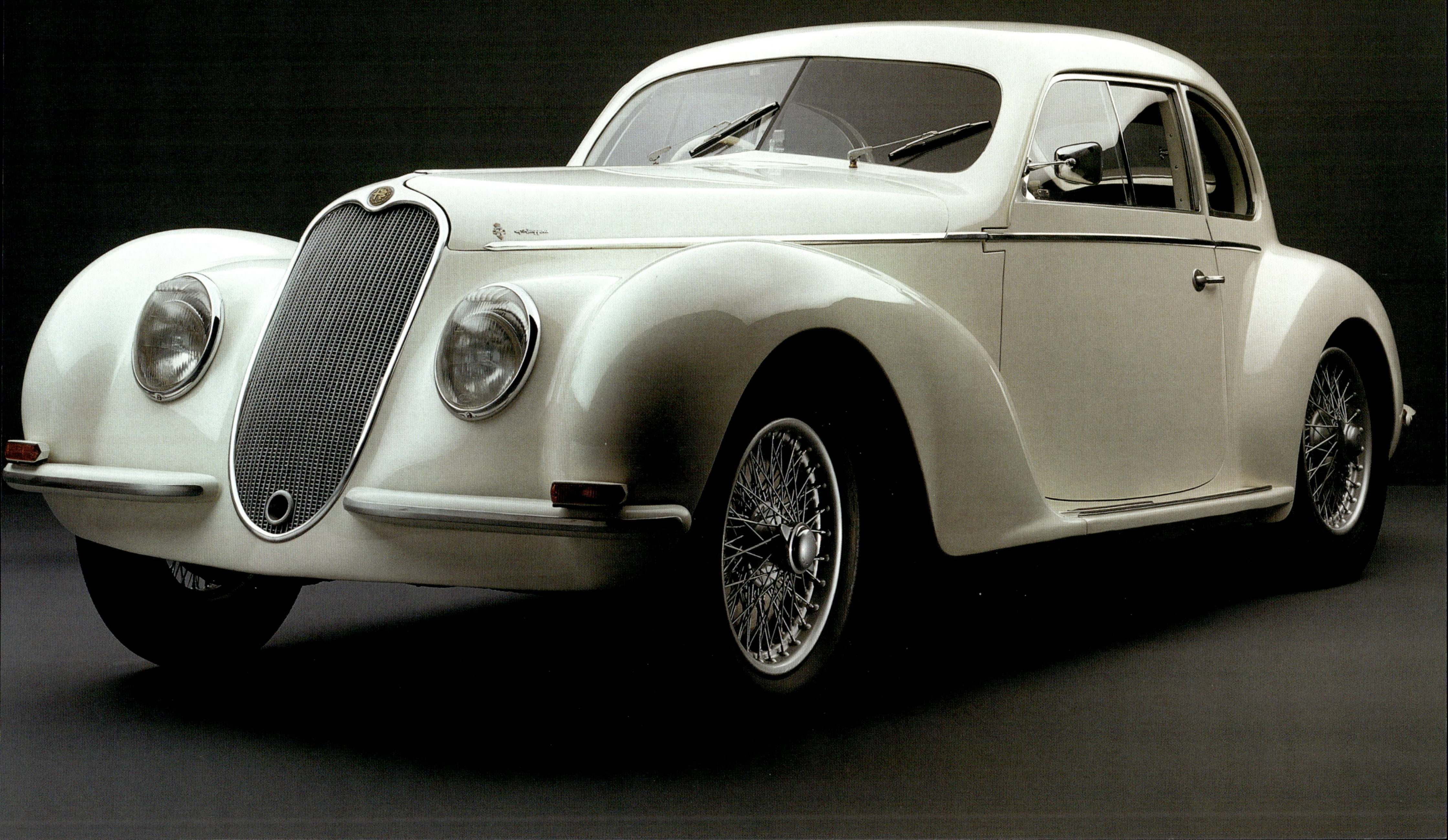

A true GT before the term was widely adopted, the Touring-bodied 8C had an outer beauty that was mirrored by the uncluttered cabin.

Alfa Romeo 6C 2500

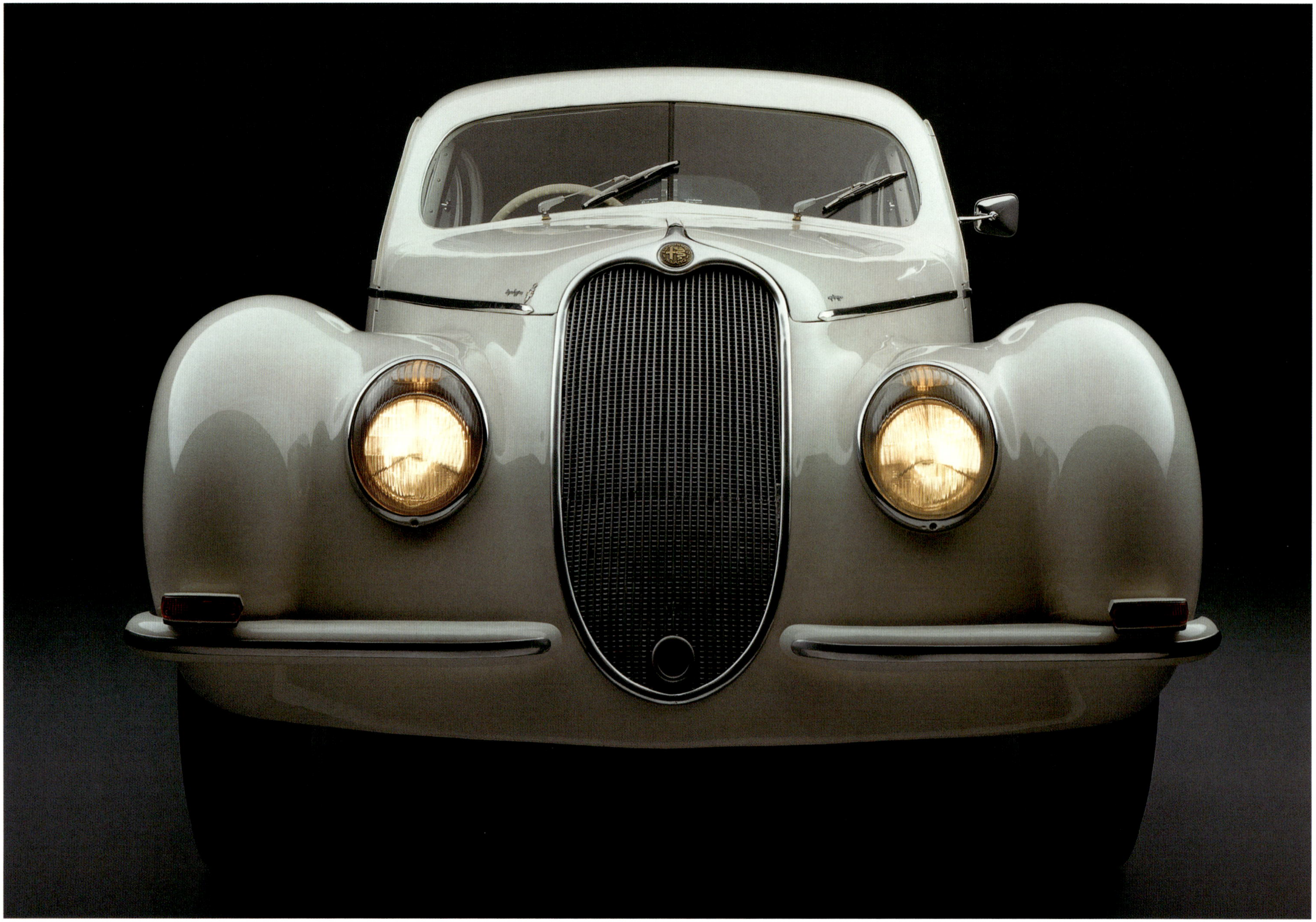

Opposite: Faired-in headlights were one of many distinctive design features that lent the Touring 8C an air of modernity.

Right: The small rear window ensured that rearward visibility was not one of the 8C's strong suits.

Alfa Romeo 6C 2500

1947 CISITALIA 202

It may have proved an unmitigated commercial disaster, but the world's motoring press was agog when Cisitalia launched the 202 in 1947. Arbiters of beauty were sent into rapture and this masterpiece of automotive design became the first car to be displayed at New York's Museum of Modern Art. Yet only 170 – including prototypes and racing cars – were ever made.

Consorzio Industriale Sportive Italia, or Cisitalia, was formed in 1939 by Piero Dusio, a former soccer star who spent the war years making uniforms for the Italian army, amassing a fortune in the process. Once hostilities were over he conceived a small racing car, the D46, using proprietary Fiat running gear. Although his original intention to create a race series for the model was unfulfilled, this single-seater proved modestly successful in local-level motor sport, also serving as a basis for a new sports-racing car that ran in the 1947 Mille Miglia, driven to second place overall by the great Tazio Nuvolari.

Of spaceframe construction – a world first – and with a body designed by aerodynamicist Giovanni Savonuzzi, the sports-racer spawned the 202 road car that same year. Turin's Pinin Farina reworked the styling, widening the rear roof section and adding vestigial tail fins, with Alfredo Vignale and Stabilimenti Farina building production coupés, later known as the Gran Sport. The former also designed a Spider variant, the 202SC, although these were built by smaller *carrozzerie*.

Sadly, Dusio overreached himself. Commissioning a grand-prix challenger from Dr Ferry Porsche left him in poverty, prompting relocation to Argentina, where he tried to reverse his fortunes with cars based on Willys Jeep chassis while retaining the Cisitalia name. At home the marque soldiered on under new ownership, although the 202 failed to find a proper foothold in the sports-car market because of its price. For what was essentially a 1.1-litre Fiat special, it lacked pace to stay with the Jaguar XK120, which cost half as much. The model lingered on until 1952, with future Cisitalias finding few takers.

Despite their outer glamour, Cisitalias made do with altogether more commonplace Fiat power.

Opposite: In the immediate post-war years Cisitalia threw the automotive world into a headspin with its daring designs. Many styling features from these hand-built sports cars were appropriated by rival manufacturers.

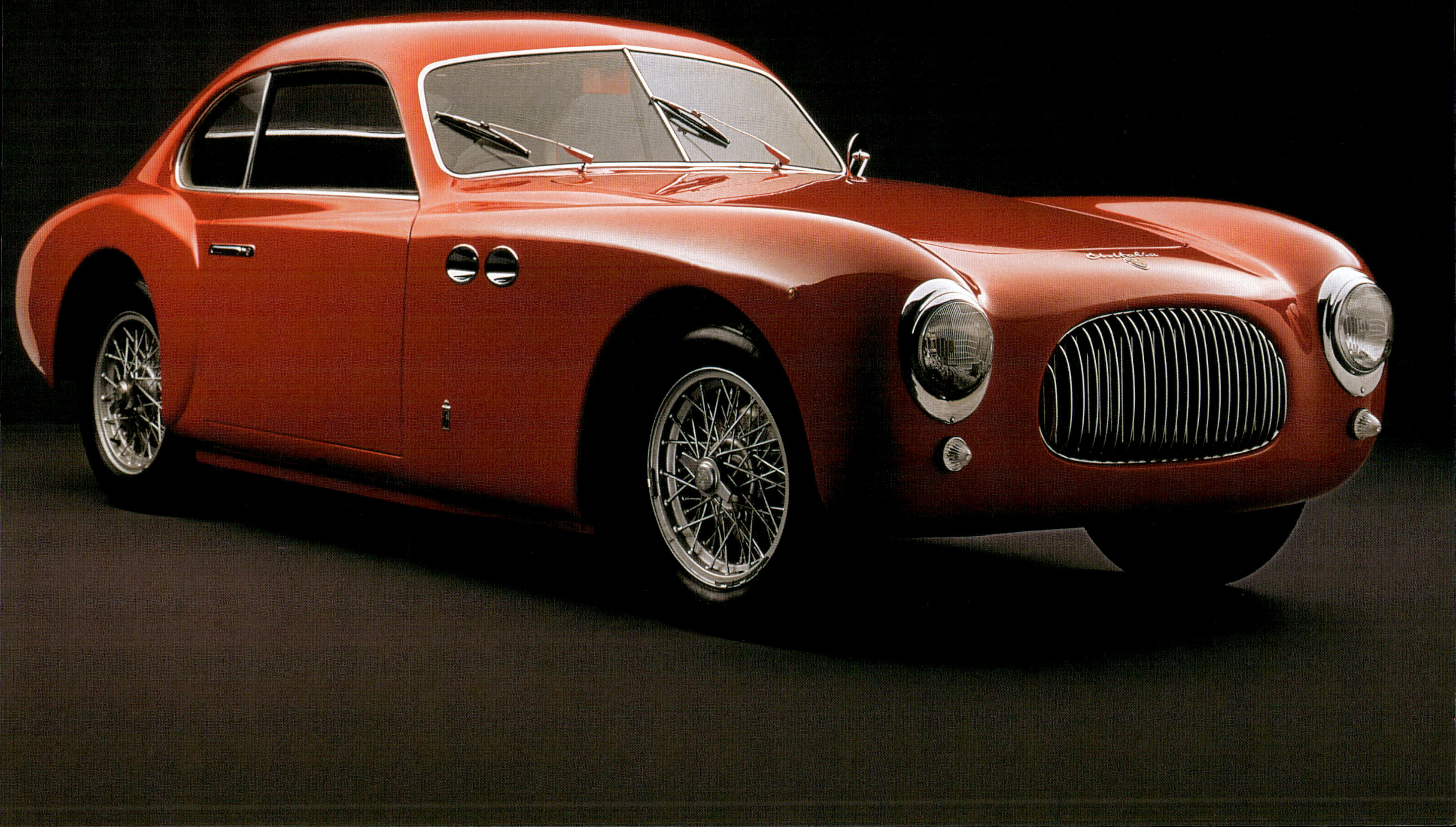

All-enveloping bodywork set the Cisitalia apart from the products of other small-scale Italian manufacturers. The car's radical styling was as much the result of rational thought as of artistic abstraction.

Cisitalia made an instant impression with this ultra-modern-looking sports-racer with its body designed by an aerodynamicist.

Vestigial tail fins were not the expression of a spirit of whimsy, as on many of the Cisitalia's American contemporaries. Here they were integral to maintaining airflow and stability.

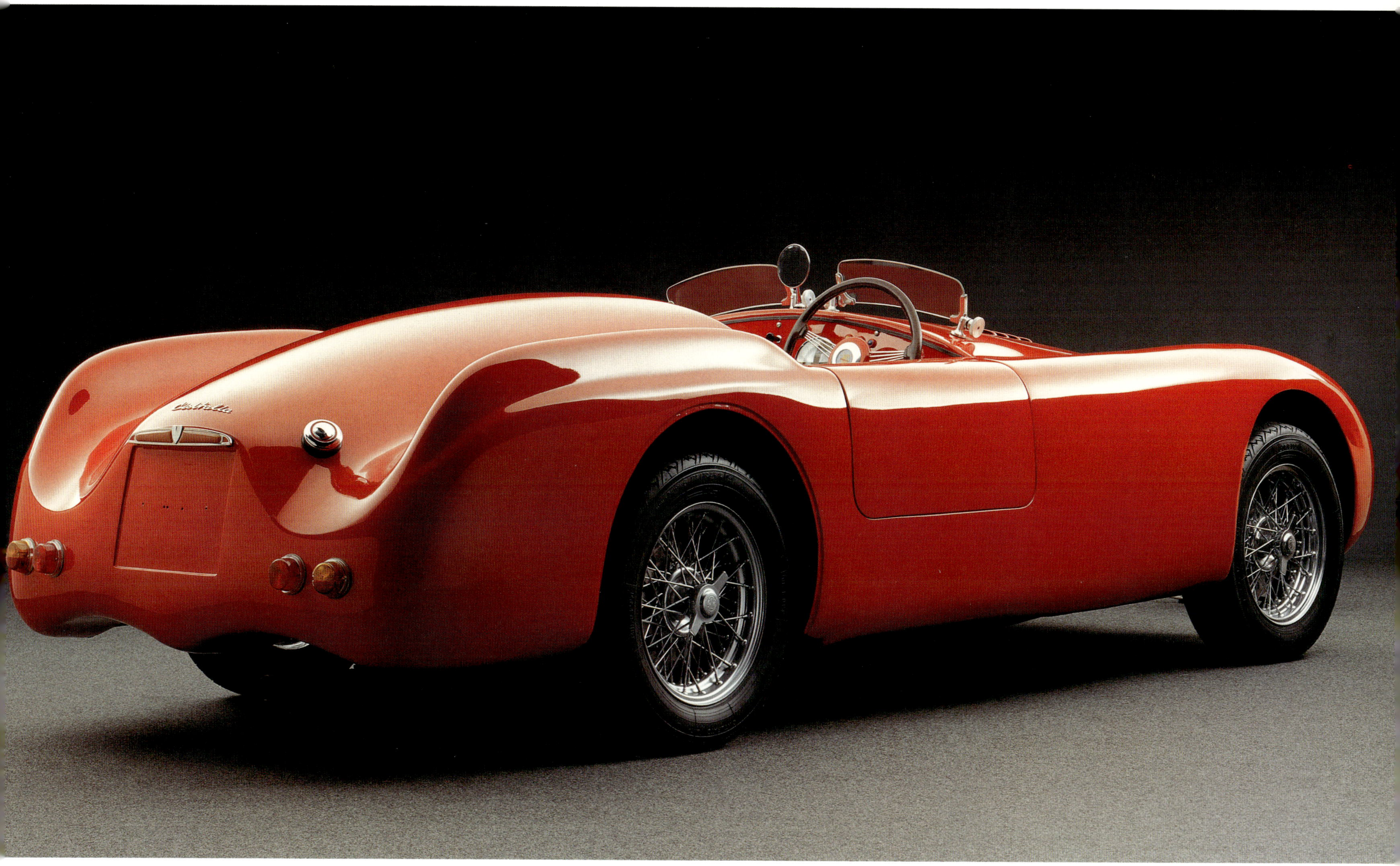

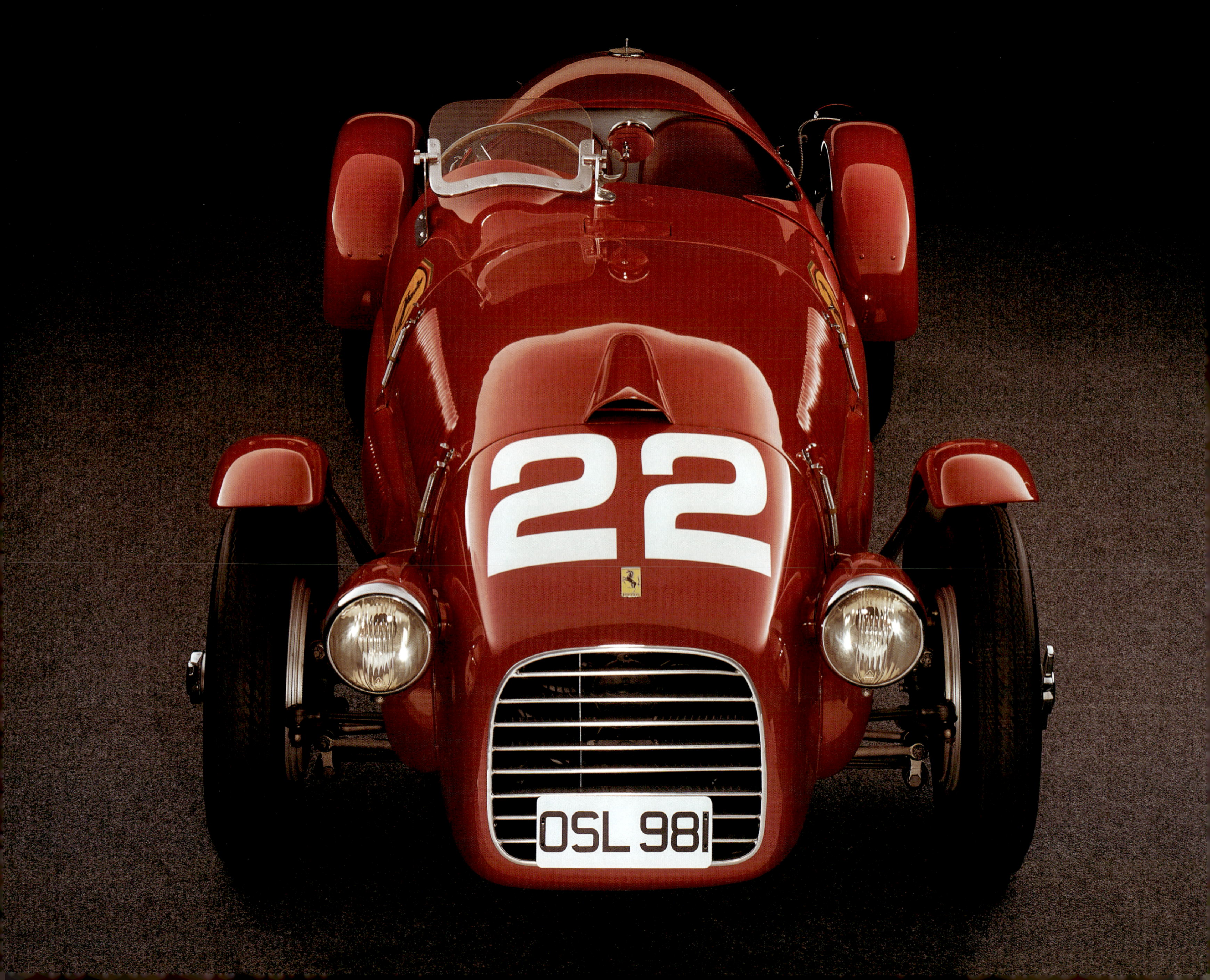
22
OSL 981

1947 FERRARI 166 SPIDER CORSA

Having spearheaded Alfa Romeo's competition programme during the 1930s, Enzo Ferrari was barred from building a car under his own name for four years under the terms of his severance. Aside from the Auto Avio 815 of 1940, of which just two were made, *Il Commendatore* would have to wait until the end of the Second World War to develop his motor-building aspirations. This car is believed to be the oldest surviving example of Ferrari's 166 Spider Corsa.

Design and development of the original Gioacchino Colombo-conceived 1.5-litre V12 engine and chassis began in 1945, but the first prototypes were not ready for another two years, this example being the third made. Franco Cortese drove the car, fitted with closed-wheel bodywork, in the Circuit of Modena meeting in September 1947, where he set the fastest lap before retiring from the race. A month later it reappeared with new *cigaro*-style coachwork and an enlarged 1.9-litre Tipo 159 engine, to be driven by Raymond Sommer in the Turin Grand Prix. The French ace scored a commanding victory, the first win of international standing for the Ferrari *scuderia*.

The car was subsequently remodelled over the winter months and sold as '002-C' to Gabriele Besana, Ferrari's first private customer. Engaging the experienced Cortese as a co-driver, Besana ran the car in the 1949 Mille Miglia, before selling it on the following year to Luigi de Filippis, brother of 1950s grand-prix driver Maria Teresa de Filippis. By now uncompetitive, the old racer soon passed to a Florentine Ferrari dealer who engaged Carrozzeria Motto to reclothe the chassis with more contemporary bodywork. In the early 1970s a protracted restoration returned the car to its original configuration.

The businesslike cockpit in this Ferrari is dominated by a vast steering wheel. As with most Italian cars, the rev counter is a prominent feature.

Ungainly aluminium coachwork hugs the chassis, with mudguards removable so that the 166 could compete as a sports car or grand-prix racer. It was later rebodied by Rocco Motto before being returned to its original outline.

The start of something big? Despite Enzo Ferrari's credentials with Alfa Romeo, few could have guessed that the 166 Spider Corsa would give birth to a legend. Ferrari has now won more grands prix than any other team in Formula One.

Ferrari 166 Spider Corsa

1948 MASERATI 4CLT

Outmoded before it had a chance to shine, Maserati's 4CLT nonetheless stands as one of the grand-prix classics. This is largely due to its status as a racing car for the privateer, both before and after the Second World War. Although lacking the resources of major rival Alfa Romeo, which had changed the rules of the game with its hugely powerful 158 in the late 1930s, the Maserati brothers were forced to abandon the ageing 6CM single-seater and produce a new design in time for the 1939 season.

The first of these twin-cam, four-cylinder racers was completed in April of that year. Featuring a special streamlined body by Stabilimenti Farina of Turin, the car was used for record-breaking attempts on the Firenze-Mare *autostrada* and then in the Tripoli Grand Prix, where it set the fastest qualifying time. A month later Englishman Peter Wakefield drove his customer example to victory in the Coppa Principessa di Piemonte with fellow Maserati aces Piero Taruffi and Franco Cortese following him home. The outbreak of the Second World War inevitably interrupted development but a revised car with reworked bodywork and a new supercharger set-up was ready by the time serious motor sport resumed in 1946.

However, a year later there was real progress: a new, lighter and stiffer chassis. The new 4CLT ('T' standing for '*Tubolare*') featured two superchargers and radically altered front suspension. Alberto Ascari won the San Remo Grand Prix in June 1948, yet further developments, including a rise in engine capacity, were not enough to seriously challenge Alfa Romeo's new 159.

By the time the official Formula World Championship was introduced in 1950, the limitations of what was an antiquated design were all too obvious. Experiments with another new chassis and suspension arrangements came to naught, with the 4CLT's best result that year being third overall in the Monaco Grand Prix.

Obsolete from the outset, the 4CLT is nonetheless a classic of its kind. Instrumentation is minimal while the gearshift sprouted out between the driver's legs.

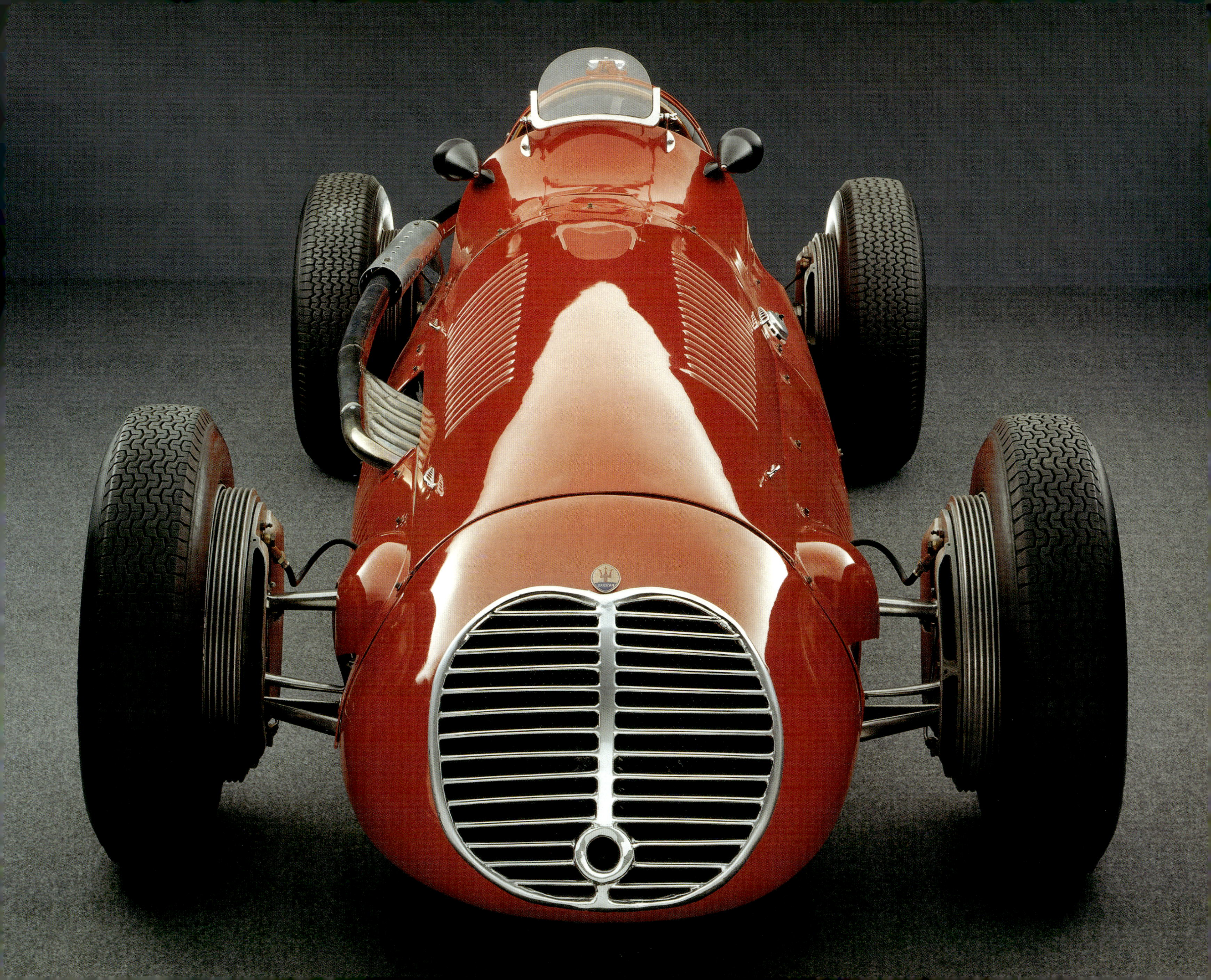

Maserati rarely built an inelegant car. However, by 1948 the 4CLT was already an antiquated design and updates of chassis and suspension simply papered over the cracks.

By the dawn of the Formula One World Championship in 1950, Maserati was outflanked and outgunned by newer designs from bigger teams, but the 4CLT was a favourite of privateer drivers.

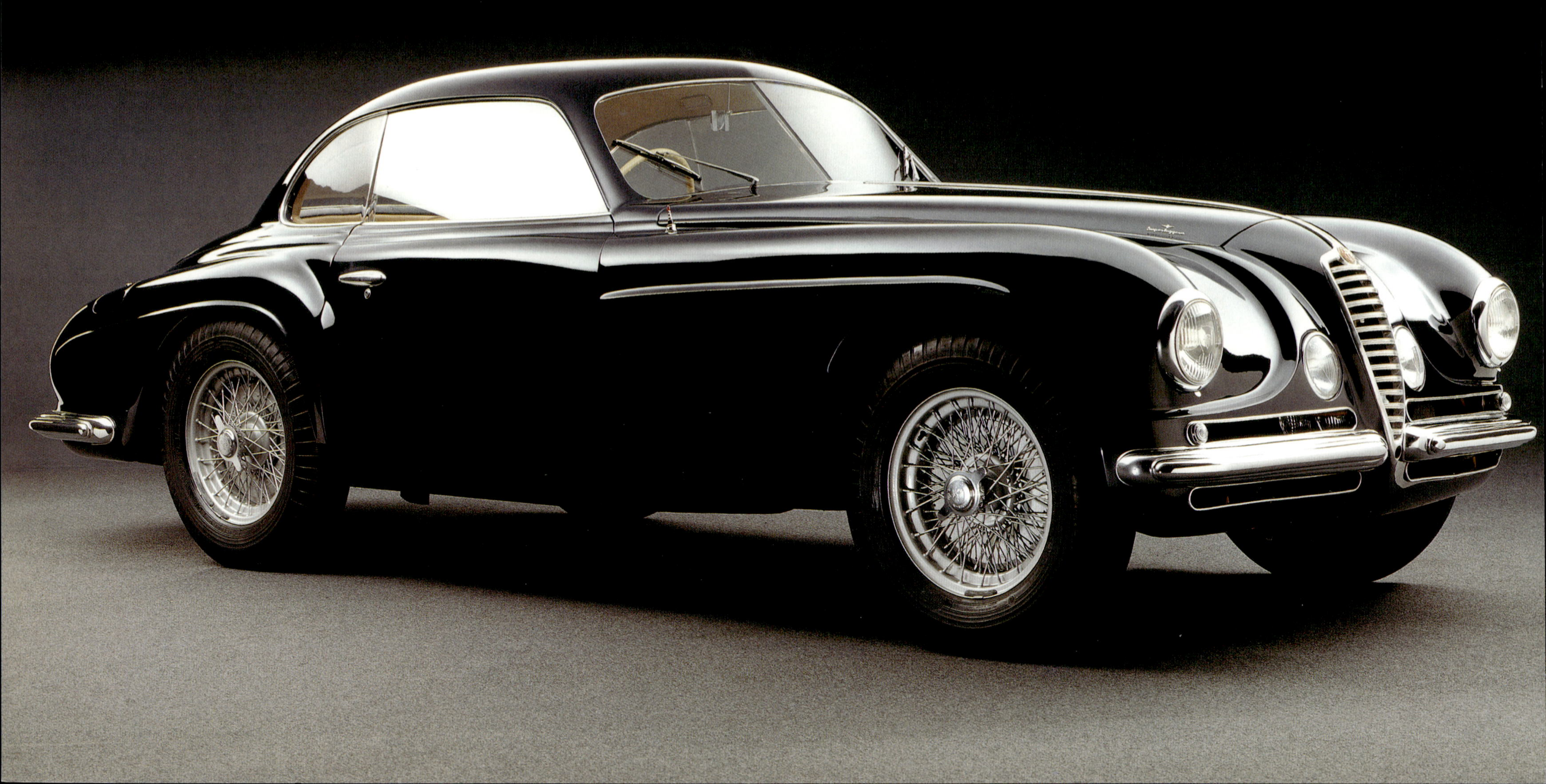

1949 ALFA ROMEO 6C 2500 VILLA D'ESTE

Nowadays, the term concours d'élégance conjures images of primped classic cars regimented on manicured lawns. But back in the heyday of coachbuilding such events were a shop window for designers and *carrozzerie*, where new styling ideas in production and prototype forms could be showcased to an informed public.

From 1929 to 1949 the Villa d'Este concours, held on the shore of Lake Como, was among the most prestigious. Alfa Romeo was often a recipient of prizes, premier awards being the Coppa d'Oro (selected by a jury) and the Gran Premio Referendum (decided by public vote). In the event's final year Alfa's sublime 6C 2500 scooped both accolades, the second – considered more important by manufacturers – being bestowed on the car bodied by Touring, a beautiful coupé known thereafter as the Villa d'Este.

This was a fitting tribute, as the 6C 2500 range – Turismo, Sport and Super Sport – marked the last generation of truly great Alfa Romeos. During the Second World War the Allies razed the firm's Portello factory because it was producing armaments, prompting Alfa Romeo to change tack and start building cars for the masses rather than continue plying its wares to the elite.

Although bodies manufactured in-house were offered for the Freccia d'Oro and GT variants of the 6C 2500, most of these formidably expensive machines (of which the Villa d'Este was the most costly) wore bespoke coachwork by the likes of Ghia, Stabilimenti Farina, Boneschi and Touring, the latter's creations being the most elegant. Creases that ran the length of the pillarless body, and long flutes trailing from the wheel arches, imbued the car with a sense of speed, even when stationary. In Sport trim, with the twin-cam engine fed by triple Weber carburettors, the Villa d'Este could reach 171 kph (106 mph) at a time when the average family saloon struggled to reach half this speed, proving it was not all for show.

Touring's sublime take on the 6C 2500 fought off rival coachbuilders' offerings to claim the Villa d'Este concours prize. It subsequently became a production model.

Left: Delicate fluting around the tail light was a trademark Touring design flourish also used on the *carrozzeria*'s Ferrari 166MM design.

Opposite: Exquisite but egregiously expensive, the Villa d'Este was among the most exclusive cars of its day. Attention to aerodynamics and a powerful engine delivered a top speed of 171 kph (106 mph).

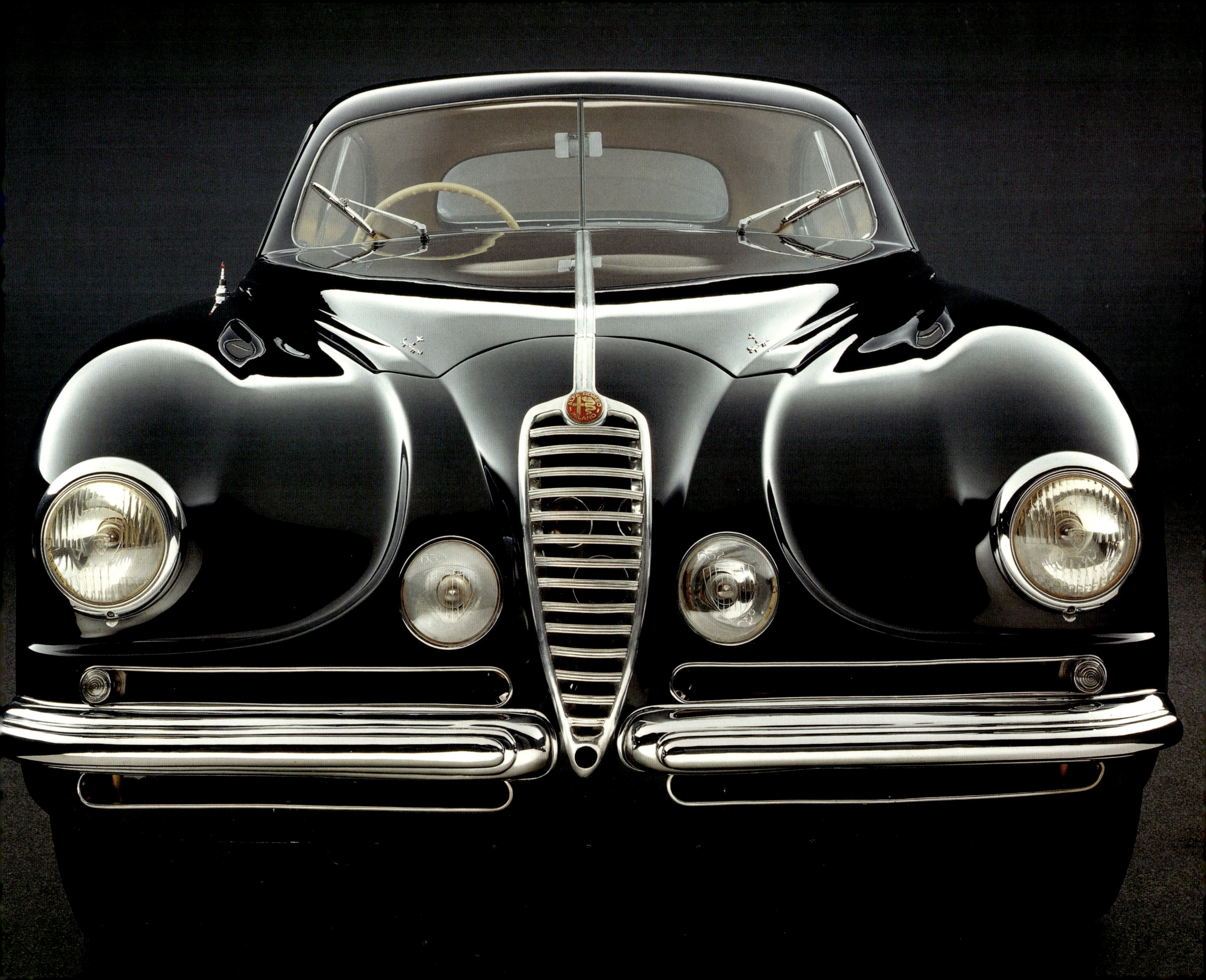

Left: Delicious detailing includes pop-out door handles, a feature that recently reappeared on the Fiat Barchetta sports car.

Opposite: A Citroënesque steering wheel adds a suitably modernist take to the Villa d'Este's cabin, although its size ensures it almost rests on the driver's lap.

Alfa Romeo 6C 2500 Villa d'Este

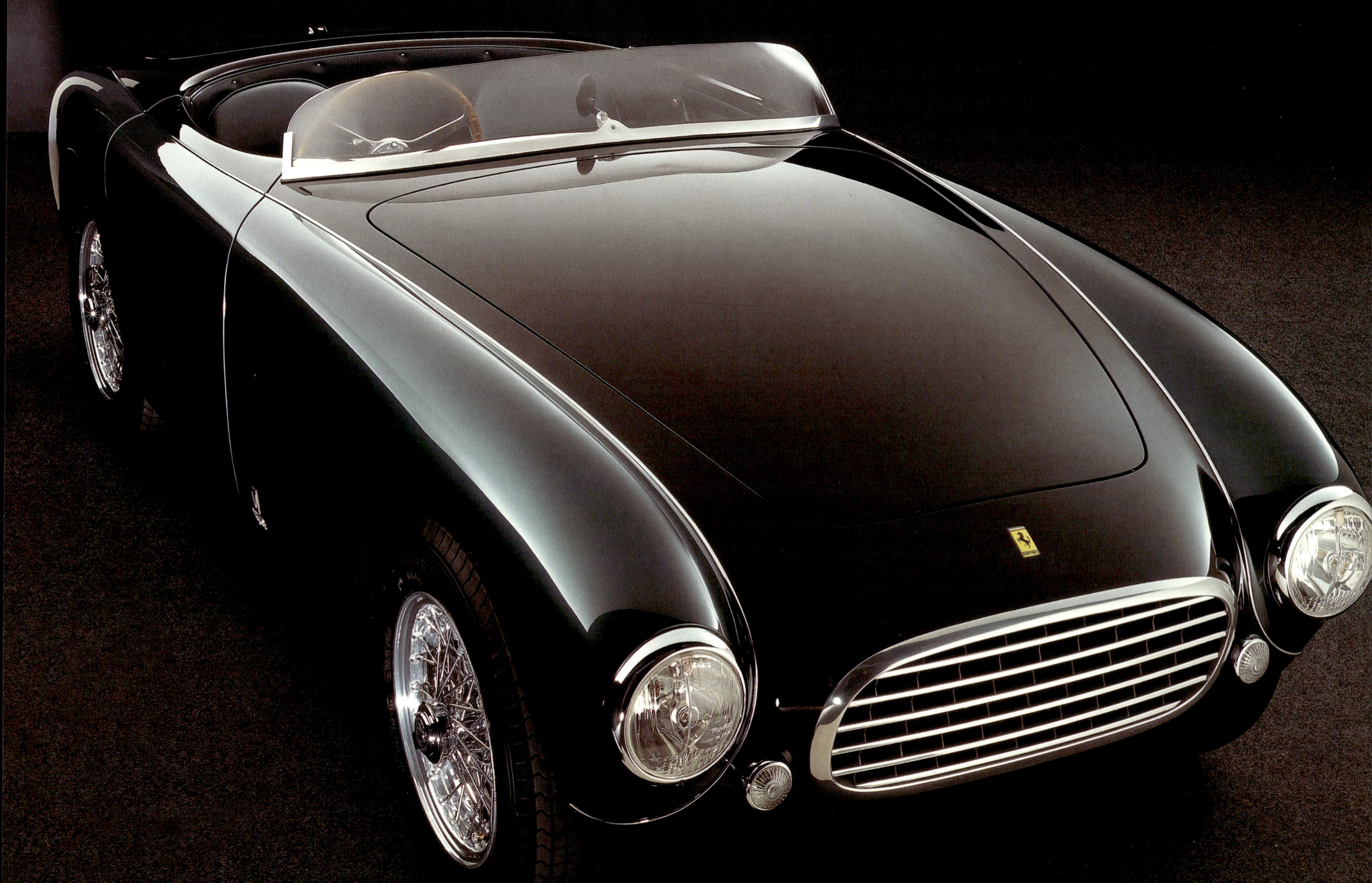

1951 FERRARI 212 EXPORT

Before the 250GT, Ferrari displayed little interest in building touring cars. Although there was a definite market, the firm tended to produce small runs to satisfy specific requests from favoured customers. One such was Count Umberto Marzotto, who, even more so than his famed brothers, had successfully campaigned Ferraris in the early 1950s.

Derived from the earlier 212 Inter, the Export featured the same V12 engine, designed by Gioacchino Colombo, in a tubular-steel frame, but had a much shorter wheelbase. This example, chassis 0090 E, was built to Marzotto's brief in March 1951 and featured coachwork by Vignale to a design by Giovanni Michelotti. Originally finished in a two-tone green colour scheme, it was among the prettiest of the breed, being devoid of any of the extraneous styling tinsel that blighted offerings from rival *carrozzerie*: there were not even external door handles or, the shallow, curved deflector being too small, any windscreen wipers. Similarly, there was almost no weather protection, despite the luxurious – by period Ferrari standards – cockpit with tan leather seats and door panels and matching carpet on the floor and transmission tunnel.

Although the car was built as a tourer, Marzotto, predictably, did not wait long to race it. On 15 July 1951 he competed in the Coppa d'Oro delle Dolomiti, finishing eleventh on the road and eighth in class. Running in the same event the following year, he was seventh overall, and a few months later won the Trieste–Opicina hillclimb. Yet the car's real significance in Ferrari lore is that it was the first of the marque ever to be road-tested by an English-language publication. *The Autocar* reviewed it in June 1951, respected journalist Gordon Wilkins commenting: "The handling is completely without vice; the response flatters the skill of the driver and brings a thrill of deep satisfaction."

The heart and soul of any Ferrari. This 212 features the classic V12 engine designed by Gioacchino Colombo: it is as beautiful as it is loud.

This achingly pretty one-off Ferrari was styled by Giovanni Michelotti and built by Alfredo Vignale. Although it was intended as a road car, there are few concessions to practicality, not least a lack of windscreen wipers. But then it did live in Italy.

114

Ferrari 212 Export 115

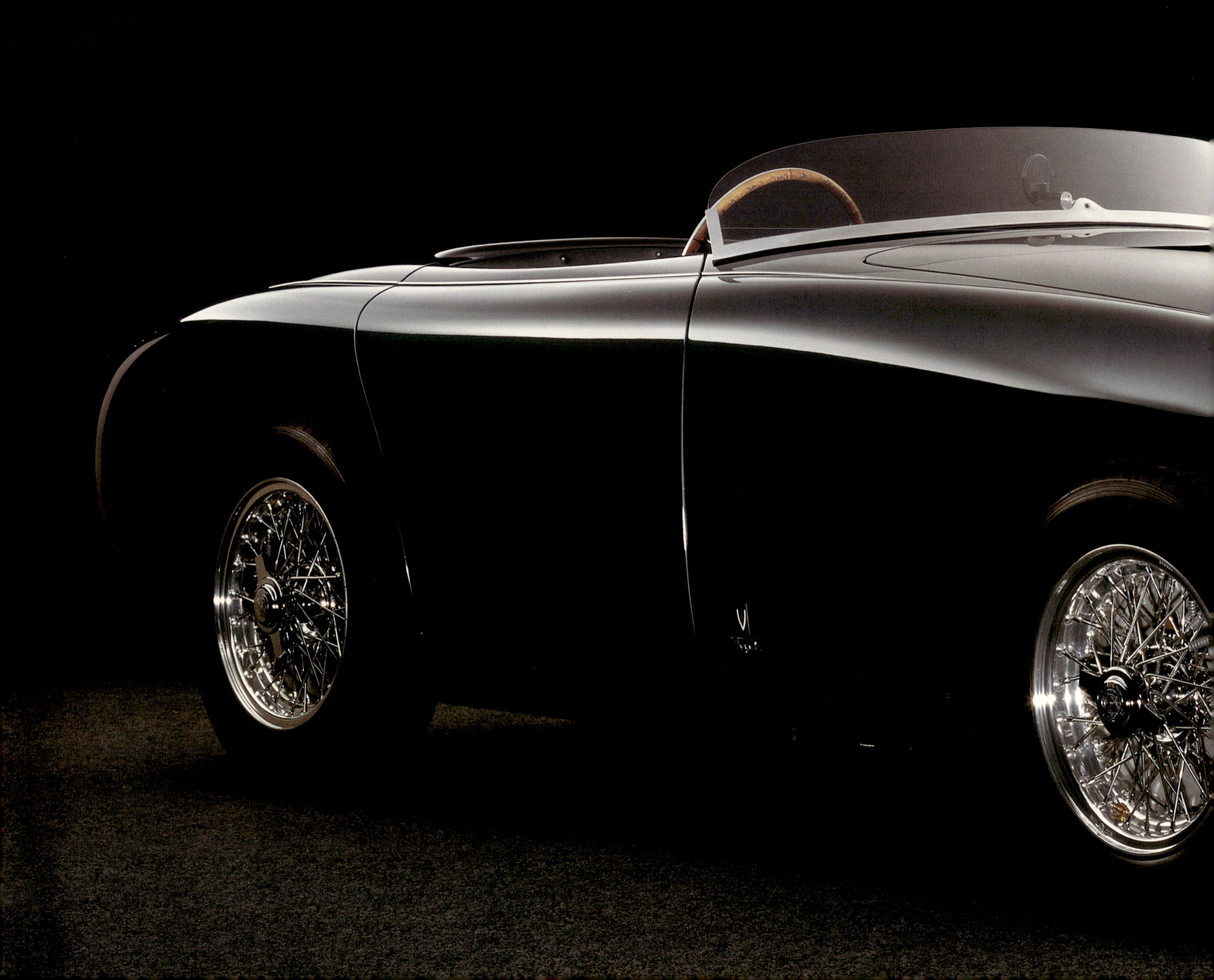

This unique custom-bodied Ferrari was ordered new by Count Umberto Marzotto, one of Italy's foremost sports-car racers of the immediate post-war years. It was intended for use as a tourer but Marzotto could not resist entering it in competitive events.

Ferrari 212 Export   117

1953 FERRARI 250MM

Amateur driver Giovanni Bracco earned his place in motor-sport history thanks to an epic drive in the 1952 Mille Miglia. Fortified by vast quantities of brandy, the industrialist chain-smoked his way to victory in the prototype Ferrari 250 Sport coupé against the might of the works Mercedes-Benz team. Ferrari honoured his heroic efforts by producing thirty-two copies of the winning car, naming the new model 'MM', after the race, to commemorate Bracco's win. This marked the firm's earliest successful attempt at building a run of cars in anything like volume. The MM also spawned the most successful line of GT racing cars to emanate from Maranello to date: the 250-series Tour de France, SWB and GTO.

Powered by an Aurelio Lampredi-designed 2963-cc V12 engine fed by three Weber carburettors, the MM was based on a tubular-steel chassis with unequal-length wishbone front suspension and a live rear axle. But it was the altogether prettier Pinin Farina Berlinette coupé version, as opposed to the open-top configuration with gawky coachwork by Vignale, that captivated. Marking the start of an enduring relationship between Ferrari and the Turin styling house, the long bonnet and sweeping fastback outline set the template for all future GTs from the Maranello factory.

This example, chassis number 0298MM, was clothed by Pinin Farina in April 1952 but differed from its sister cars in having a slightly longer nose that aped the then-current 500 F1/F2 single-seater. Predictably finished in Italian Racing Red, it was sold new to Luigi Giuliano of Rome for 3,500,000 lire. Unlike most other MMs, this car led a sheltered life, future owners including a film company that used it to chauffeur stars around Italy. Having been used only sporadically in its intended role as a competition car, it has never been crashed, restored or physically altered.

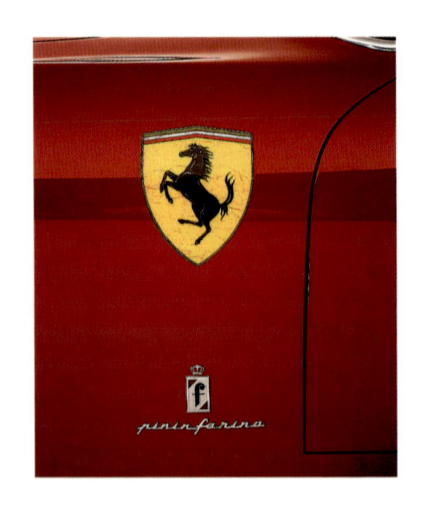

Pinin Farina and Ferrari, the car builder and the *carrozzeria*, have been inextricably linked for over five decades, producing some of the most dazzling cars ever seen.

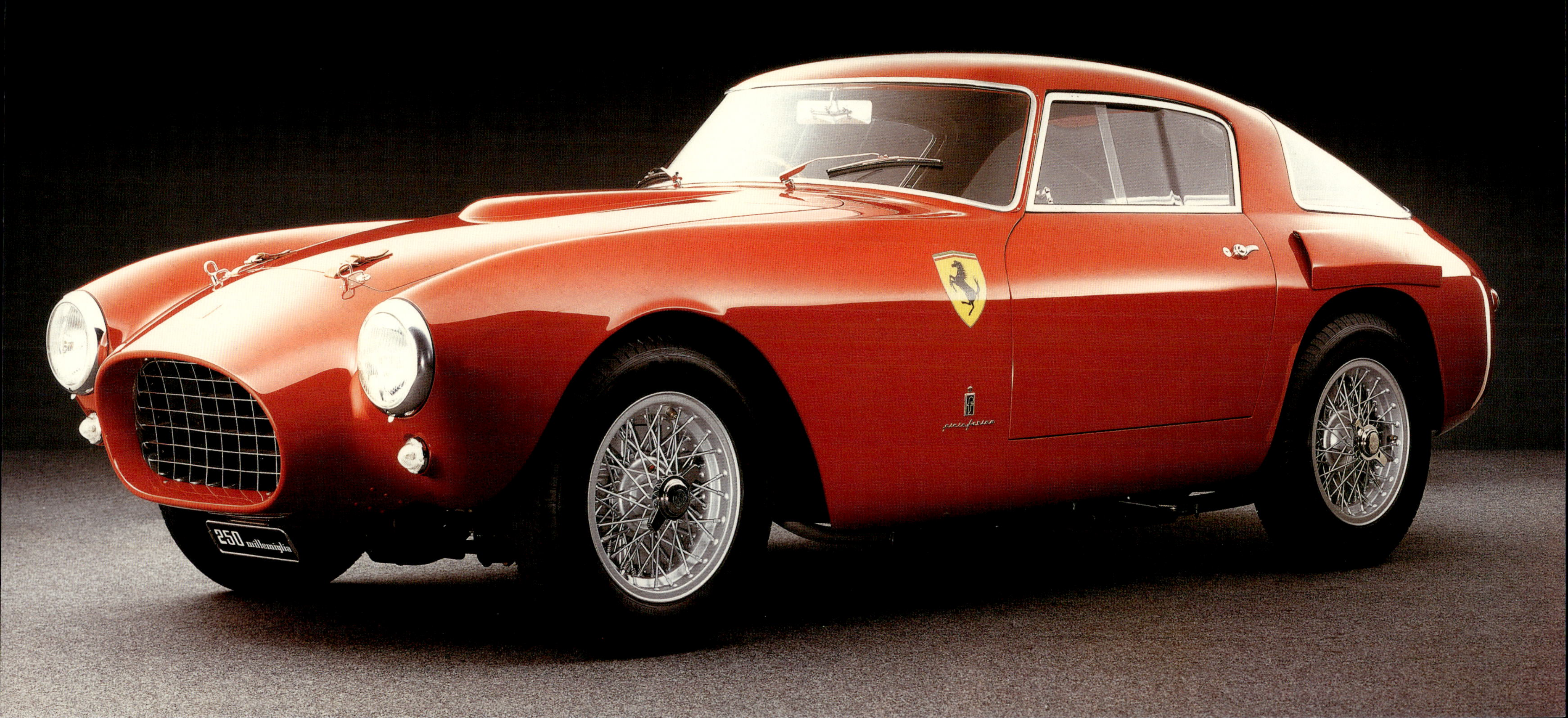
250 millemiglia

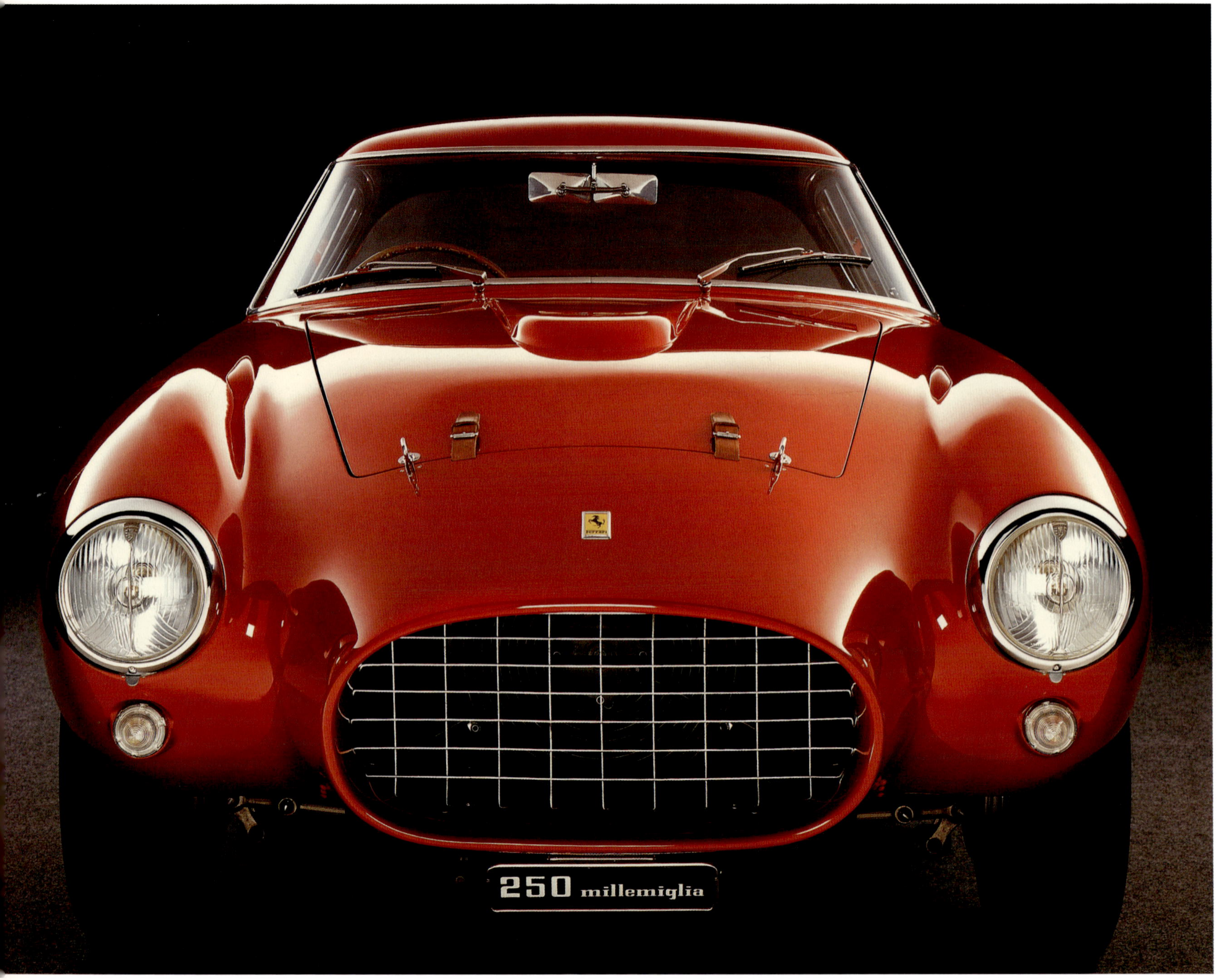
250 millemiglia

Opposite: The classic egg-crate grille became a Ferrari staple during the 1950s. The MM sired a successful line of 250-series models including the Tour de France, SWB and GTO.

Left: Unadorned and functionally elegant, the 250MM's hind view is dominated by the quick-release filler cap sited at the base of the rear screen.

Ferrari 250MM 121

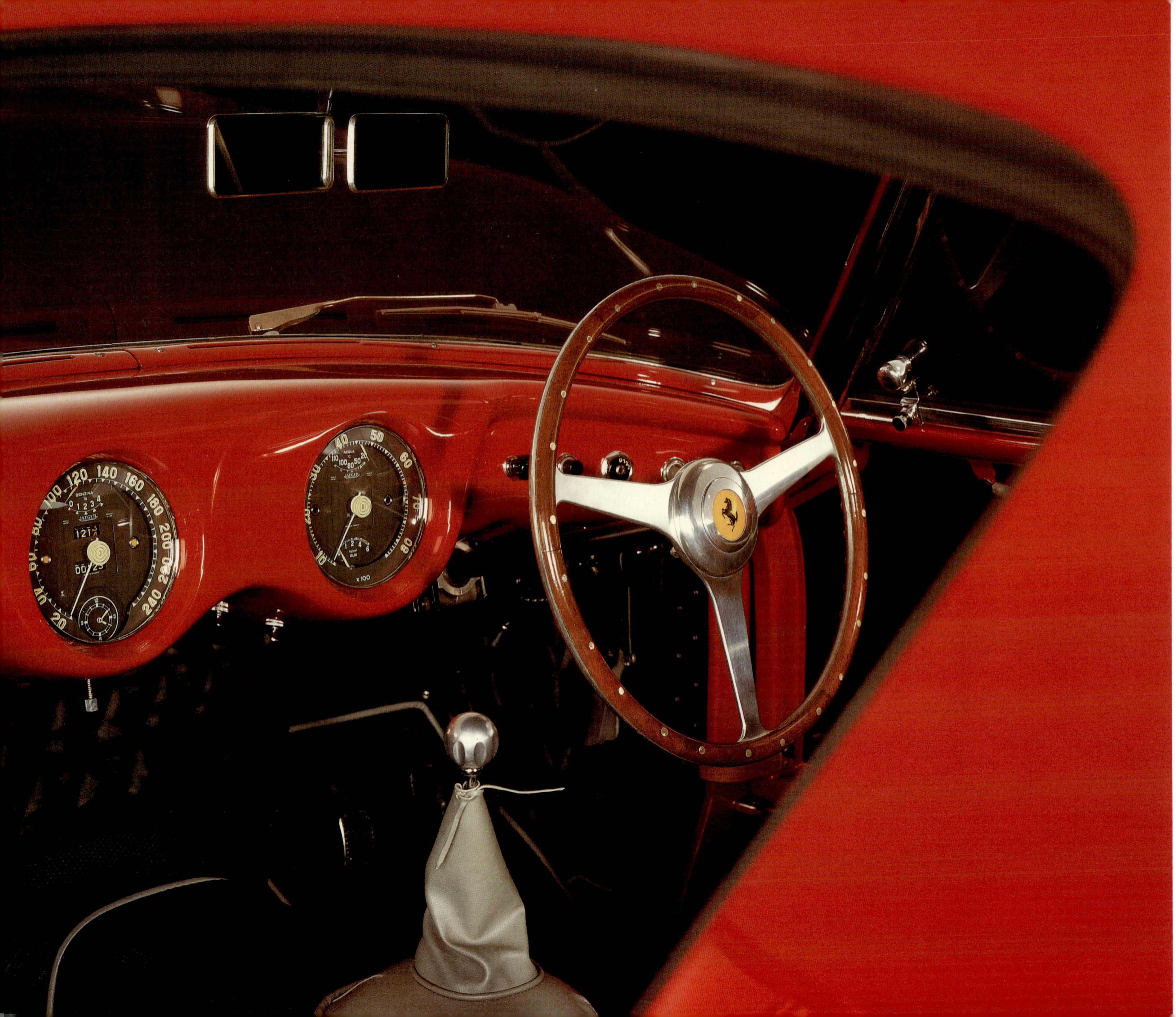
JAEGER
BENZINA
ACQUA
JAEGER
X 100

Opposite: The 250MM was cramped, as befits any period GT racer, so it is hard to believe that this car was used to chauffeur movie stars around Italy.

Left: The Aurelio Lampredi-designed V12 engine was mounted far back in the tubular chassis to assist weight distribution. This view is dominated by the three large Weber carburettors.

Ferrari 250MM 123

1954 ALFA ROMEO GIULIETTA SPIDER PROTOTYPES

During the early 1950s Alfa Romeo was desperately in need of a volume product. The debt-ridden marque seemed to be facing a bleak future until someone hit on a novel method to raise funds. It would hold a lottery and winners would receive the new Giulietta saloon car, or Berlina, due for release in 1955. All very well, except that continued delays were making production of the Berlina far from likely. With a scandal brewing, Alfa engaged Carrozzeria Bertone to build a coupé variant using existing components in time for the 1954 Turin Salon as a means of appeasing angry ticket holders. The lucky winners went home happy, and now the only problem was that demand for the pretty Sprint proved overwhelming, so it became a production car.

Naturally, there followed calls for an open version, but Alfa Romeo's management was not convinced there would be sufficient demand. Austrian-born, New York-based car dealer Max Hoffman thought otherwise. Having been largely responsible for introducing European sports cars – and the Volkswagen Beetle – to post-war North America, he was convinced there was a market for a Giulietta Spider. So the project was put out to tender, with Franco Scaglione styling two Bertone prototypes and Pinin Farina being allocated three chassis, of which this ivory car used two as a result of being constantly changed.

Each basing their cars on shortened Sprint platforms with all-alloy, 1290-cc, twin-cam, four-cylinder engines, both contenders met the brief. Hoffman's major concern was that the definitive production car should feature wind-up windows – unlike most British roadsters of the period. Pinin Farina's concept won the contract, although not without alterations before it was ready for public consumption. Bertone's offering was considered too difficult to make in volume. Given that production of the Sprint had the tiny coachbuilder calling on the assistance of every body shop in and around Turin, this was perhaps as well.

Bertone's approach to the Giulietta Spider was more radical than Pinin Farina's. The extreme curvature of the bodywork would have made construction in volume expensive, which is one of the reasons why it lost out in the final reckoning.

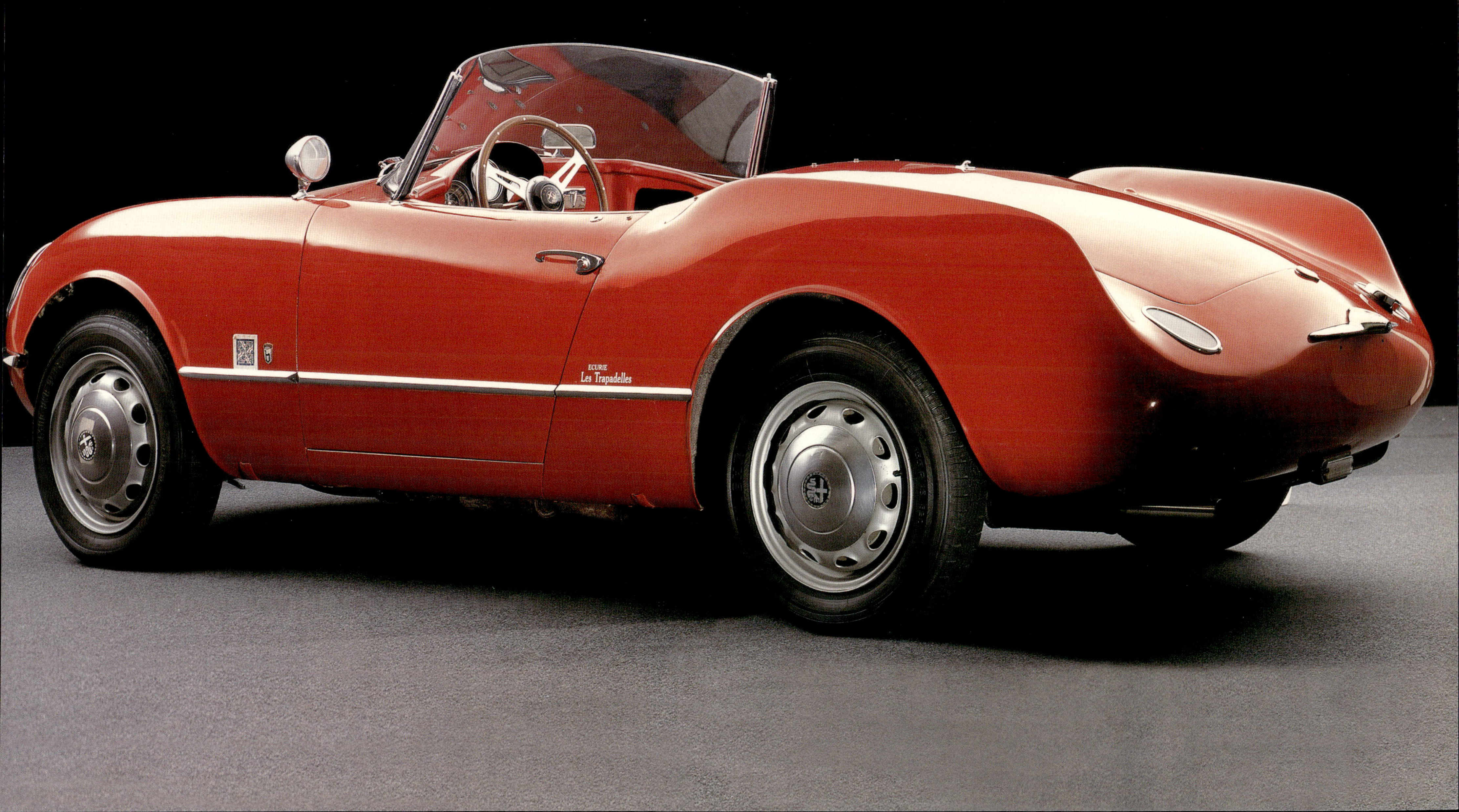
ECURIE
Les Trapadelles

Left: A curvy tail and pronounced tail fins were common to many designs by Bertone stylist Franco Scaglione in the 1950s, notably on the Anglo-American Arnolt-Bristol.

Opposite: The faired-in headlights behind Perspex covers on Bertone's offering foreshadowed the Alfa Romeo Duetto Spider of the following decade.

126

Alfa Romeo Giulietta Spider prototypes

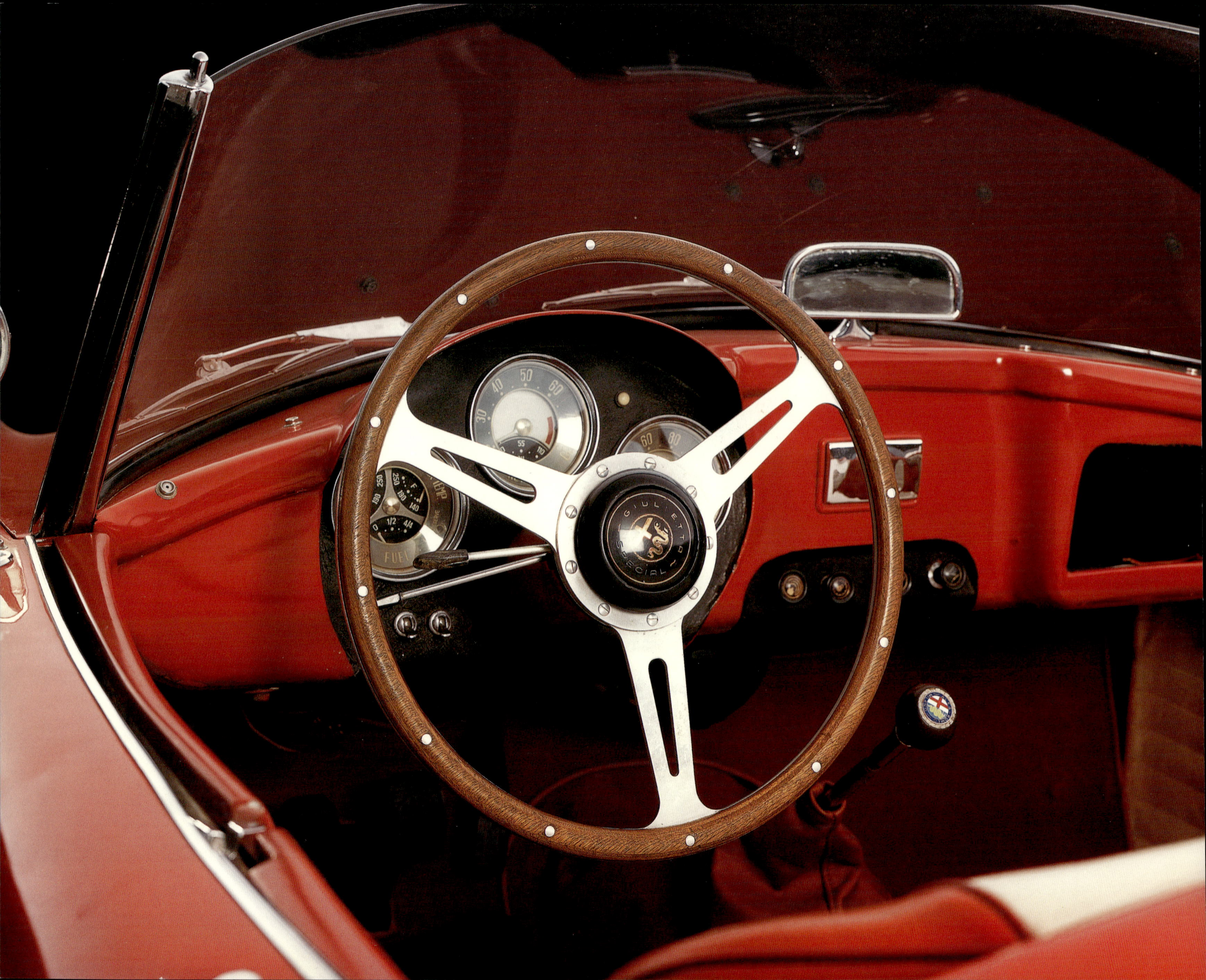
FUEL

Opposite: Despite the outer wildness, the Bertone Spider's uninspired cabin comes as a bit of a disappointment, with sparse instrumentation clustered behind the Nardi steering wheel.

Below: The Bertone Giulietta was styled by Franco Scaglione, the firm's free-spirited design chief. Although it shared several styling cues with some of his earlier concept cars, it is a little dumpy in profile.

Above and opposite: Aside from the wrap-around windscreen and sliding side glazing, there are few obvious clues to help differentiate between Pinin Farina's Giulietta prototype, seen here, and the production version.

Alfa Romeo Giulietta Spider prototypes

1954 ALFA ROMEO 2000 SPORTIVA

Before car manufacturers cottoned on to the value of heritage as a marketing tool, prototypes and show cars tended to live brief lives. Once they had been pushed to their limits on test tracks, or had done the rounds of the automotive catwalks, most were sent to the crusher, with only sepia-tinged images serving as a reminder that they had ever existed. Somehow the two Sportiva coupés escaped such a fate but their origins remain shadowy.

Alfa Romeo's 1900 effectively saved the Milan marque, the original four-cylinder saloon being launched at the Turin Salon in 1950. Within a few years the range blossomed into more glamorous versions, along with a four-wheel-drive off-roader. With a background steeped in competition, the 1900 soon formed the basis for a motor-sport programme, the C52 Disco Volante (flying saucer) and 6C 3000 racers finding little success save for Juan Manuel Fangio's brilliant – if fortuitous – second place in the 1953 Mille Miglia.

Closely related to these racing variants, four Sportivas are widely believed to have been made: two Spiders and two coupés. Only the coupés survive, the first of these being a test mule, the second a show car that debuted at the 1956 Turin Salon. All four were beautifully engineered with a spaceframe chassis, De Dion rear axle and the regular 1900 unequal-length wishbones and coil-sprung front suspension; power came from the basic 1900 engine but with a light-alloy cylinder head on top of the cast-iron block. The sublime styling was the work of Bertone's troubled genius Franco Scaglione, previously responsible for Alfa's wild triumvirate of BAT (Berlina Aerodinamica Tecnica) aerodynamic studies. Sadly, just as quickly as the Sportiva arrived, the project was dropped before the car ever raced.

The classic wood-rim, alloy-spoked steering wheel offers all the GT racer reference points. The Sportiva was to have raced but the two coupés that were built never ventured near a circuit.

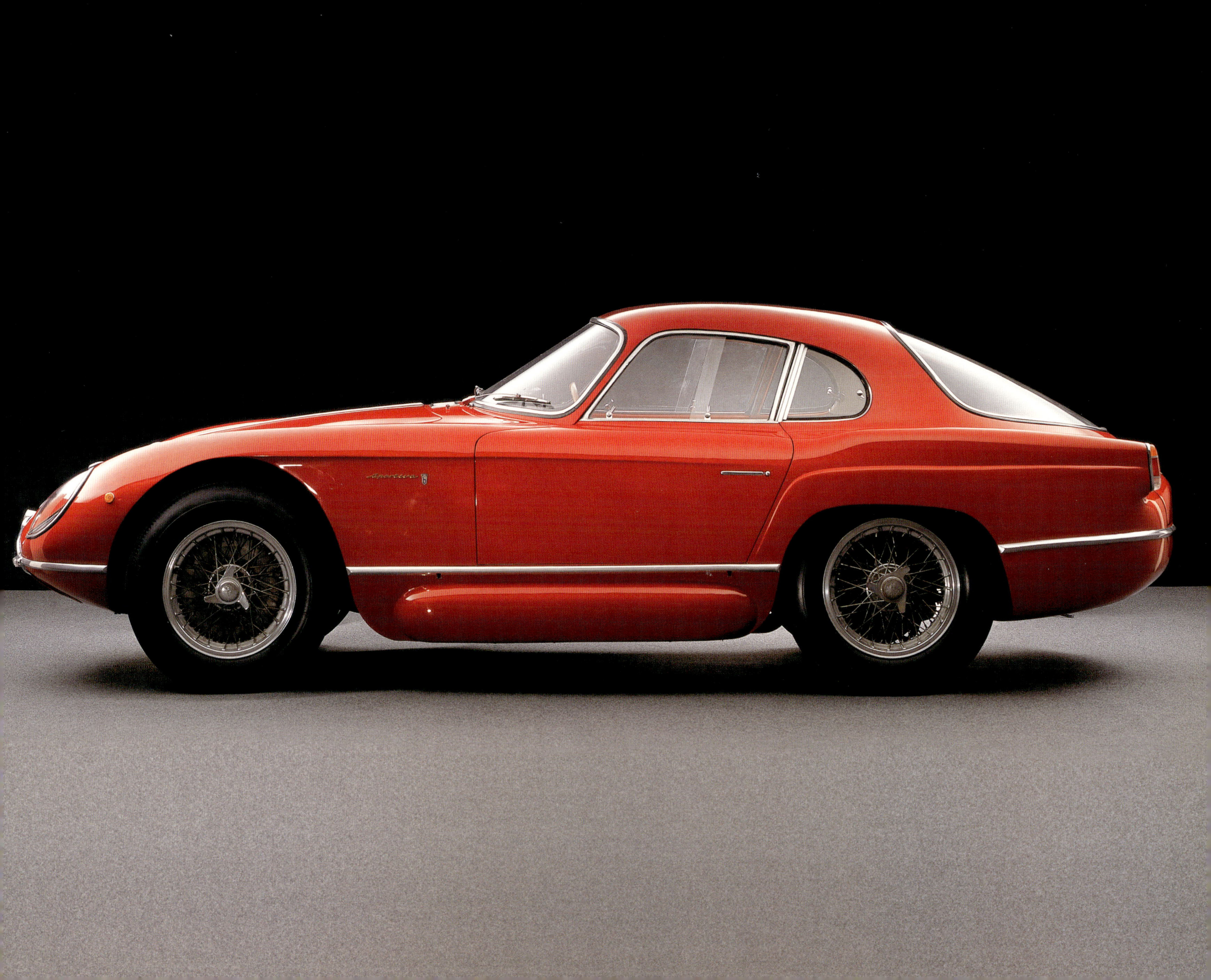

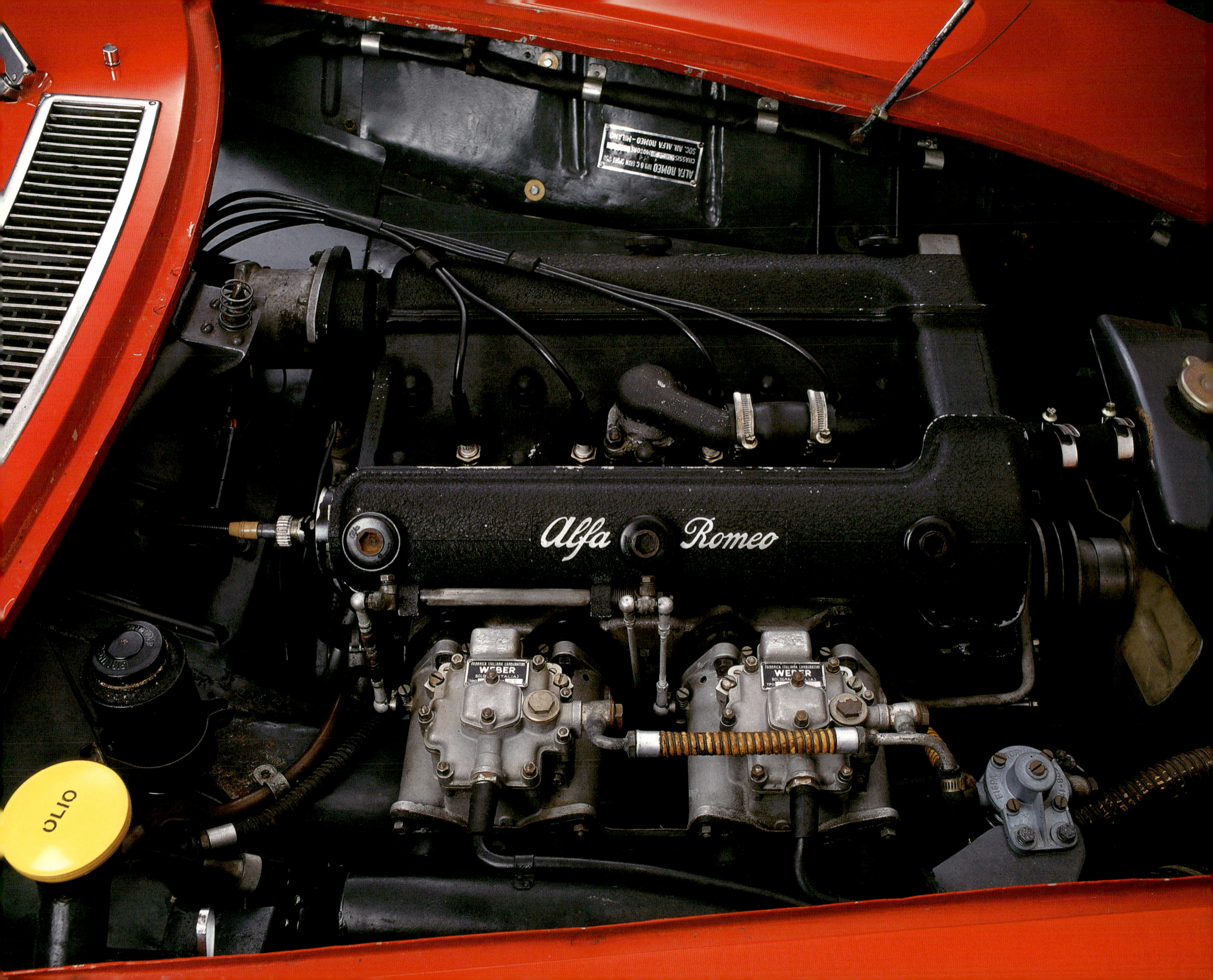
Alfa Romeo
WEBER
WEBER
OLIO

Opposite: The Sportiva's four-cylinder engine owed its architecture to less exotic variations of the 1900 family, but here with a light-alloy cylinder head atop the cast-iron engine block.

It's a tragedy that only two Sportiva coupés were ever made. Franco Scaglione's outline is still captivating, but the car's shadowy beginnings and premature end ensure that few have seen one up close.

Alfa Romeo 2000 Sportiva

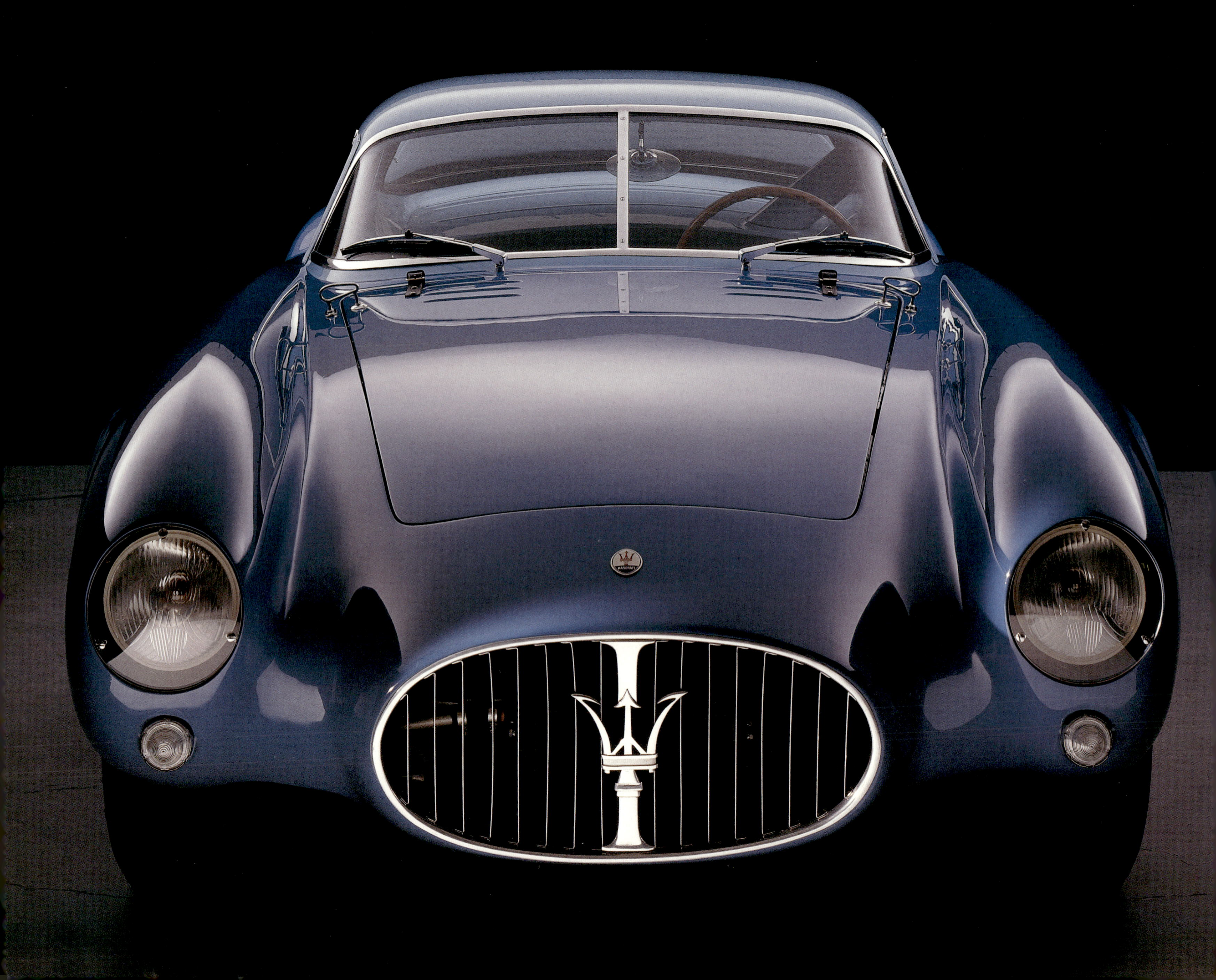

1954 MASERATI A6GCS/53

Conceived by former Ferrari designer Gioacchino Colombo, the inelegantly named A6GCS/53 was effectively a two-seat road-going version of the A6GCM Formula Two car – from a time when this was the premier racing category. The all-alloy, 2-litre, twin-cam, four-cylinder engine produced 170 bhp, which ensured a top speed of 237 kph (147 mph).

The model's competition career began in 1953, with overall and class wins across Europe and the USA. It is believed that fifty-four were made to 1955, most bodied by small *carrozzerie* Fantuzzi or Fiandri, although Pietro Frua is known to have built two Spiders and Alfredo Vignale a single example. Yet it was Pinin Farina that received the plaudits for its variation on the theme, just four of these radically modern coupés being made.

This was all the more remarkable in that the Turin styling house had an exclusivity deal with Ferrari, barring it from working with the Bologna firm; it would not design another Maserati until 2003. That Pinin Farina clothed an A6GCS/53 was down to Maserati's Rome dealer, Guglielmo Dei, who needed a closed version for customers who wanted better weather protection when racing. That it was an agent, rather than the manufacturer, who commissioned the cars' construction handily circumvented the agreement with Ferrari.

This car, chassis 2057, was first shown at the 1954 Turin Salon and was the only one of the quartet made with a split front windscreen and two-tone colour scheme. The first owner, Pietro Palmieri, entered the car in the Giro di Umbria only to find the cabin heat so intolerable that he had the body removed and replaced with an open *barchetta*-style affair. Remarkably, the original body survived and was later rescued by Maserati historian Franco Lombardi, who arranged its restoration.

Louvres in the rear glasshouse were a nod to the problem of dissipating in-car cockpit heat, which is said to have been unbearable. This explains why the roof was removed at one point.

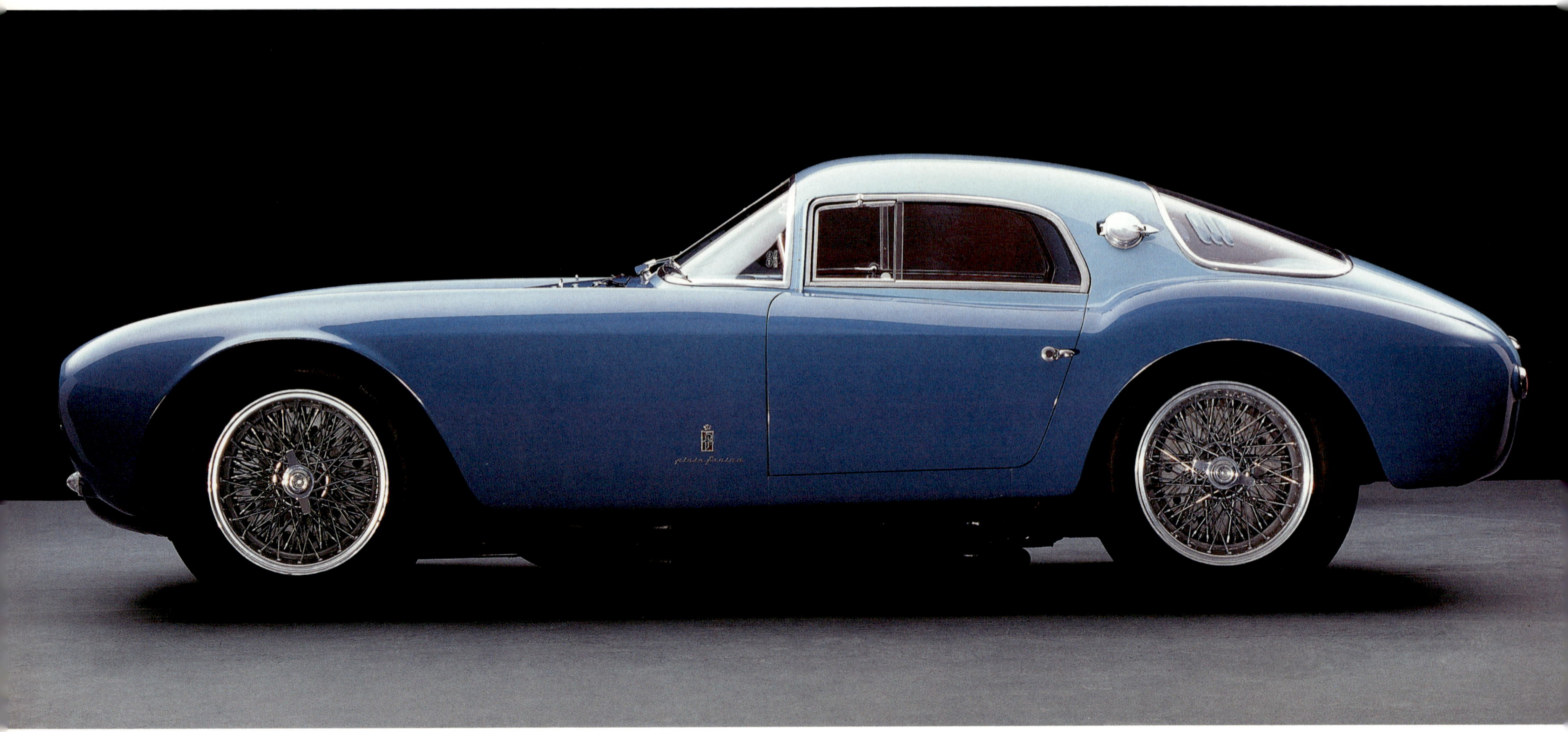

Opposite: Pinin Farina created this dazzling confection despite an exclusivity deal with arch-rival Ferrari. The car was created on behalf of an agent for a racing client.

Below: Pinin Farina retained the regular A6's near-ovoid grille, flanked here by tunnelled-in headlights. The low roofline and gently upswept rear flanks lent the car an aggressive stance.

Maserati A6GCS/53 139

Duo-tone paintwork was an oddity for a racing car in this period, especially an Italian one. The rear bodywork is similar to Pinin Farina's Ferrari 250MM design.

Opposite: A vast steering wheel fronts a minimalistic dashboard. The cabin is said to have been cramped because of the extremely low roofline.

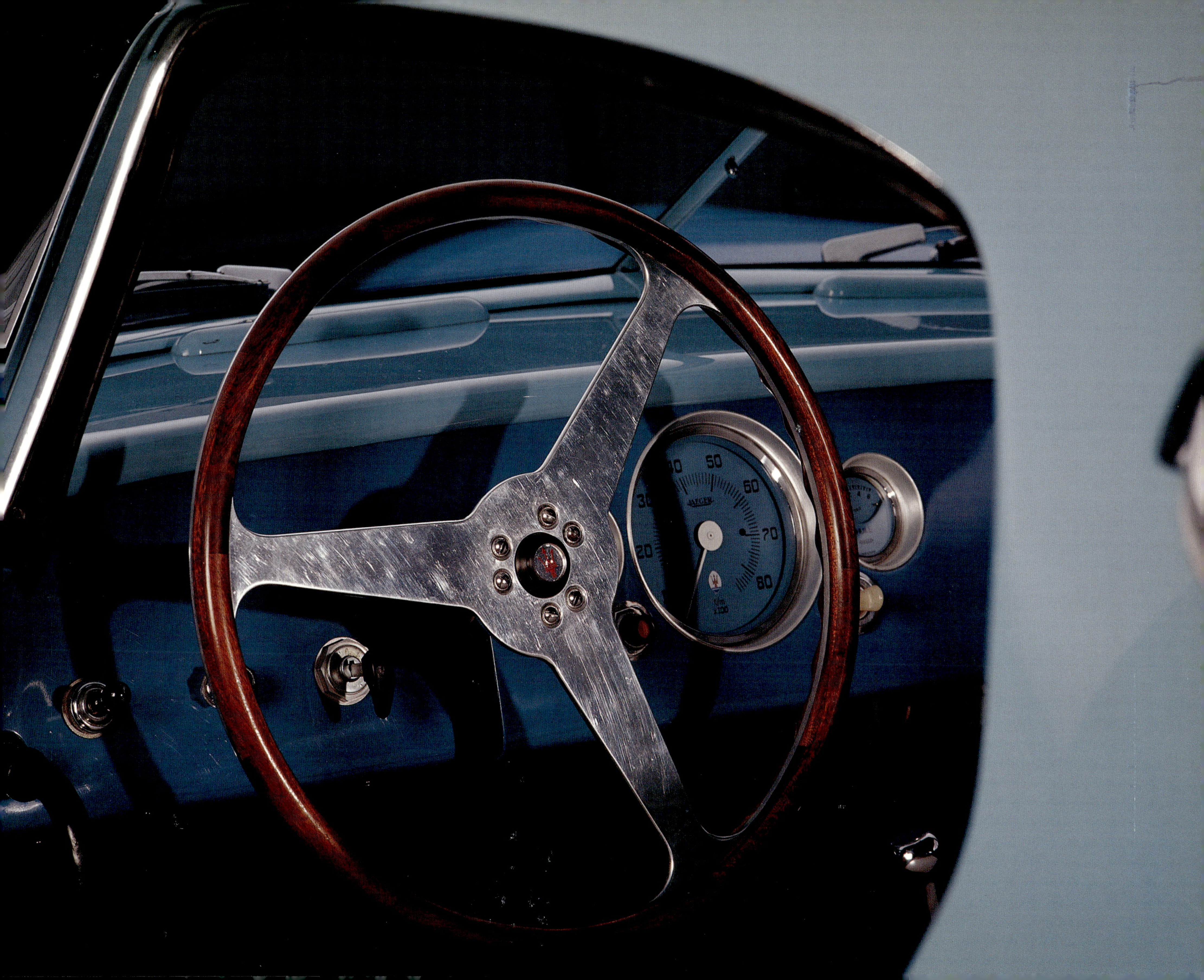
50
60
70
80
20
JAEGER

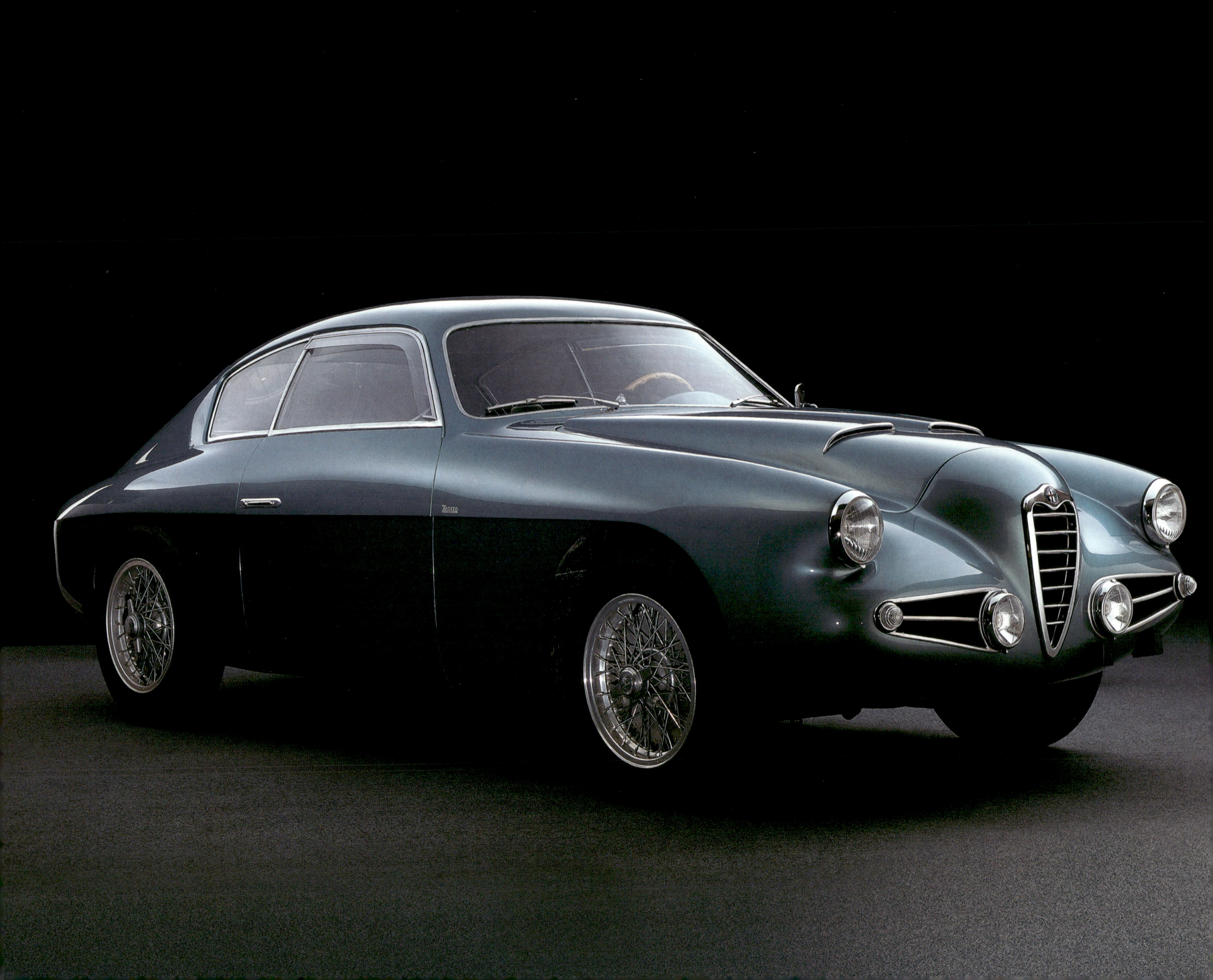

1955 ALFA ROMEO 1900 SSZ

The sublime 1900 saloon marked Alfa Romeo's first dalliance with mass production. With its twin-cam, four-cylinder engine and light, unitary body, the *'Millenove'* proved a fine-handling car that inevitably attracted numerous coachbuilders, Touring being the factory-sanctioned favourite. The tiny firm of Zagato rebodied a 1900 for racer Vladimiro Martinengo in 1954. Although intended from the outset as a one-off, the car soon received official approval after Alfa Romeo engineer Consalvo Sanesi took the prototype for a 'shakedown' run, to identify problems, and raved about it to the management. Even so, the *'Esse-Esse Zagato'* was always going to be made in tiny numbers owing to the firm's size.

As was typical of Zagato's output during the 1950s, the 1900 SSZ was highly distinctive. No individual is credited for the styling, although it is believed that Ugo Zagato worked from a rough sketch by long-time collaborator Fabio Luigi Rapio. On to the existing monocoque was added a box-section structure with the ultra-light aluminium coachwork welded to it. The most distinctive feature was the nose area. The lofty engine necessitated an elevated bonnet line rather than the desired low, tapered effect. Zagato's solution was to segregate the engine by means of a pronounced bulge, with other sharp bonnet lines breaking away to the 'corporate' – that is, used across the range – grille. The result was an aerodynamically efficient coupé that weighed 100 kg (454 lb) less than the equivalent Touring-bodied car. Predictably, the model proved highly competitive on the track, future Formula One driver Joakim Bonnier winning the 1956 Swedish Grand Prix (for sports cars) in his example.

Very much made to order, only forty SSZs were built to 1958, the final car a *'lusso'* (luxury) edition with chrome accessories and special interior trim. Zagato also produced two open Spiders, with the familiar nose 'hump' less prominent than on the competition cars.

1955 OSCA MT4-2AD COUPÉ

The history of the Italian motor industry is awash with acronyms, among the more fêted being OSCA. This should have been OSCAFM but the last two letters were wisely dropped as this nomenclature was judged unpronounceable. Yet it is 'FM' that is significant, as it stands for 'Fratelli Maserati'.

The *fratelli* in question were Ernesto, Bindo and Ettore, survivors of the original 'gang of four' who had founded the firm that bore their name in 1926. Alfieri, the sibling who by all accounts was the guiding force, died in a racing accident in 1932. Five years later the finance-deprived brothers sold out to Omar Orsi and remained under contract for a further ten years.

Their relationship with the new master was apparently less than harmonious and they departed once the agreement expired. From a disused part of the original Maserati factory in their home town of Bologna, they built small-series racing cars under the alias Officina Specializzato per la Costruzione di Automobili – Fratelli Maserati SpA. Their first model, the MT4 (Maserati Type 4) was introduced in 1948, aimed at the 1100-cc racing class that was popular in Italy at the time. After unsuccessfully dabbling in Formula One, the brothers wisely stuck mainly to sports cars, a fully enclosed MT4 1450 *barchetta* being driven to victory in the 1954 Sebring 12 Hours by Stirling Moss and Bill Lloyd.

At this time four MT4-2AD, to give the full designation, chassis were supplied to outside coachbuilders: three to Vignale and one – the car shown here – to Frua. Although primarily built for competition, this Giovanni Michelotti-styled coupé was sold to a Frenchman who never raced it, the car later finding its way into the hands of a reclusive Swiss collector. After his death it was sold off and, after minor titivation, was auctioned in 2005 for $507,500.

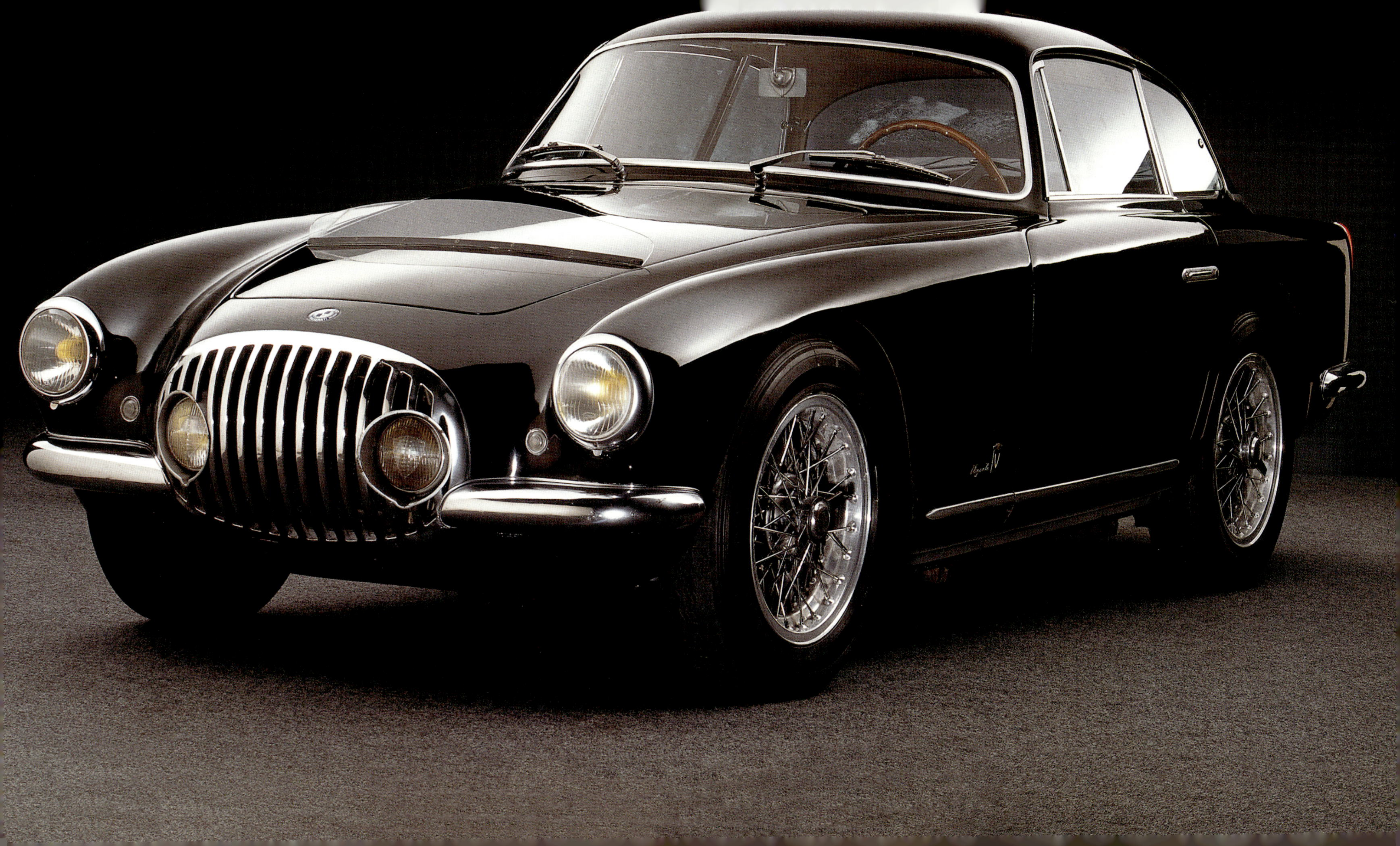

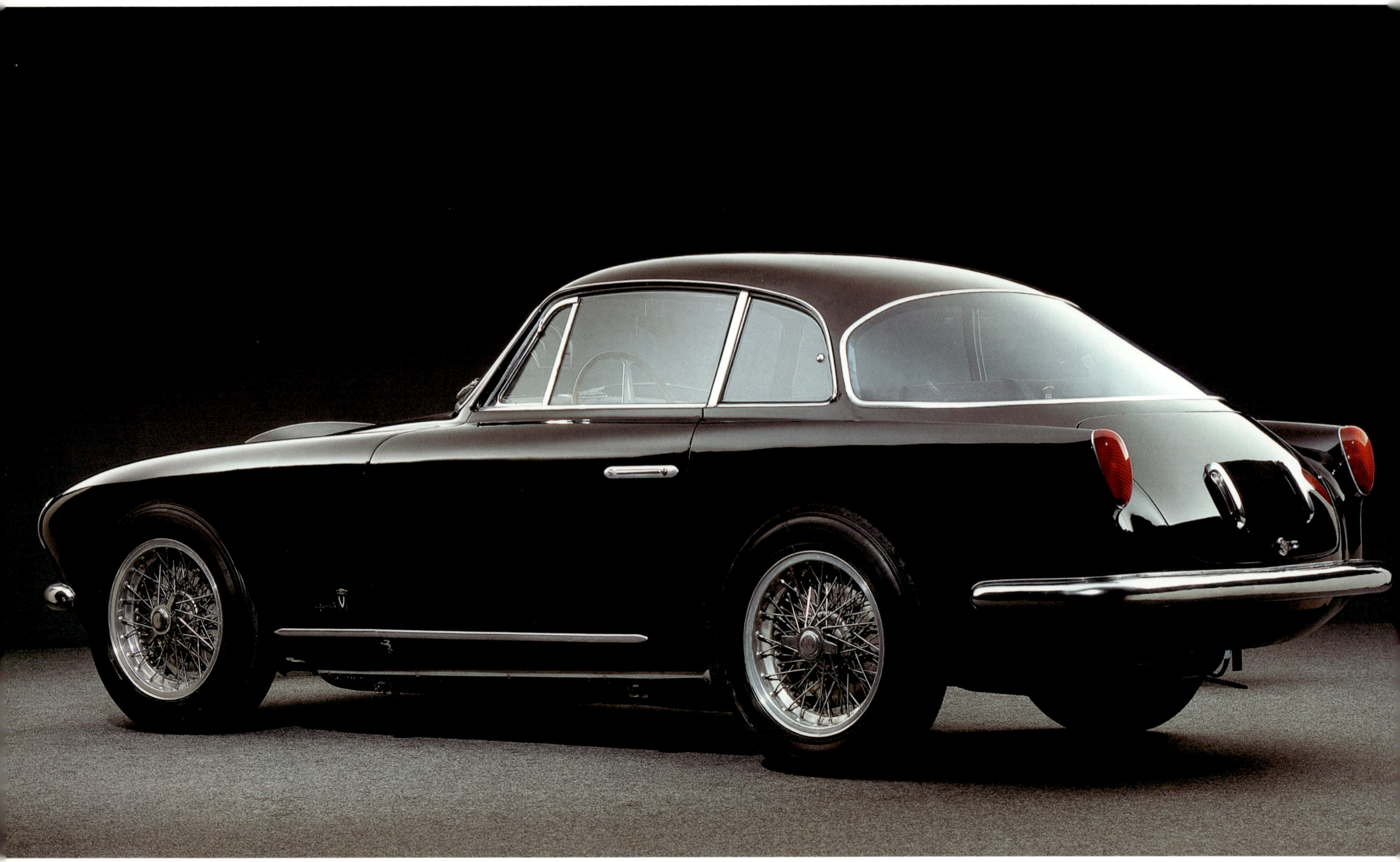

Opposite: Built to compete in motor sport, this OSCA never saw action on the circuits, spending much of its life with a reclusive Swiss collector.

Right: The frontal treatment of this highly distinctive coupé showcased OSCA's then regular corporate grille but with inset driving lights.

OSCA MT4-2AD Coupé   147

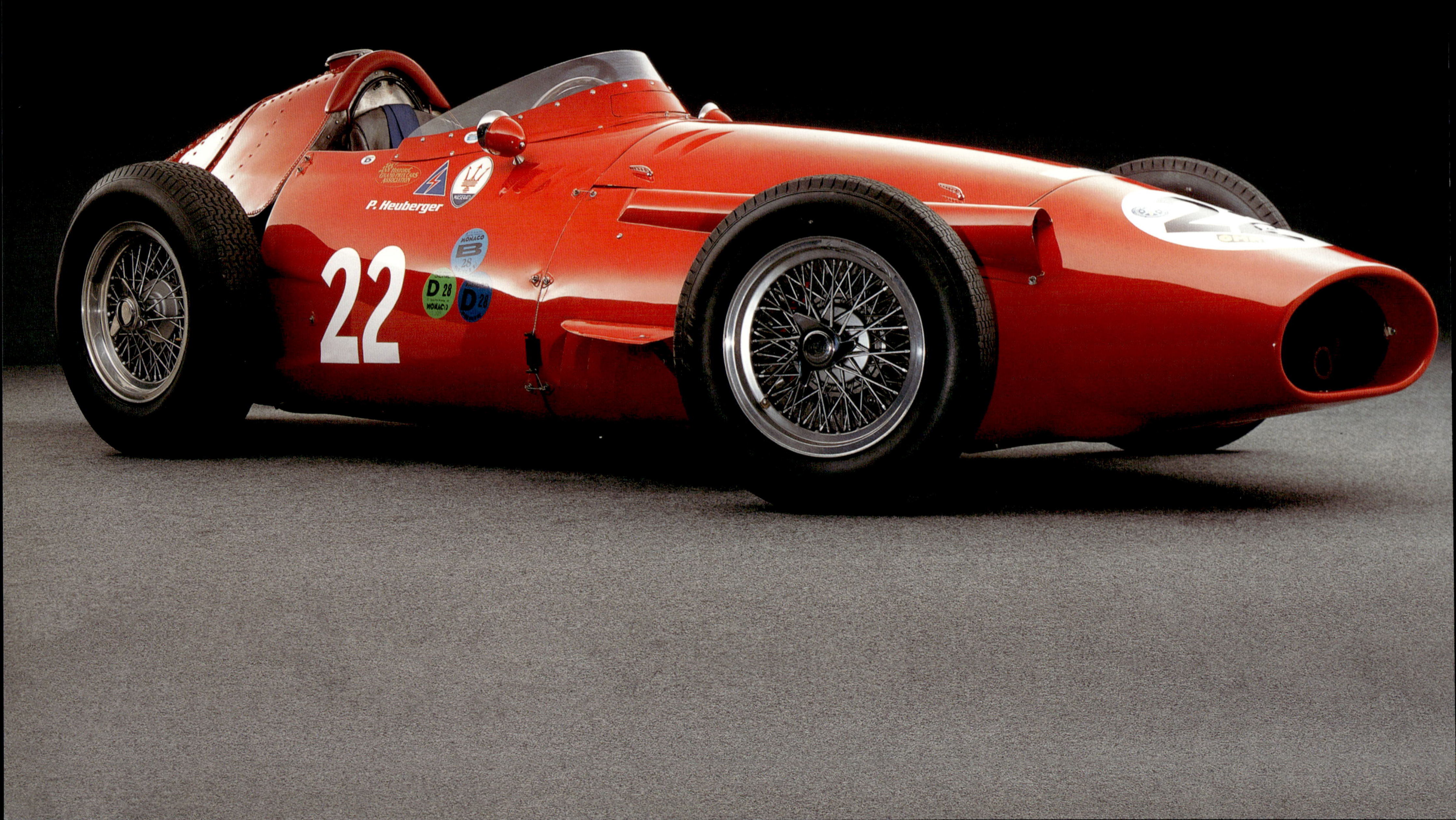
P. Heuberger
22

1956 MASERATI 250F

Given that it was the privateer entry of choice in mid-to-late-1950s grand-prix racing, it is not surprising that Maserati's iconic 250F has the distinction of making more race starts than any other car in Formula One history: 277 from forty-six World Championship rounds between 1954 and 1960. Since the modern practice is for teams to construct a new car each year, this record is likely to stand for ever.

Maserati's return to top-flight motor sport followed the introduction of a new formula for the 1954 season. Regulations stipulated 2.5-litre normally aspirated or 750-cc supercharged engines, the Bologna squad poaching Ferrari's chief designer, Gioacchino Colombo, and engineer Valerio Colotti to produce the new car. Both functional and elegant, the resultant 250F – the name was shortened from the original designation, 250/F1 – consisted of a multi-tubular chassis with independent-wishbone front suspension and a De Dion arrangement at the rear. Power came from a 2490-cc straight-six, based on the firm's existing A6SSG unit and producing 270 bhp at 8000 rpm.

Initially Maserati intended to supply cars to customers to race in lieu of retaining a proper factory team, and, with no other manufacturer offering a competitive 2.5-litre car for privateers, there was plenty of interest. Yet, by the start of the season, works cars were run under the Officine Alfieri Maserati banner for Juan Manuel Fangio and his protégé Onofre Marimon, with the former winning the Argentinian and Belgian Grands Prix before jumping ship to join the Mercedes-Benz team.

It would be another two years before a 250F would triumph at championship level, with Stirling Moss victorious at Monaco and Monza. The following year Fangio returned to the fold to score four wins on the way to his fifth and final World Driver's title. A V12 variant in 1957 had proved no more competitive than the old six-cylinder version but there was not enough time to develop the car further. Maserati was placed under controlled administration before the year was out, leaving the 250F the last grand-prix car to be built in its entirety by the firm.

Maserati's classic 2.5-litre straight-six engine powered the 250F to motor-sport glory for much of the 1950s. Although the firm would return to Formula One as an engine supplier during the following decade, the 250F was the last grand-prix car to be built in its entirety by the Bologna firm.

Left: The 250F is widely considered to be one of the prettiest grand-prix cars of all time, many examples continuing their competition careers to this day in historic events. When a V12 engine was tried late in the car's development life, the nose area was extended.

Opposite: Like most racing cars, the 250F was not styled as such, its form being dictated by the positioning of the running gear. The pointed tail area housed the fuel tank.

Maserati 250F   151

Left: The iconic grand-prix car of its era, the 250F is indissolubly linked with the great Juan Manuel Fangio, who scored six of the model's eight wins in World Championship Formula One racing.

Opposite: The cabin was typical of any period GP car: no speedo; a large steering wheel to brace the driver as much as to help steer in those days before seatbelts; and a near-vertical seating position.

TOURS
X 1000
JAEGER
OFF
BENZINA
OLIO
MASERATI
MOTORE Nº 2526
TIPO 250F
MODENA
(ITALY)
HISTORIC
GRAND PRIX CARS
ASSOCIATION

1957 FERRARI 250 TESTA ROSSA

Following a tragedy at Le Mans in 1955 when more than eighty people died after Pierre Levegh's Mercedes-Benz plunged into the crowd, changes were slowly drafted in an aim to curb speeds, the World Championship for sports cars engine capacity being lowered to 3 litres in time for the 1958 season. Typically, Ferrari had been preparing for such an eventuality.

The *scuderia* had already raced a four-cylinder Testa Rossa ('Red Head', named after the engine's scarlet cam covers) in 1956 and 1957, before introducing a 3-litre V12-powered prototype in time for the 1957 Nürburgring 1000-km (620 miles) race. A second car was then readied for Le Mans the same year, which gave race goers their first look at this wild sports car with its 'pontoon fenders'.

Described by coachbuilder Sergio Scaglietti as a 'Formula One car with fenders', the Testa Rossa sported cut-outs around the front wheels that were intended to aid brake cooling, although in time the 'works' racers reverted to more conventional bodywork. This was apparently done at the behest of drivers who felt the cutaway shape made the cars unstable at speed, although this notion has long been refuted: the nineteen customer cars made retained the controversial styling.

When the 1958 season opened at Buenos Aires, Argentina, in late January, the definitive Testa Rossa was driven to victory by Peter Collins and Phil Hill, the duo winning the Sebring 12 Hours two months later. Luigi Musso triumphed in the Targa Florio in May with Olivier Gendebien, the latter joining Hill to seal the title with victory in the Le Mans 24 Hours the following month. Of the five championship rounds that year, the factory Testa Rossas failed to prevail only once en route to the crown, with Stirling Moss and Jack Brabham winning the Nürburgring 1000-km (620 miles) event in their Aston Martin: Ferraris came in second, third, fourth and fifth.

The Testa Rossa borrowed some of its architecture from current Grand Prix cars, not least the protruding nose, home here to auxiliary driving lights.

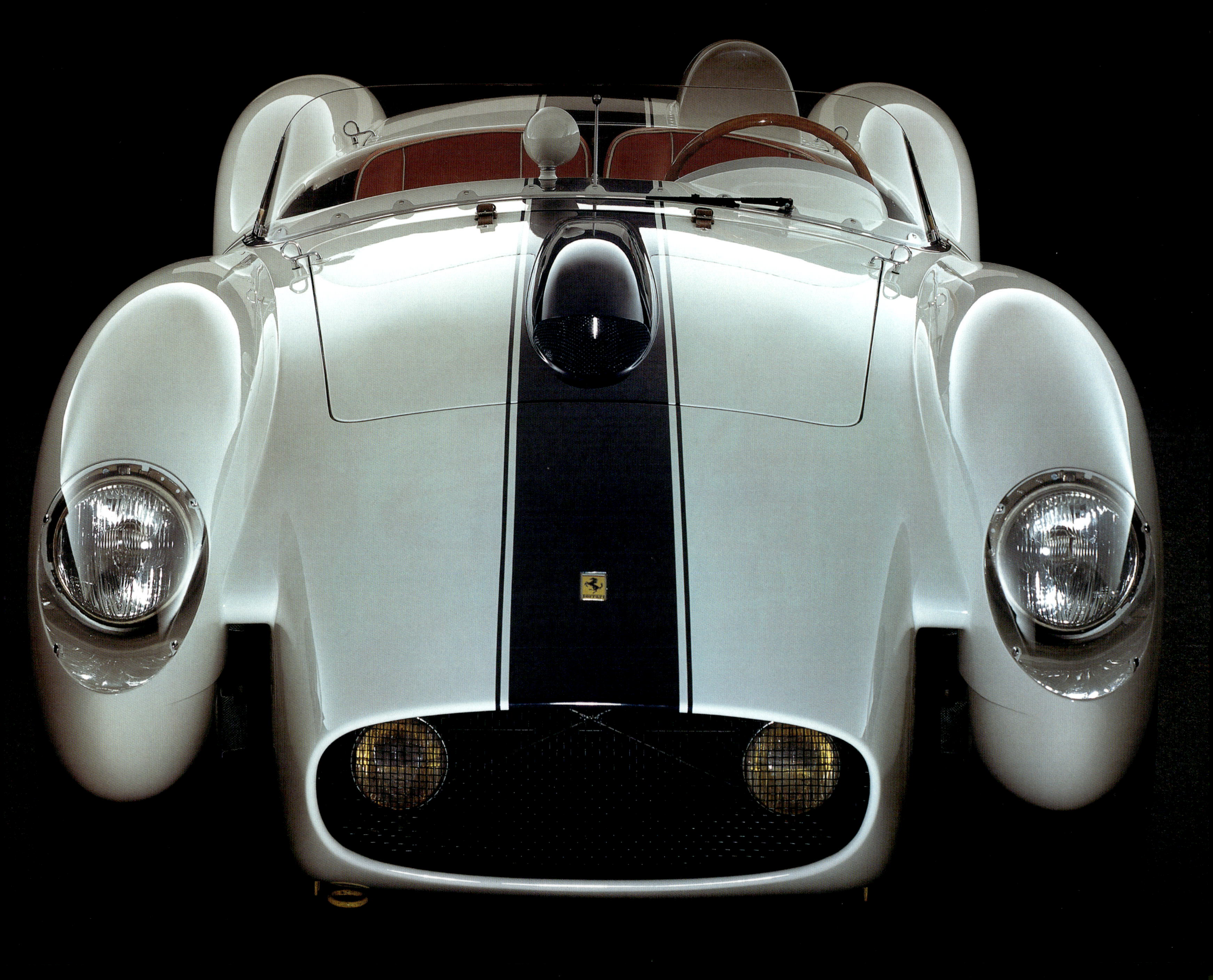

Sergio Scaglietti created the Testa Rossa's outline by eye. It remains one of the most easily identifiable of all racing cars thanks to its 'pontoon fenders', although the factory-run racers possessed more conventional outlines.

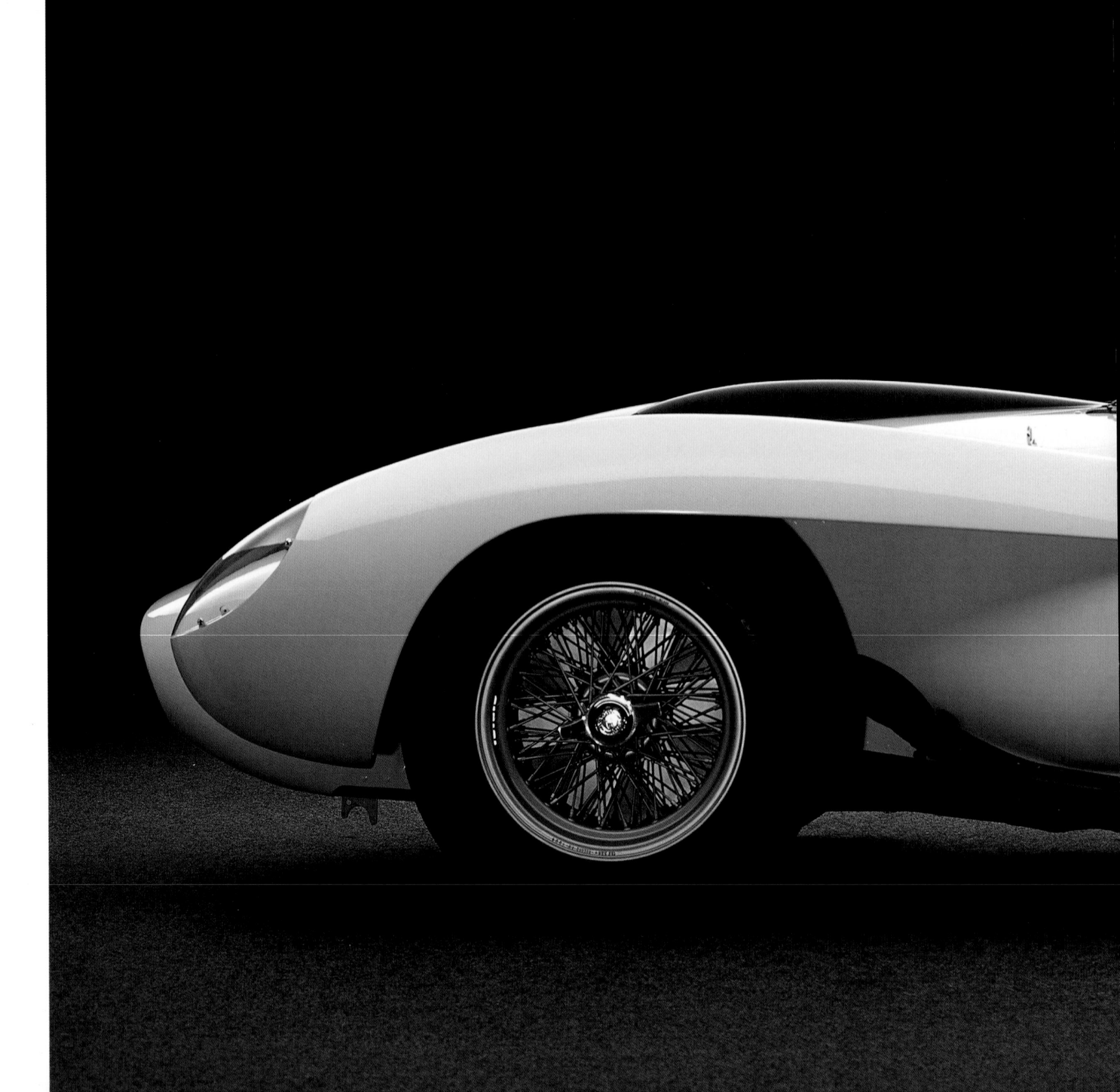

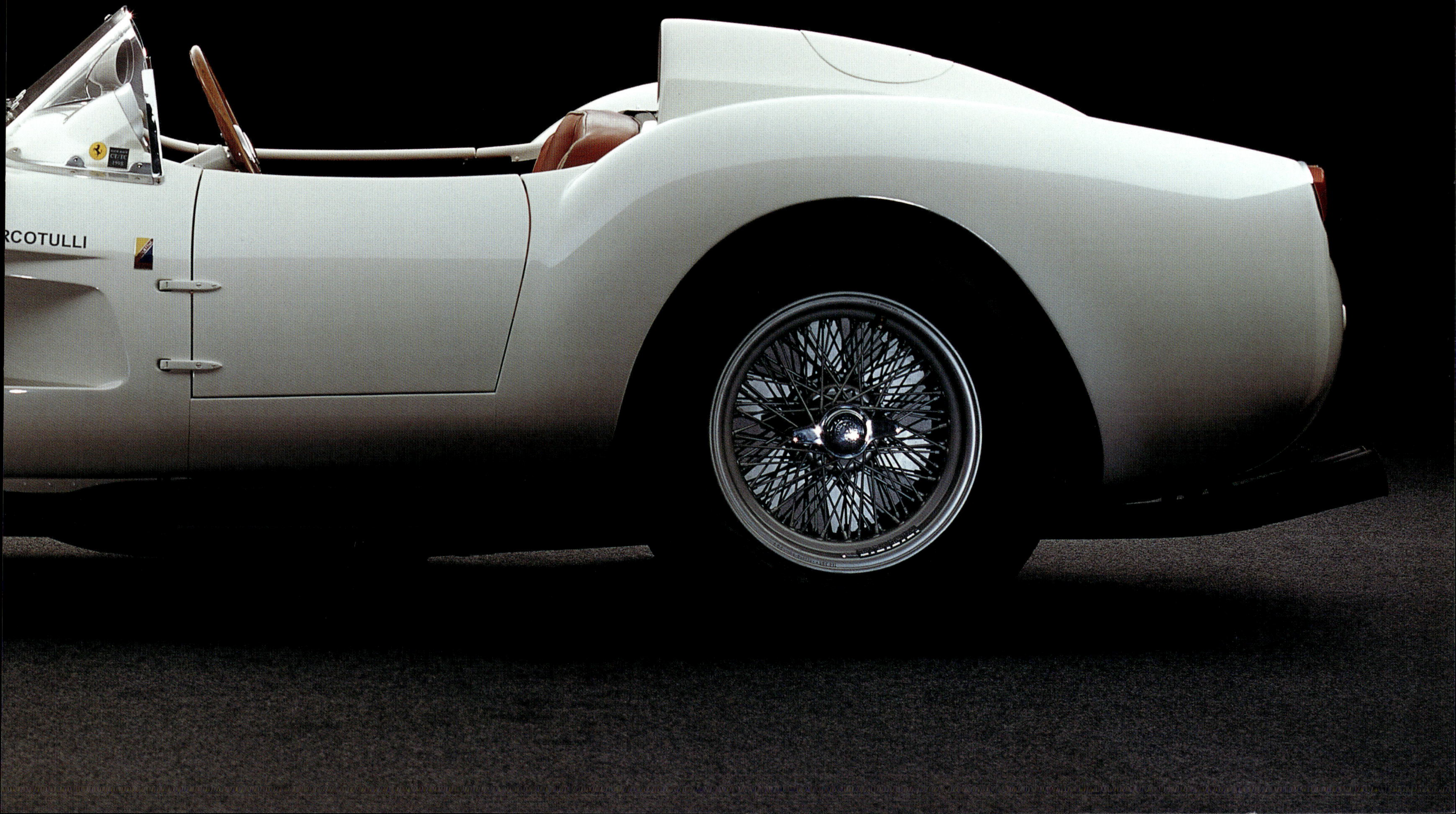
RCOTULLI

M. MARCOTULLI

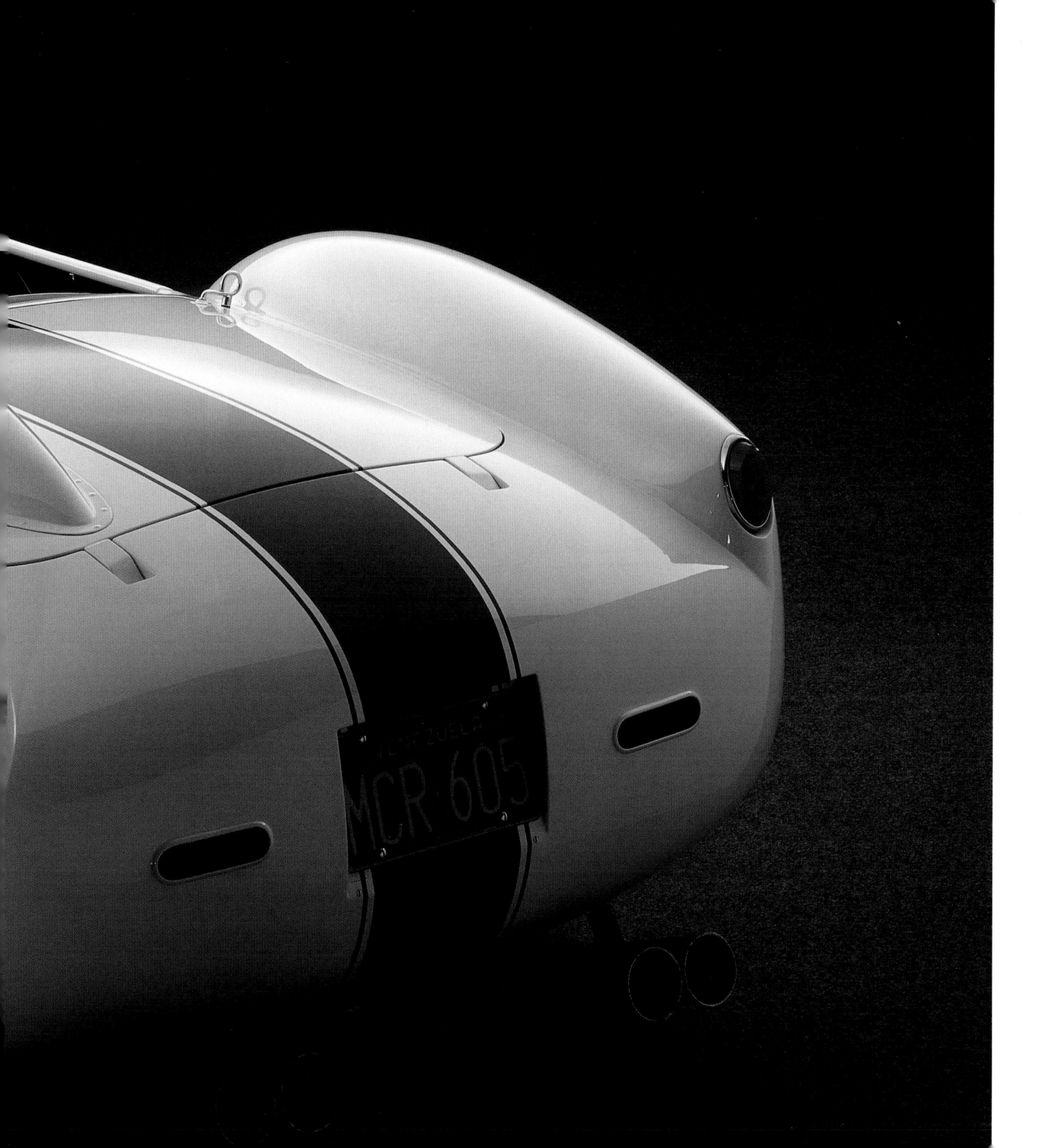

With its long bonnet, rakish wing line and aggressively hunched hind treatment, the Testa Rossa exudes animalistic aggression.

Ferrari 250 Testa Rossa

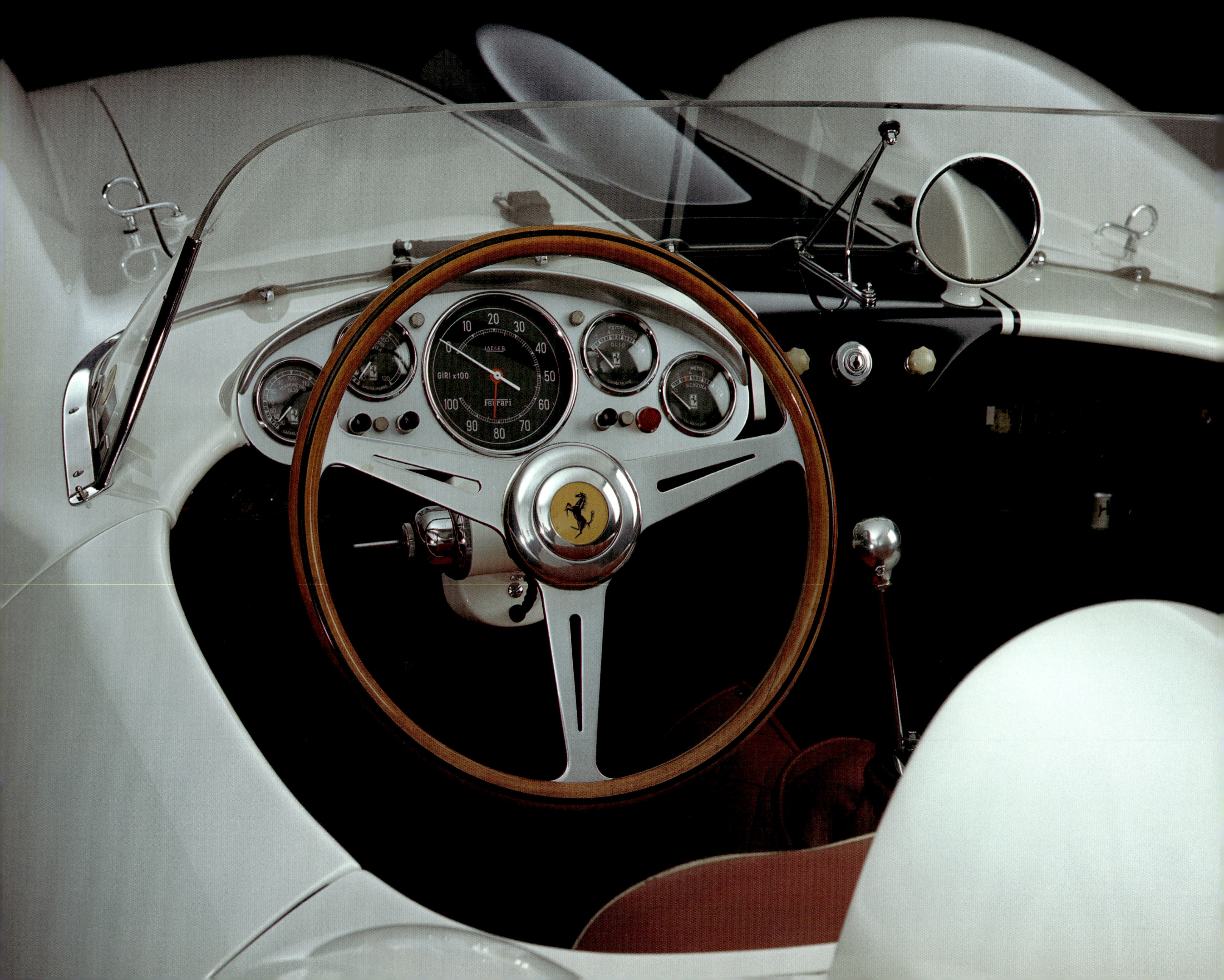

JAEGER
GIRI x100
Ferrari
OLIO
BENZINA

Opposite: The racing driver's office. A classic Nardi wood-rim steering wheel fronts a cluster of instruments. There's nothing superfluous: just all the information the driver needs.

Right: The dominant sports-car racer of the late 1950s, the Testa Rossa won four of five major international races in 1958 alone, including the Sebring 12 Hours and the Sicilian Targa Florio.

Ferrari 250 Testa Rossa 161

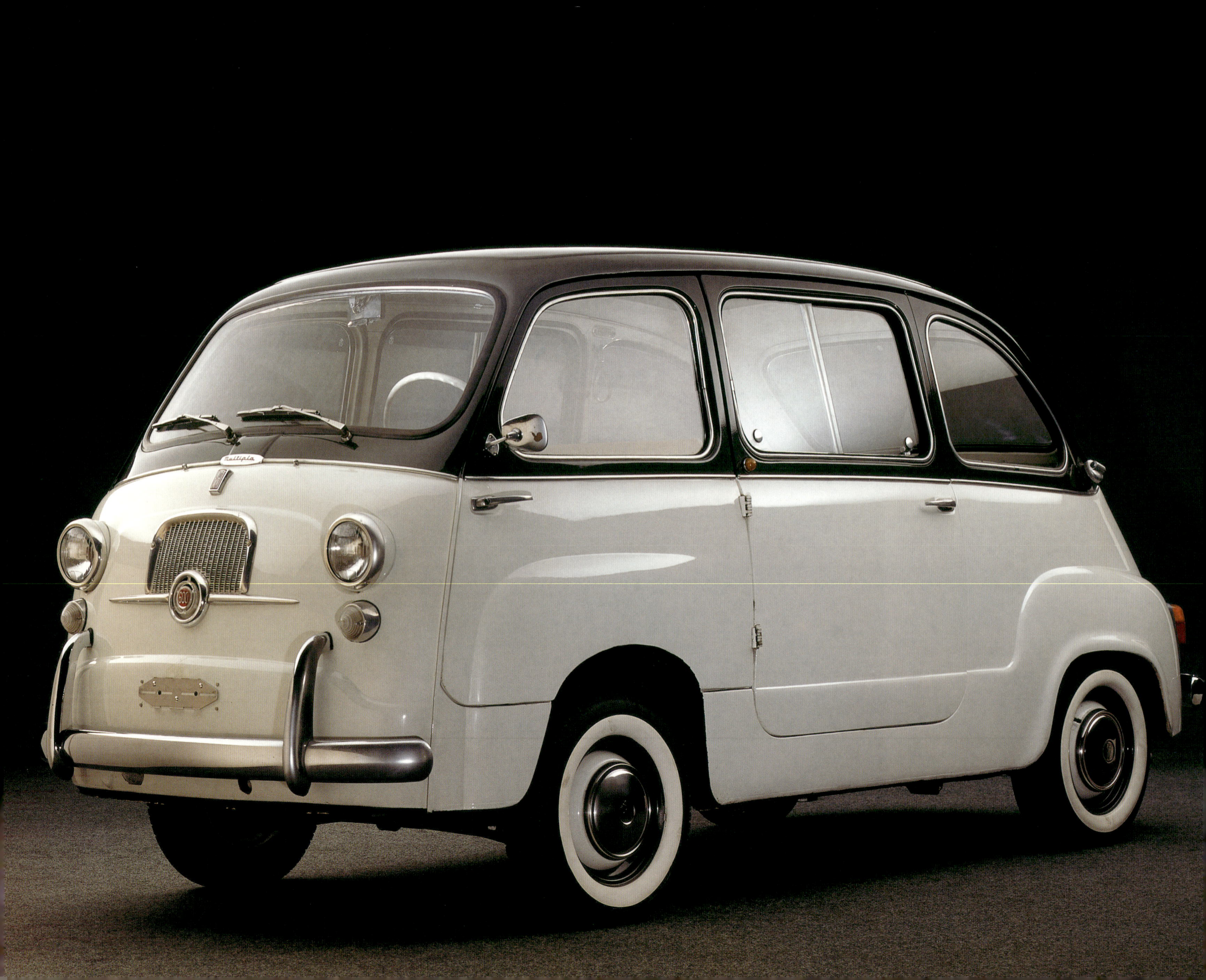

1957 FIAT 500 AND MULTIPLA

Prompted by economic austerity in the immediate post-war years and the ebbing popularity of its ageing Topolino, Fiat launched its small, utilitarian 600 at the 1955 Geneva Salon to rapturous applause. This 633-cc, rear-engined saloon, conceived by Dante Giacosa, generated huge interest in Italy, having been designed to seat four in comfort while being offered at the affordable price of just £265, cheaper even than the 500C Topolino it replaced.

Realizing the potential of the 600's platform, Fiat introduced a highly distinctive variation on the theme at the Brussels Motor Show in January of the following year. The Multipla, which housed three rows of seats, plus luggage space, was arguably the world's first people carrier (although the pre-war Stout Scarab would qualify if it had entered volume production). Yet, at 3540 mm (11 ft 6 in.) from bumper to bumper, it was only 254 mm (10 in.) longer than the 600 while retaining the same wheelbase. Despite its cab-forward styling and difficult-to-negotiate rear-hinged doors over the front wheels, the Multipla overcame initial customer resistance and around 150,000 were built over the following ten years.

Yet Giacosa's crowning achievement was the 500 Nuova, Fiat's 'city car'. General construction of the 500 followed on from the 600 but the new baby, diminutive in the extreme, had an air-cooled, 479-cc, twin-cylinder engine housed in the rear. Some 230 mm (9 in.) shorter than the 600, it was a miracle of rational design that would remain in production from 1957 until 1975, by when more than 3,000,000 had been made. The 500 also spawned coachbuilt and highly tuned variations from Monterosa, Lombardi, Moretti, Siata, Giannini and, most famous of all, Abarth. More recently, Fiat has raided its back catalogue, the new Roberto Giolito-styled Trepiuno aping the 500's cheeky good looks in a retro package.

With the introduction of the Multipla, Fiat ushered in a new breed of automobile – the people carrier. Fiat revived the name in the 1990s with an equally unusual variation on the theme.

Left: The baby Fiat offered minimal instrumentation and its stark cabin was in keeping with the economy-car rationale. The lack of a fuel gauge was known to cause problems; a warning light came on when fuel had run out.

Opposite: Fiat redefined the small car with the 500. The small twin-cylinder engine provided modest performance but the car's tiny stature allowed surprisingly high cornering speeds.

Fiat 500 and Multipla   165

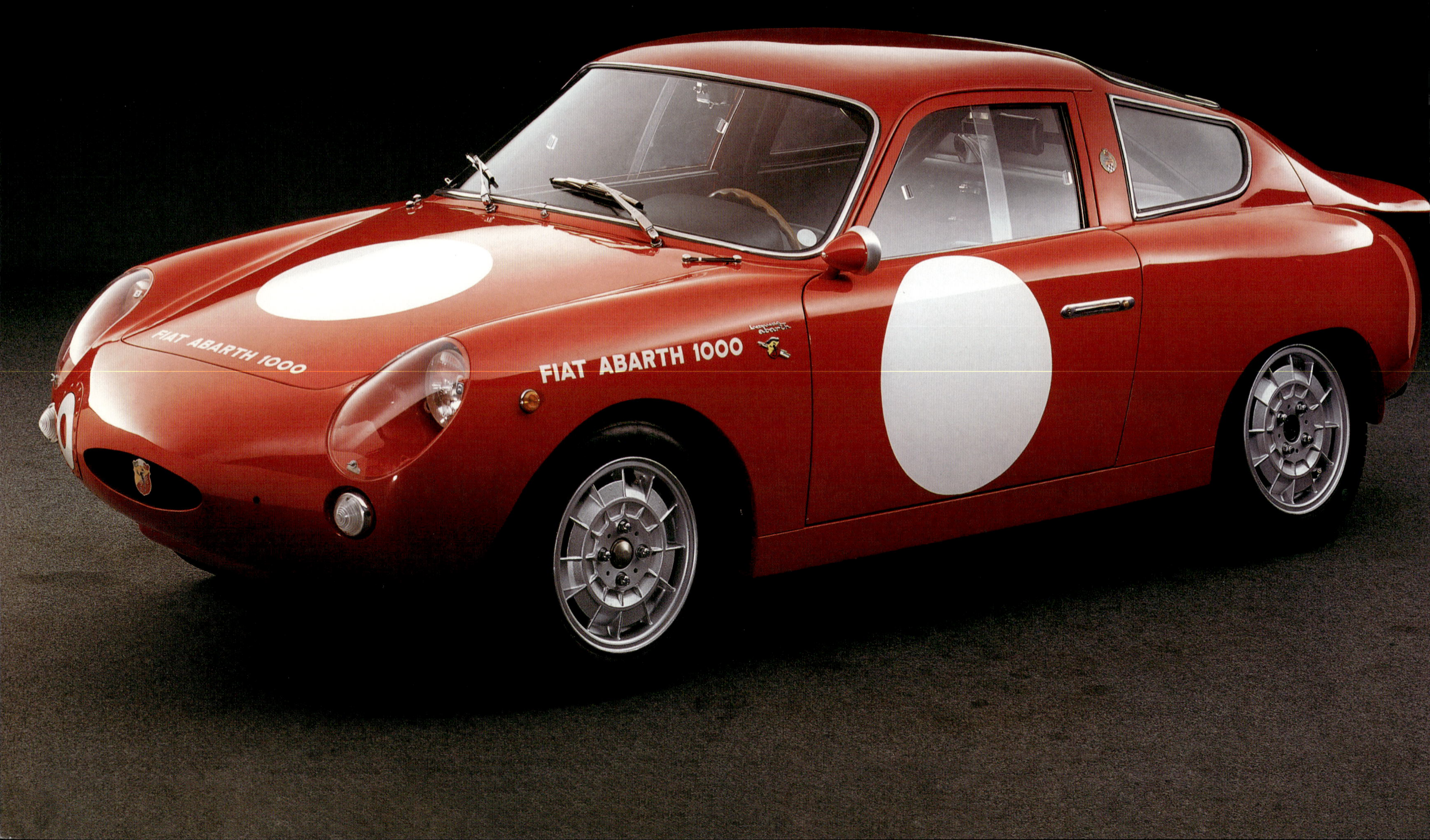
FIAT ABARTH 1000
FIAT ABARTH 1000

1959 ABARTH 750

Known as 'the Sorcerer', Carlo (Karl) Abarth was capable of extracting seemingly impossible amounts of power from the smallest of engines. The Austrian-born tuning wizard founded his eponymous firm on performance-enhancing exhaust systems while simultaneously becoming a car manufacturer in his own right.

This former motorcycle racer was made an Italian citizen in 1945, initially eking out a hand-to-mouth existence selling bicycles. However, his technical nous soon led to his becoming embroiled in the ill-starred Cisitalia grand-prix project, out of the ashes of which he formed his own company in 1949. Although Abarth was building racing cars in only tiny numbers, his tuning parts for small Fiats soon attracted positive press reports and led to him producing his 750-series coupés. Taking the Fiat 600's platform and running gear as a basis, Carlo increased engine capacity to 747 cc, achieving a power output of 47 bhp at 6000 rpm. Also benefiting from streamlined and ultra-light Zagato coachwork – the whole car weighed just 535 kg (1179 lb) – the 750 swiftly proved a natural contender for class honours in sports-car racing from its introduction in 1955.

The winner of 750-cc Grand Touring honours in the 1957 Mille Miglia and countless other minor successes, the 750 was continuously updated, no two cars seeming identical. In time came a twin-cam variant devised by former Ferrari designer Gioacchino Colombo and further increases in engine capacity, including the 1000, shown here, resulting in yet more victories in races, rallies and hillclimbs. From 1958 there was even greater incentive for Abarth, as the firm received a financial reward from Fiat for every success garnered with its products. The Turin giant must have been paying out a lot, for that first year there were forty-nine wins and almost twice as many the following season.

1959 FIAT 8V DÉMON ROUGE

At a time when the company's output was weighted towards small, utilitarian machines, the arrival of Fiat's 8V in 1952 came as a shock. What began as an after-hours project for a select band of engineers proved too good to remain a prototype and the management allowed it to enter limited production.

At the heart of the 'Otto Vu' was a 1996-cc V8 set in a tubular chassis with the steel bodywork welded to it. Specialist sports-car manufacturer Siata was said to have played a role in its design, which would explain why it was allowed the use of the engine for a car of its own invention. Unusually, the 8V featured all-round independent suspension – then sill quite a novelty – along with a fully synchronized four-speed transmission. The car soon attracted the attention of the competition fraternity, 8Vs taking an outright win in the 1952 Pescara 12 Hours, along with consecutive class honours in the Mille Miglia from 1955 to 1957. Yet, with the 8V costing twice as much as a Jaguar XK120, which matched it for pace, only 114 of these highly exclusive coupés found a home.

Styled by Giovanni Michelotti and constructed by Alfredo Vignale in 1955 – three years after the chassis was made – the Démon Rouge marked the zenith of the 8V. With its panoramic Plexiglas roof that gave panoramic visibility with full weather protection, and vestigial tail fins atop the rear wings, this most exotic of all Fiats took the prize in the Campione d'Italia concours d'élégance on its public debut. Just one car was ever made and after its show career ended it passed to Count Zanon, future patron of Formula One star Ronnie Peterson.

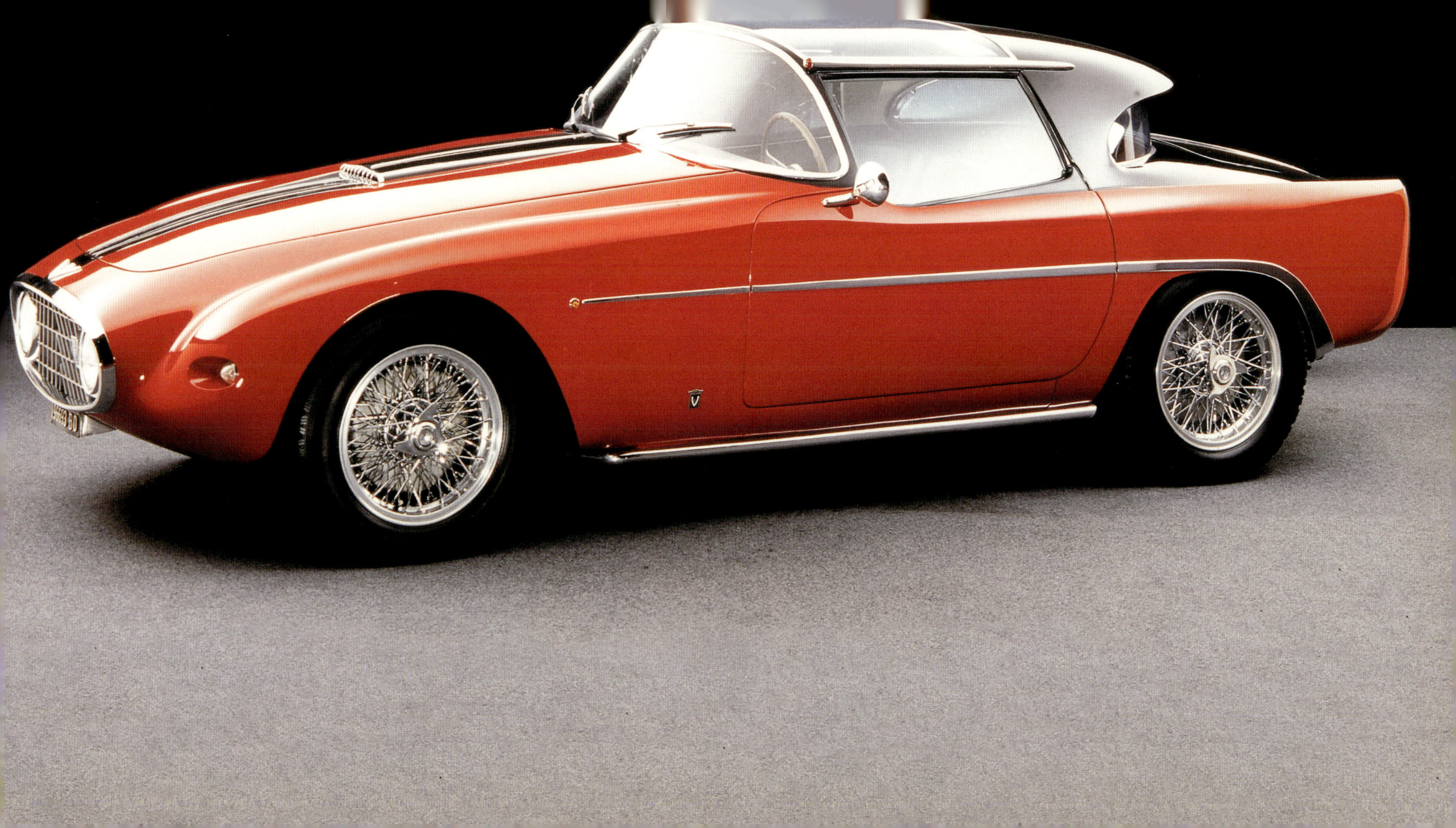

1959 LANCIA FLAMINIA ZAGATO SUPER SPORT

Lancia's sublime Flaminia employed soberly attractive styling with almost unassailable build quality. Introduced at the 1957 Geneva Salon, the new saloon continued to build on the marque's legendary engineering pedigree but against a backdrop of continued commercial failure. Predictably, it was not long before specialist *carrozzerie* began to fill out the model range, among the more idiosyncratic of the factory-sanctioned offerings being those made by Zagato.

Unveiled at the 1958 Turin Salon, the Zagato Sport was based on a substantially shortened Flaminia platform with a wheelbase of 2250 mm (99 in.). Although more than capable of the occasional credibility chasm, Zagato produced a well-balanced design, the aerodynamic coupé featuring the Terrazzano di Rho-based coachbuilder's trademark 'double bubble' roof treatment – a carry-over from its racing involvement – and headlights faired in behind Plexiglas covers.

Inside, the regular Flaminia instruments were retained within Zagato's own dashboard design, the low roofline making the Sport cramped when compared with the saloon. Weighing in at 1320 kg (2910 lb), the car was not as light as it looked but was still capable of 180 kph (112 mph) from 119 bhp. Around ninety-nine were made to 1960 before a facelift brought a switch to vertical headlights and technical upgrades in line with the regular Flaminia, including a 140-bhp 3C engine and, in time, a larger-displacement 2.8-litre unit.

The ultimate iteration was the Super Sport. Restyled by new recruit Ercole Spada (later design chief at BMW), it featured a return to recessed headlights and a new shapely hind area in place of the original sloping tail. With aerodynamics superior to those of its predecessors, and 148 bhp, this gorgeous *gran turismo* was capable of 209 kph (130 mph). Some 526 Zagato Flaminias of all types – including two competition models, one with a lightweight *tubolare* chassis – are believed to have been made, this example's first owner being the Italian screen legend Marcello Mastroianni.

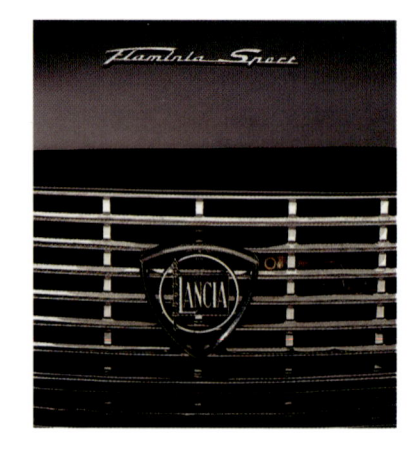

Zagato's relationship with Lancia has resulted in some of the most beautiful – and ugliest – GTs yet seen. The Super Sport is undoubtedly among the former, being a car fit for a silver-screen star.

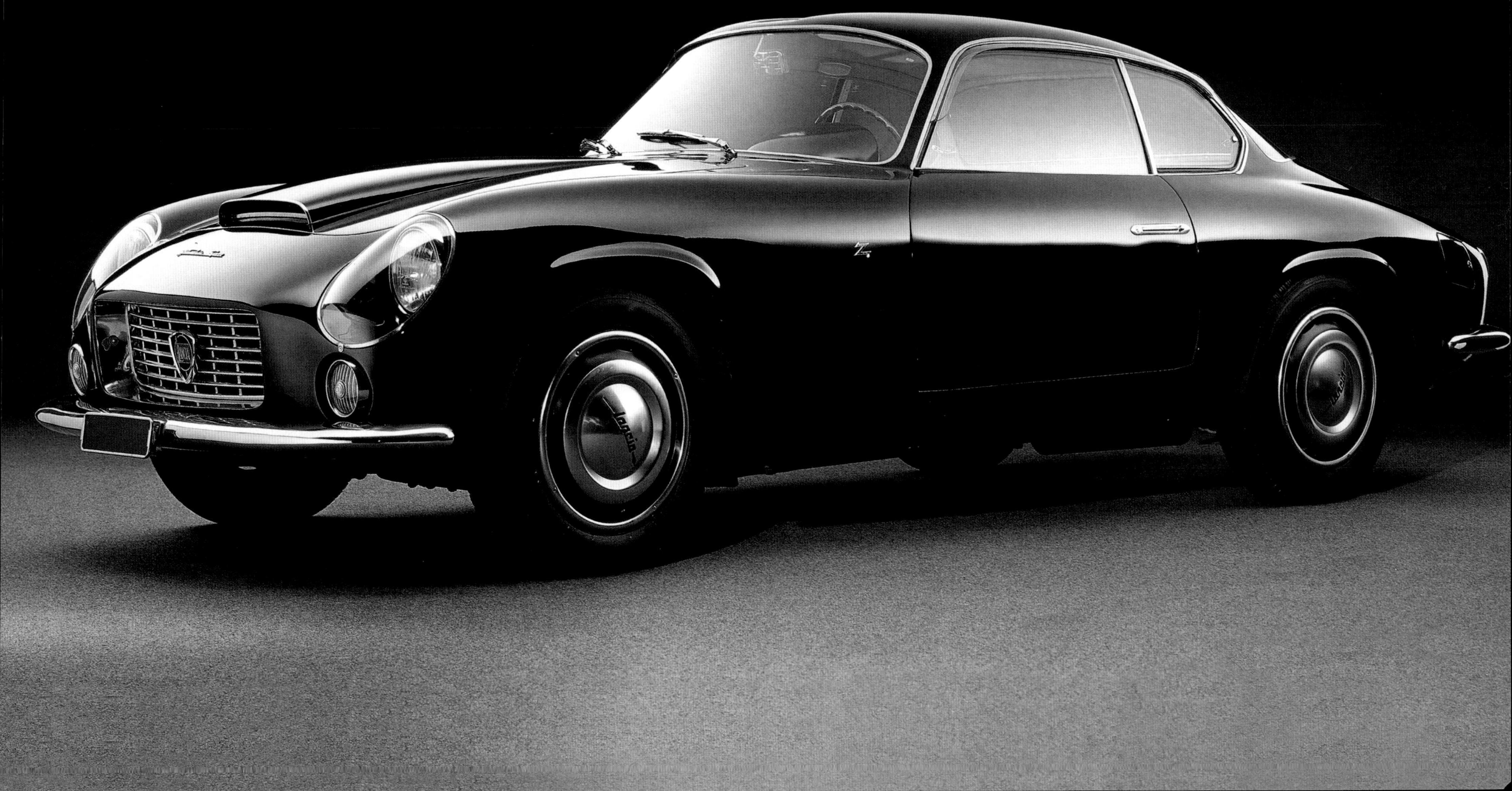

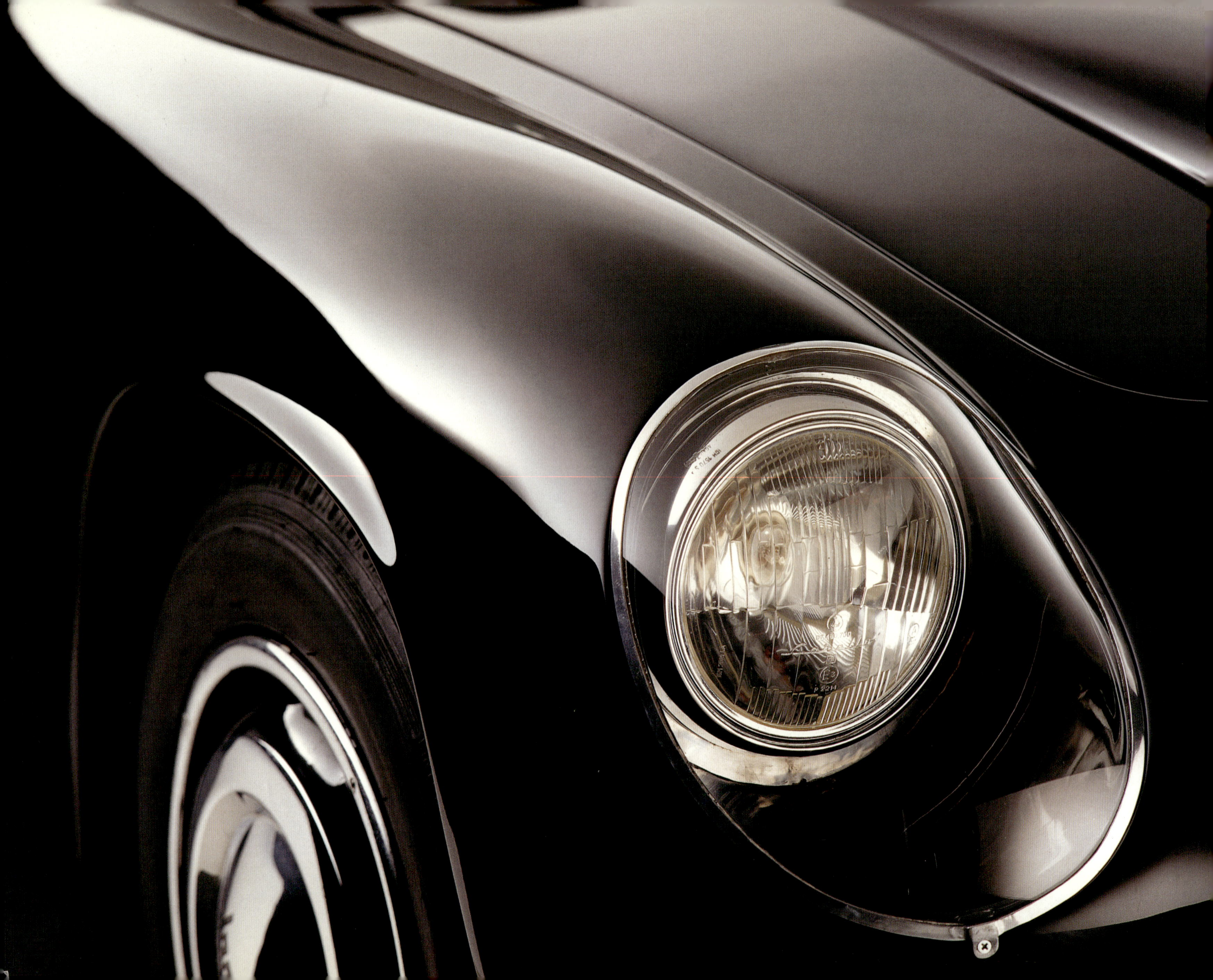

Opposite: Faired-in headlights featured glass cowlings for superior aerodynamics. With its background in bodying competition cars, Zagato had a strong grasp of streamlining.

Left: BMW's future head of design Ercole Spada restyled the Zagato Flaminia's hind treatment; a more bulbous affair than the cropped original. The distinctive 'double bubble' roof was originally a motor-sport-orientated styling trick, giving decent headroom for drivers wearing helmets.

Lancia Flaminia Zagato Super Sport

Left: Zagato was so happy with the frontal treatment of the Super Sport that it later reworked it for British manufacturer Bristol. Inset headlights behind Perpex covers were a carry-over from earlier Flaminia racers.

Opposite: Zagato's delicious Super Sport retained the regular Flaminia's instrumentation, mounted in a bespoke dashboard. The overall effect mirrored the outer dazzle.

174

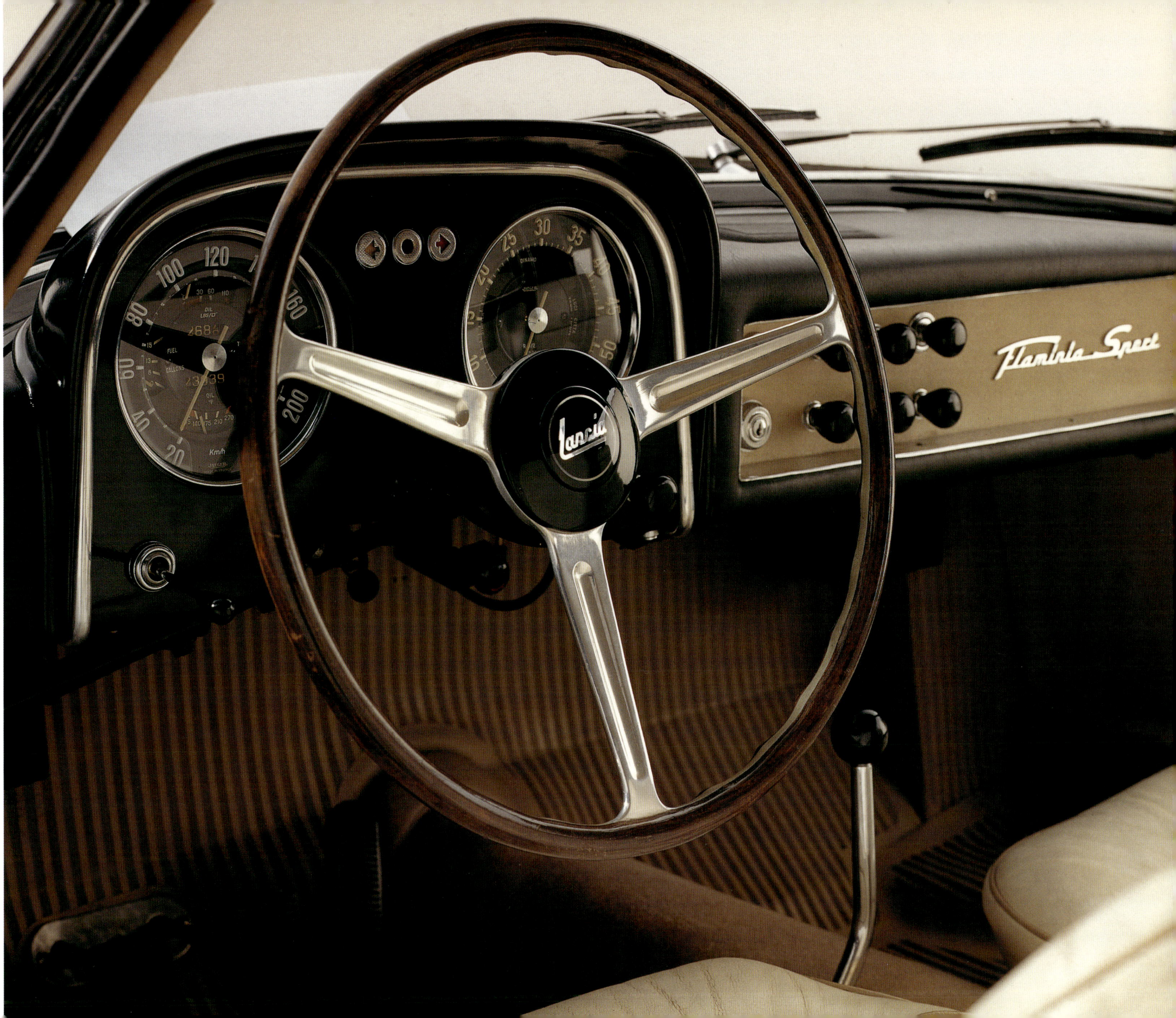
Lancia
Flaminia Sport

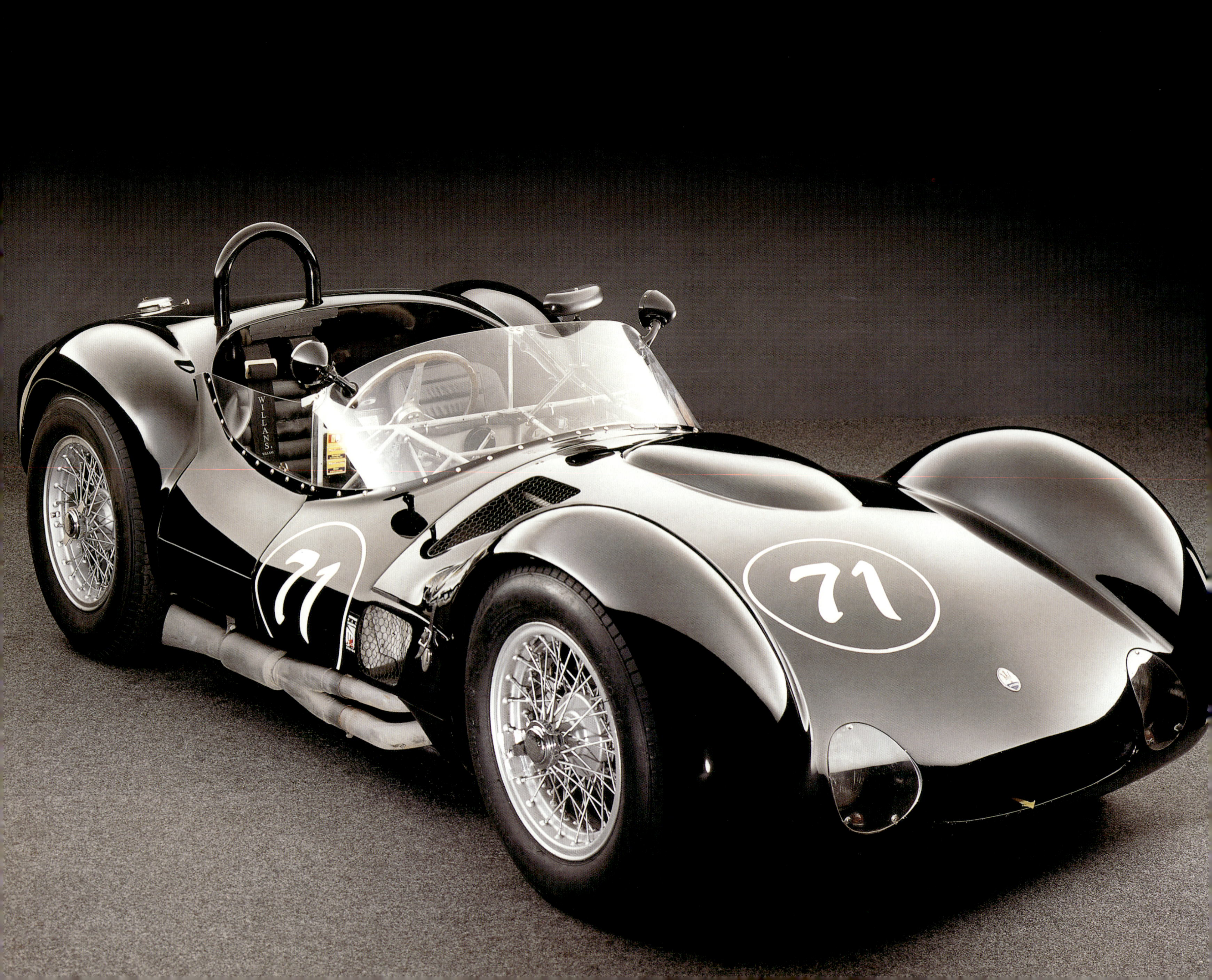
71
WILLANS.
71

1959   MASERATI TIPO 61 BIRDCAGE

Given that Maserati's 1957 motor-sport programme had been its greatest ever, with Juan Manuel Fangio winning the Formula One Drivers' Championship at the wheel of a 250F, news that the Bologna marque was withdrawing from competition at the end of the season came as a profound shock. A business deal between Maserati's paymaster the Orsi family and Argentina's Péron regime had turned sour, leaving the firm staring bankruptcy in the face. It recovered in time, but the creation of any new racing car had to be funded by customers: some twenty-two were found to subsidize the Tipo 60/61 Birdcage.

Designed by the brilliant Giulio Alfieri, this highly unusual sports-racer earned its epithet thanks to the use of more than 200 individual tubes welded together to form an ultra-light structure that supported the 2-litre, four-cylinder engine, transmission and suspension, the De Dion-type rear end aping that of the 250F grand-prix car.

Stirling Moss gave the Tipo 60 its maiden win in the 1960 Delamare-Deboutteville Cup, which supported the French Grand Prix at Rouen, but demand from customers soon led to enlargement of the engine to 2890 cc. Although heavier than the outgoing model thanks to a bigger crankshaft and outsized brakes, the revised Tipo 61 now posed a threat to the dominant Ferrari 250 Testa Rossa in the premier class of the World Sports Car Championship and the Sports Car Club of America's D-Modified category, where Gus Audrey won the title in 1961 and Roger Penske claimed the same honours the following year.

Yet in European endurance events the Birdcage never realized its potential. Lloyd 'Lucky' Casner's Camoradi team won the 1960 Nürburgring 1000-km (620 miles) race with Stirling Moss and Dan Gurney driving, Gurney joining Casner for a successful follow-up a year later but the car's fragility cost the team victories elsewhere.

A good example of form following function, the Birdcage was not a work of great beauty. However, it did prove competitive, although poor reliability robbed it of many victories.

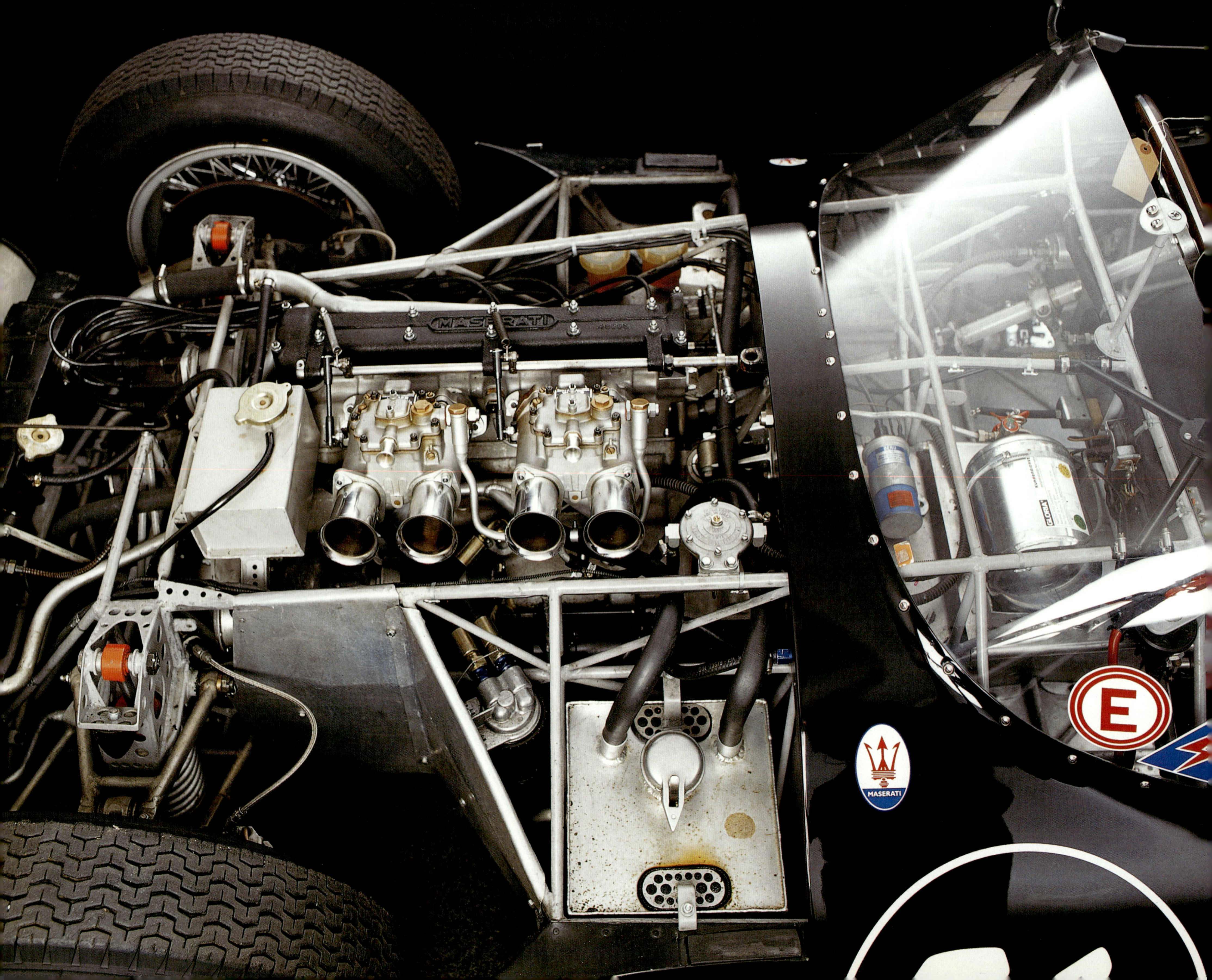
MASERATI
E
MASERATI

Opposite: The small four-cylinder engine was housed far back in the multi-tubular frame for better weight distribution. Maserati made no attempt to conceal the framework, which continued into the cabin area.

Right: The Birdcage was perhaps the most idiosyncratic of all 1950s sports-racing cars. Conceived by the great Giulio Alfieri as a customer racing car, it proved hugely successful at national level in the USA.

Maserati Tipo 61 Birdcage

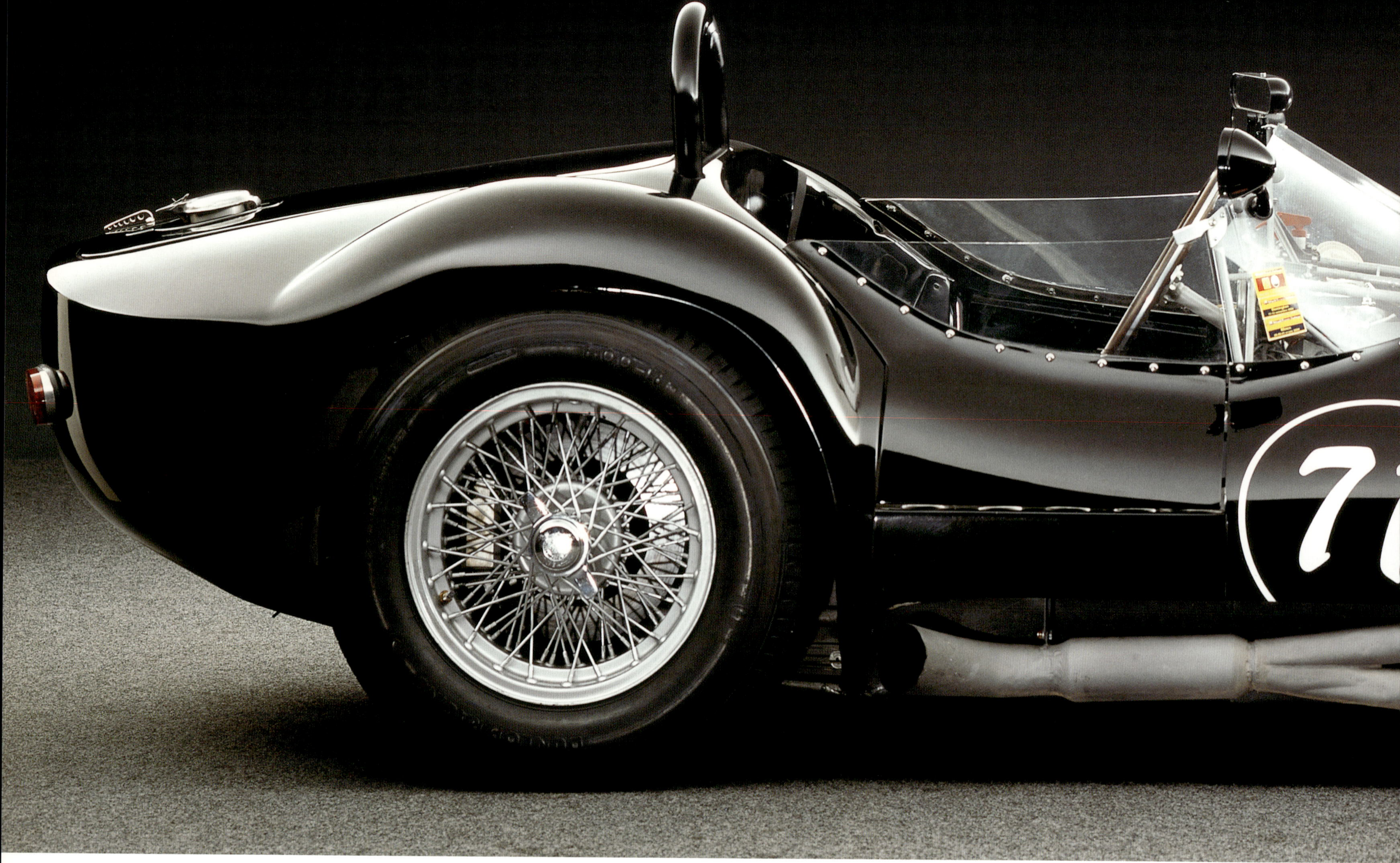

Decades on from the model's career in front-line motor sport, the Birdcage is now favoured by the historic racing fraternity, short sprint events suiting the car better than the long-distance events that it competed in originally.

Maserati Tipo 61 Birdcage 181

1960 FERRARI 250GT SWB

Smudging the boundaries between road and racing car, the 250GT SWB graphically illustrated its duality of character when it was driven by Stirling Moss in the 1960 Tourist Trophy. Lapping Goodwood en route to victory aboard Rob Walker's fully road-equipped version, Moss bided his time twiddling the radio dials between music stations and Raymond Baxter's live race commentary for the BBC. Had he chosen to, there was no reason why he could not have driven home in the car afterwards.

First shown at the 1959 Paris Motor Show, the model was given its suffix 'SWB' because its wheelbase was, at 2400 mm (94.5 in.), some 200 mm (20 in.) shorter than that of proceeding 250-series models, the aim being to improve cornering agility. The SWB's other novelty was the introduction of all-round Dunlop disc brakes for the first time on a Ferrari, six years after Jaguar had pioneered their use at Le Mans. Offered in a number of guises, the car was the sportsman's ideal, with aluminium coachwork and a high-compression, 280-bhp, 3-litre V12 engine, although more were sold in Lusso (luxury) trim with heavier steel bodywork (alloy doors, bonnet and boot), leather upholstery and de-tuned 240-bhp engines. Fastest of all were the SEFAC (Società per Azioni Esercizio Fabbriche Automobili e Corse) 'hot rods', with monstrous Weber carburettors, larger intake valves and gossamer-thin bodywork.

One of the last truly hand-built production Ferraris, the SWB had one other great strength: its styling. Penned at Pinin Farina and built by Scaglietti – it is doubtful that any two cars were ever identical dimensionally – it had not a single jarring line, no gimmickry or quickly dated addenda: just a purity of form that still captivates. In total, 165 cars are believed to have been made to 1962, by which time Moss had notched up back-to-back TT wins. Other scalps taken by the SWB include the 1960 Tour de France and the Paris 1000-km (620 miles) race at Montlhéry, along with the following year's GT class of the Constructors' Championship.

Ferrari's short-wheelbase variant of the long-running 250 series was among the last of the breed to be competitive while remaining a convincing road car. Add breathtaking beauty and you have one of the greatest of all Ferraris.

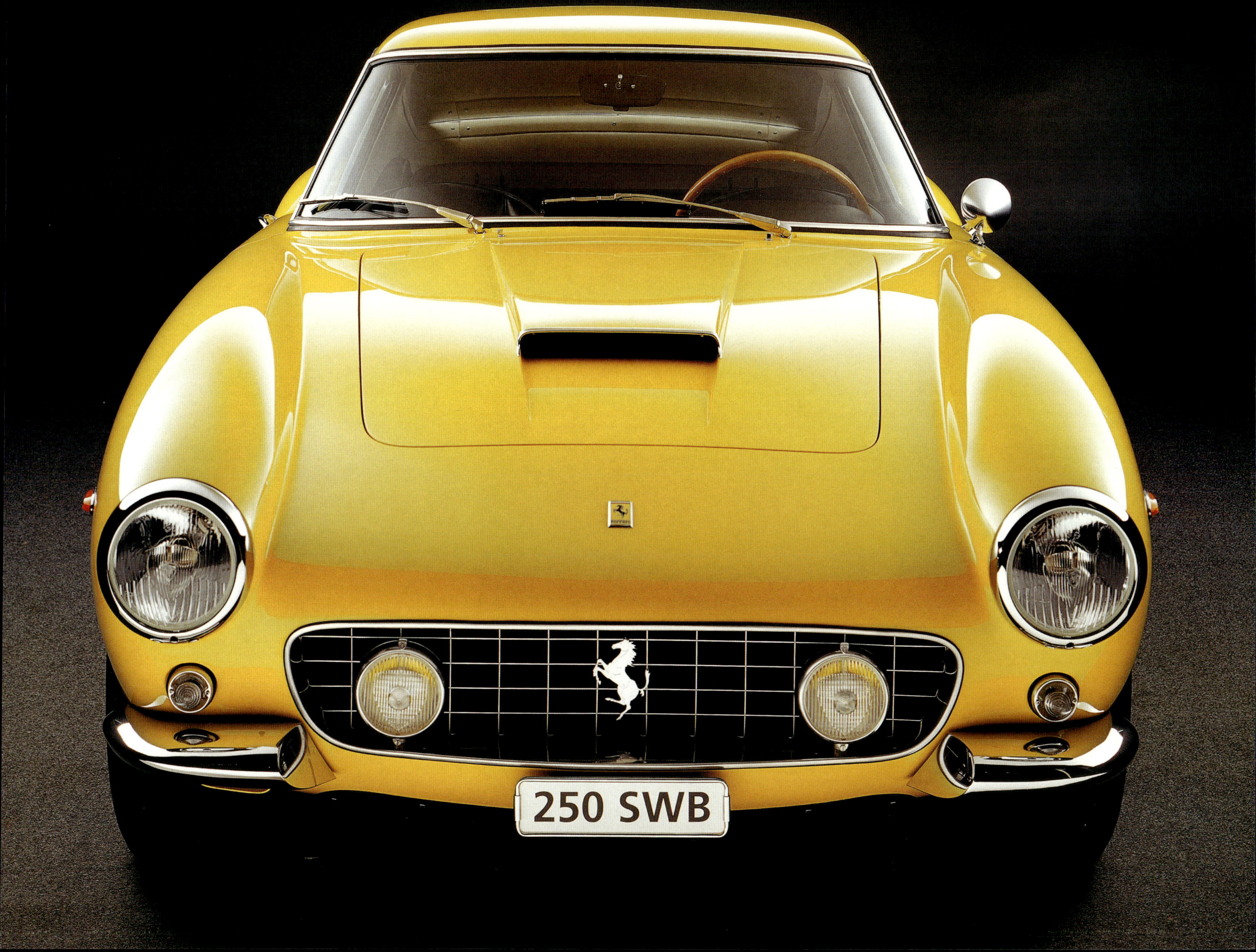
250 SWB

Left: The bodywork of the 250GT SWB was crafted by Sergio Scaglietti's famous *carrozzeria*. The car was offered with the choice of steel or aluminium coachwork

Opposite: Minimal use of chrome jewellery served to highlight the SWB's perfect proportions. Attractive Borrani wire wheels were a Ferrari constant.

Ferrari 250GT SWB 185

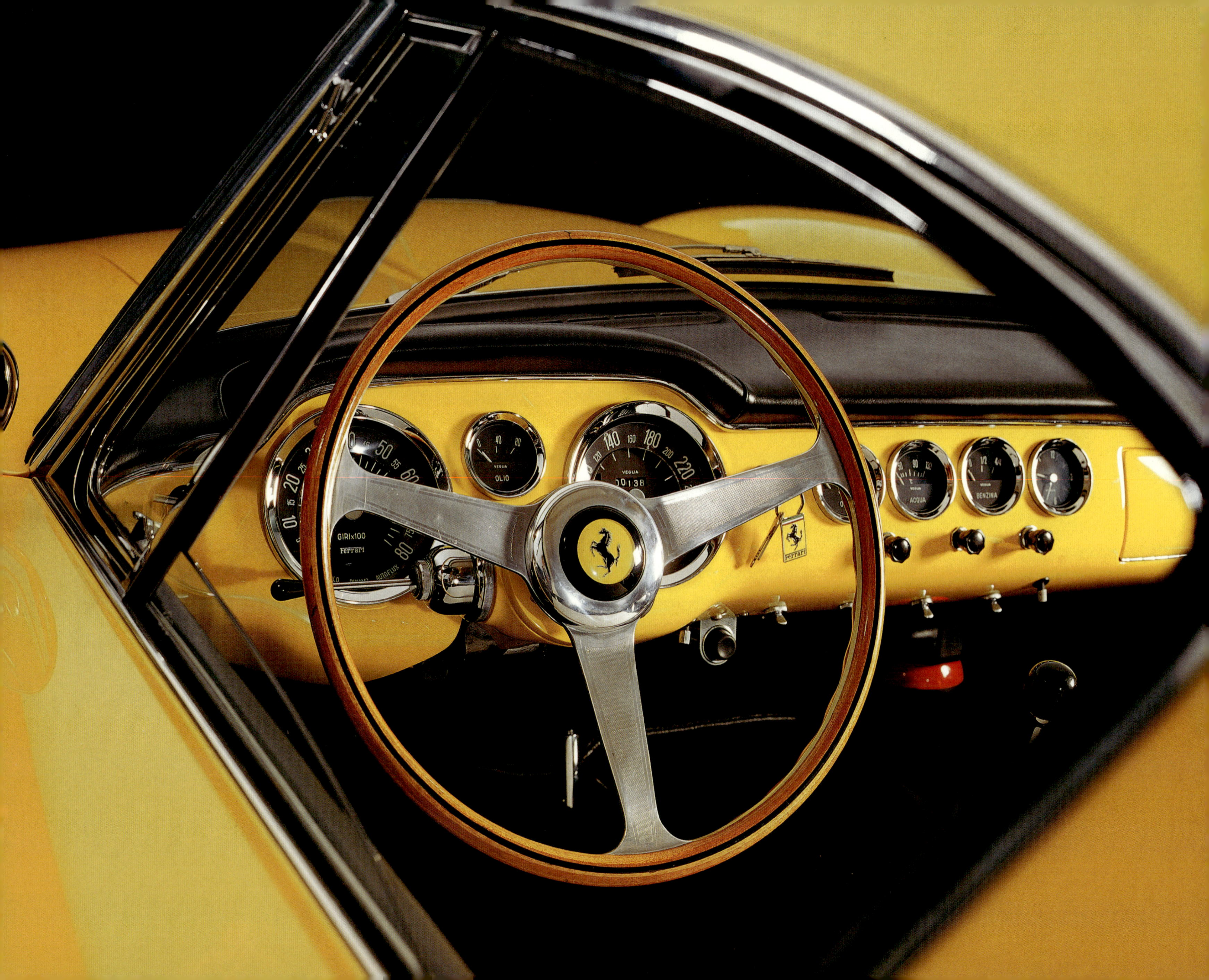
OLIO
ACQUA
BENZINA
GIRIx100
Ferrari

Opposite: In a cabin that was as chic as the outer silhouette, the metal dashboard was painted in body colour and fronted by a traditional Nardi wood-rim steering wheel.

Right: The 3-litre V12 engine was offered in varying states of tune. Entry-level road cars had 240 bhp, outright racers 40 bhp more. And it sounded as glorious as it looked.

Ferrari 250GT SWB   187

1961 FERRARI 400 SUPERAMERICA CABRIOLET

Given its proud model name, it is ironic that this hyper-glamorous strain of Ferrari never did conquer America. From 1959 to 1964 the most powerful production car to bear the badge of the Cavallino Rampante (prancing horse) was the 400 Superamerica. First presented in coupé form at the Turin Salon in November 1959, it had a designation that broke with Ferrari's tradition of indicating the individual cylinder displacement, '400' referring to overall engine capacity. This was a clever ploy, as most potential customers believed it could produce 400 bhp, whereas the seldom circulated factory sales literature claimed 340 bhp.

Powered by a 4.9-litre V12 engine conceived by Aurelio Lampredi that owed its basic design to earlier grand-prix engines, the 400 Superamerica had a shortened 250GT chassis on to which was fitted Pinin Farina's elegant Aerodinamico coachwork. Each example differed in detail as this was an exclusive coachbuilt car tailored to each buyer. The Cabriolet version was first displayed at the Geneva Motor Show in March 1961, where it was royally upstaged by the new Jaguar E-type. With North America as its target market, the model ultimately proved a flop as US customers did not exactly rush to embrace the open version, preferring instead the existing 250GT Cabriolet. From 1962 a longer-wheelbase Series II model was offered but this too failed to find favour and just ten Cabriolets of each type were crafted by Pinin Farina (plus an eleventh by Scaglietti).

The car shown here, chassis 2331 SA, was completed in March 1961 and featured on Pinin Farina's stand for the model's Geneva debut. Originally finished in metallic ivory, it was sold to a doctor from Milan, who returned the car to the Turin *carrozzeria* to be repainted in Blue Antille Savid and given a new leather interior. For a car that singularly failed in its intended market, the 400 Superamerica is now highly sought after, this example presently residing in a Ferrari collection in New York.

No two 400 Superamericas were ever alike. This car was the first of a limited series. Aimed at the Stateside market, it proved a flop in its intended marketplace, although examples are highly sought after today.

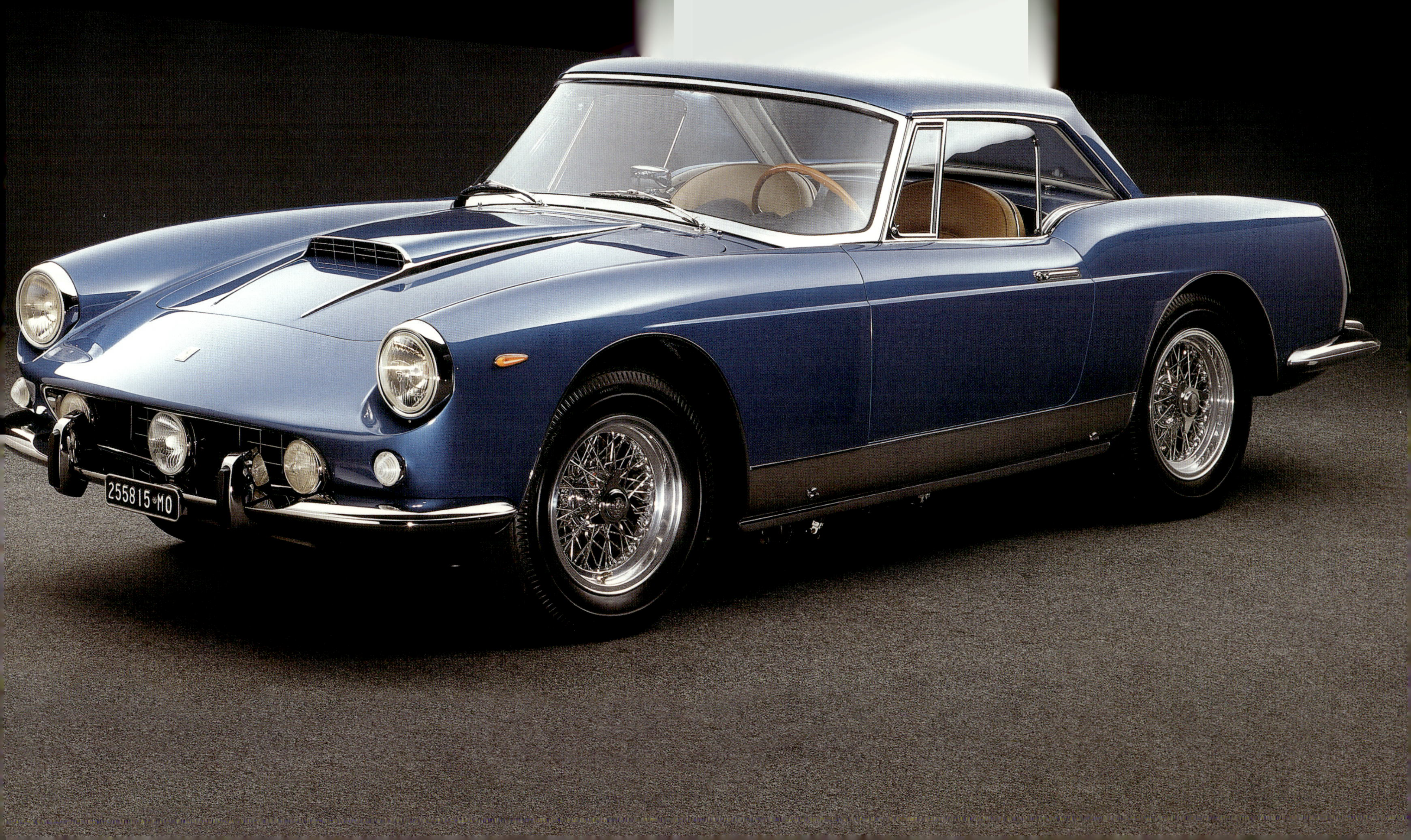
255815 MO

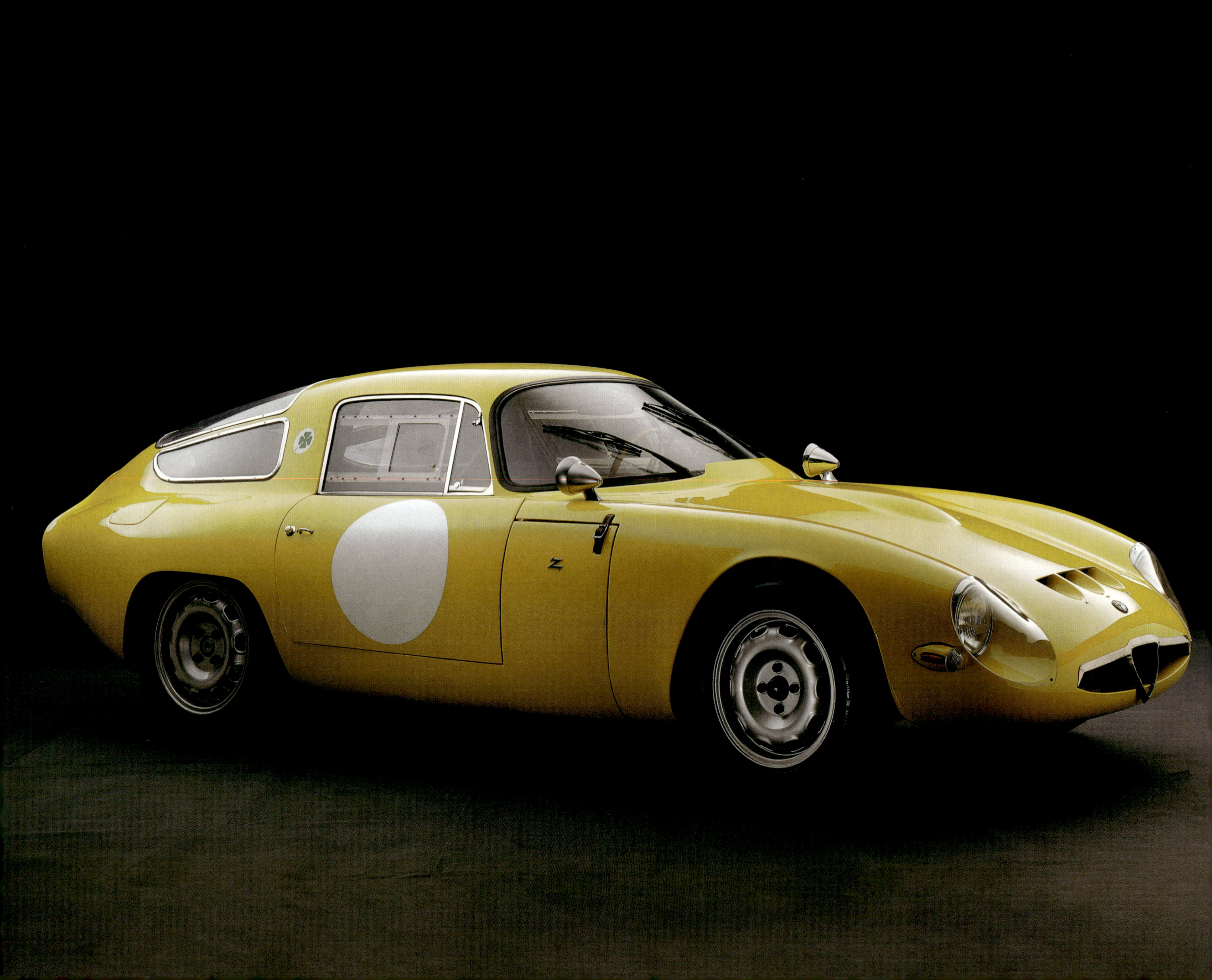

1962 ALFA ROMEO GIULIA TZ1

By the dawn of the 1960s Alfa Romeo had long since pulled out of front-line motor sport, concentrating instead on production-car-derived machines such as the Tubolare Zagato (retrospectively known as the TZ1). The construction of this pretty coupé, aimed at privateers, was entrusted to the Chizzola brothers, whose Udine-based Delta (later Autodelta) concern produced the first car in time for the 1962 Turin Salon. Based on a lightweight tubular frame with a 1570-cc, twin-cam, four-cylinder engine and five-speed gearbox from the Giulia saloon, it went into production the following year with a list price of 3,334,000 lire.

Unusually, much of the manufacturing process was farmed out, with Ambrosini de Passignano sul Trasimeno building the chassis and Zagato the fragile aluminium body. Styled by the *carrozzeria*'s self-taught head of design, Ercole Spada, the car's lithe form featured a low frontal area and cropped tail for superior aerodynamics. With 112 bhp in standard form, and as much as 150 bhp when tuned by Virgilio Conrero, the 640-kg (1411 lb) device soon proved its dominance in its class, with a debut win at Monza in November 1963 for future Ferrari F1 star Lorenzo Bandini. The TZ1 would go on to collect class honours in the Targa Florio, Le Mans 24 Hours, Tour de France and Nürburgring 1000-km (620 miles) races.

At the end of 1964 Alfa Romeo sought an autonomous competition department, Autodelta being amalgamated with the parent company two years later, by which time the TZ1 had been usurped by the lower, wider and glass-fibre-bodied TZ2. By the end of the decade Alfa Romeo returned to the International Championship for Manufacturers with the Tipo 33. Around 110 TZ1s were made, their ease of replication meaning that today several cars share the same chassis number.

1963 FERRARI 250GTO

It was one of the most blatant cheats ever perpetrated in motor sport. For 1962, the CSI (Commission Sportive Internationale) decreed that the International Championship for Manufacturers would be replaced by one for GT cars. Ferrari took a more lateral approach to rule interpretation than its rivals and built an out-and-out racer instead: the 250GTO.

Regulations stated that 100 cars needed to be built to meet homologation requirements. Ferrari made just thirty-nine GTOs ('O', preposterously, standing for 'Omologato') from December 1961 to May 1964, the *scuderia* claiming that as it was merely a 'mildly modified' variation of the 250GT SWB, of which the requisite number had been built, and was therefore an evolutionary model. Aided and abetted by race organizers wanting Ferraris on their grids, the firm succeeded with its strategy.

Although based on the existing 250GT SWB tubular-steel chassis, the GTO was longer, lower and 250 kg (551 lb) lighter. The model used the earlier car's 3-litre, V12 engine, designed by Aurelio Lampredi, which produced 295 bhp. During the three years the GTO was campaigned, it won twenty of twenty-eight World Championship rounds, finishing second in fifteen and third in nine.

Yet, even more than its racing credentials, it is the car's unequalled proportions and bestial elegance that make it one of the greatest of all Ferraris. And one of the most coveted. Viewed as a commodity, the GTO is as desirable as cars get, one Japanese collector paying $15 million in the late 1980s for the example in which Jean Guichet won the 1964 European GT Championship. With demand outstripping supply, it is not surprising that innumerable replicas have consequently been made using running gear sourced from lesser Ferrari models.

The GTO's rear air duct served to dissipate heat from the brakes. The subtle upturned lip atop the cropped tail added downforce.

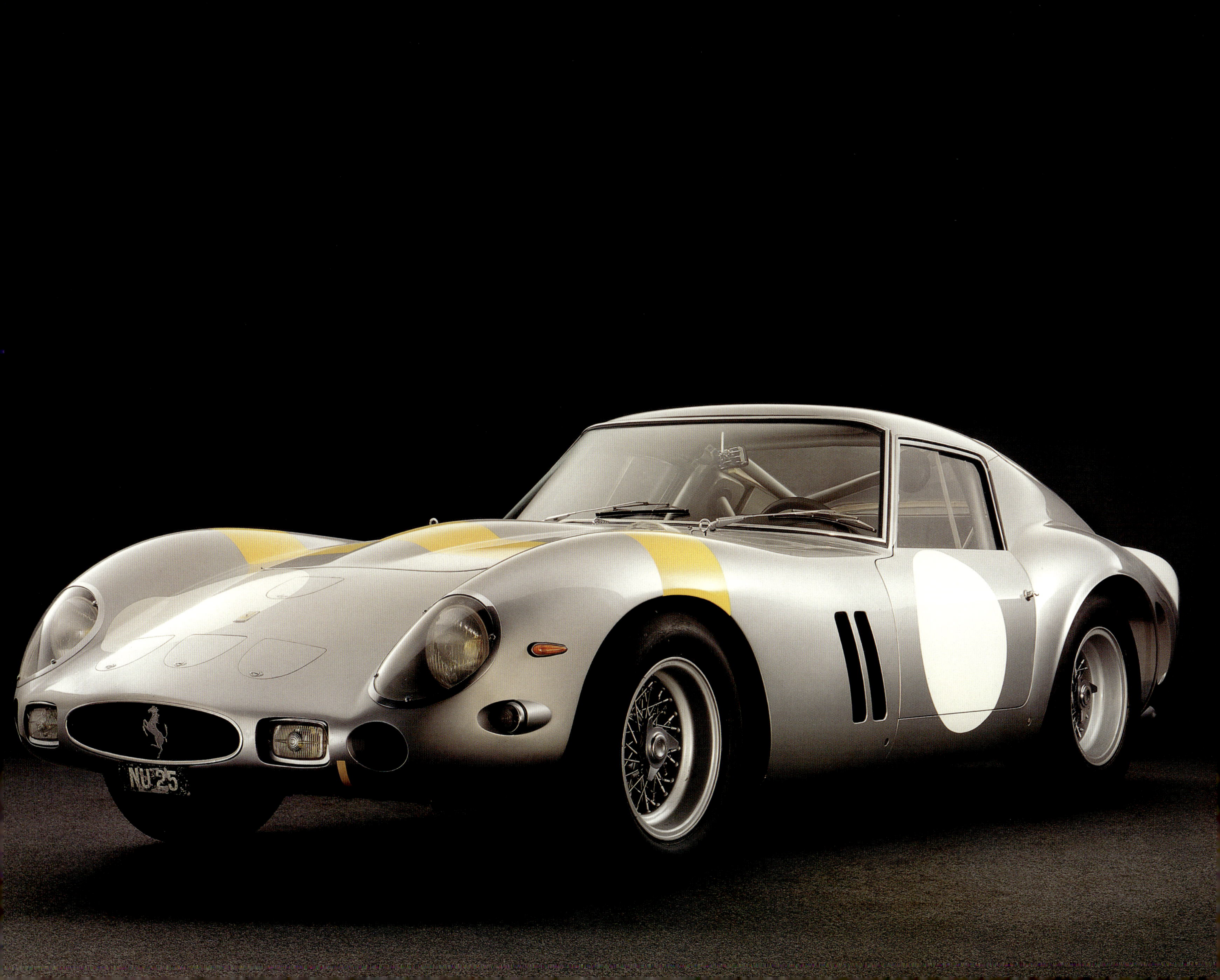
NU 25

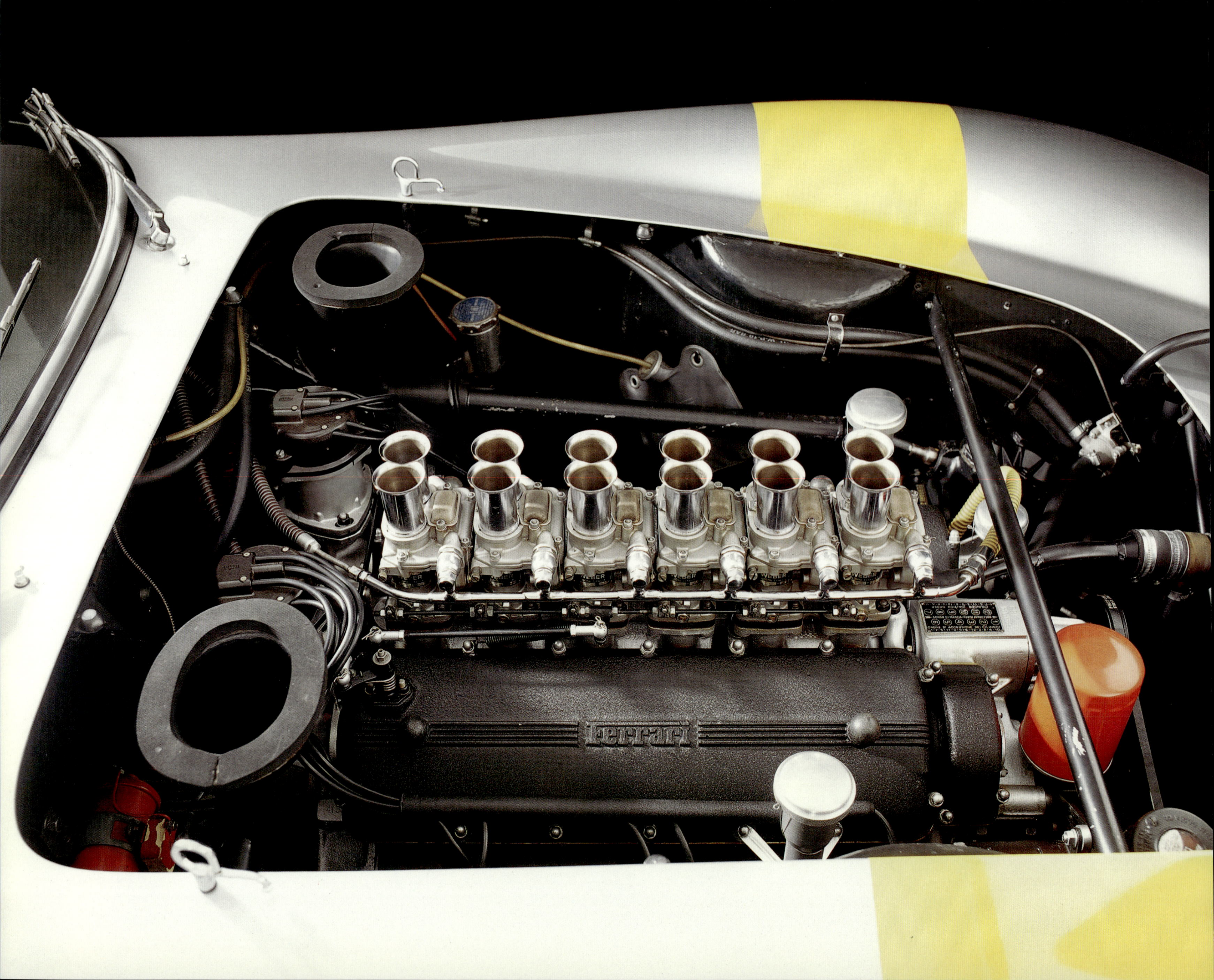
Ferrari

Opposite: The classic 3-litre V12 engine was carried over from the 250GT SWB but was made more powerful still. It was mounted farther back in the frame to help agility.

Below: The iconic GTO silhouette was not styled so much as allowed to evolve. Ferrari later claimed that the car was created simply out of fear of Jaguar's new E-type sports car.

Ferrari 250GTO   195

1964 FERRARI 250 LUSSO

Marking the zenith of Ferrari's illustrious 250-series dynasty, the GT Berlinetta Lusso possessed a seductive form that broke away from Pinin Farina's 1950s 'cubist' period. Although this is very much a road car – 'lusso' meaning luxury, after all – the Turin styling house combined totemic elements of Ferrari's racing heritage in one glorious package. The shark-nose profile hinted at the F1 and Dino sports-racing cars, while the roofline and side glazing treatment were reminiscent of the 330 Le Mans coupé.

The Lusso was not quite ready for the opening of the 1962 Paris Motor Show, but the response when it finally appeared on Ferrari's stand was overwhelming, the motoring press going into raptures. After a marathon drive from Milan to Le Mans and back, Count 'Johnny' Lurani gushed in *Auto Italiano Sport*: "the 250GT Berlinetta thoroughly confirmed its right as the most exceptional high performance sports car in existence – the very best in the world".

By Ferrari standards, the Lusso's 3-litre V12 produced a relatively modest 250 bhp and this, probably optimistic figure, was 50 bhp lower than the 250GTO racer's power output. From that car the Lusso borrowed its independent double-wishbone and coil-sprung front suspension. The rear end was suspended by a prosaic live axle on semi-elliptical springs with trailing arms and a Watts linkage. The biggest deviation from the GTO was the positioning of the engine, which was placed several inches forward to increase cabin space, in part to counter the intrusive width of the four-speed transmission.

Bodied in steel (with alloy only for the bonnet, door skins and boot) by Scaglietti, the car's 1486-kg (3276 lb) heft blunted performance by comparison with its competition brethren, yet it could still sprint from 0 to 161 kph (0–100 mph) in seventeen seconds and had a top speed of 233 kph (145 mph). During the Lusso's two-year lifespan around 350 were made, only twenty-three in right-hand drive.

One of the most elegant of all 1960s Ferraris, the 250 Lusso was also a Pininfarina design landmark. Latterly it has been criticized for not matching the handling proficiency of other 250-series cars, but it was never intended as a racing car.

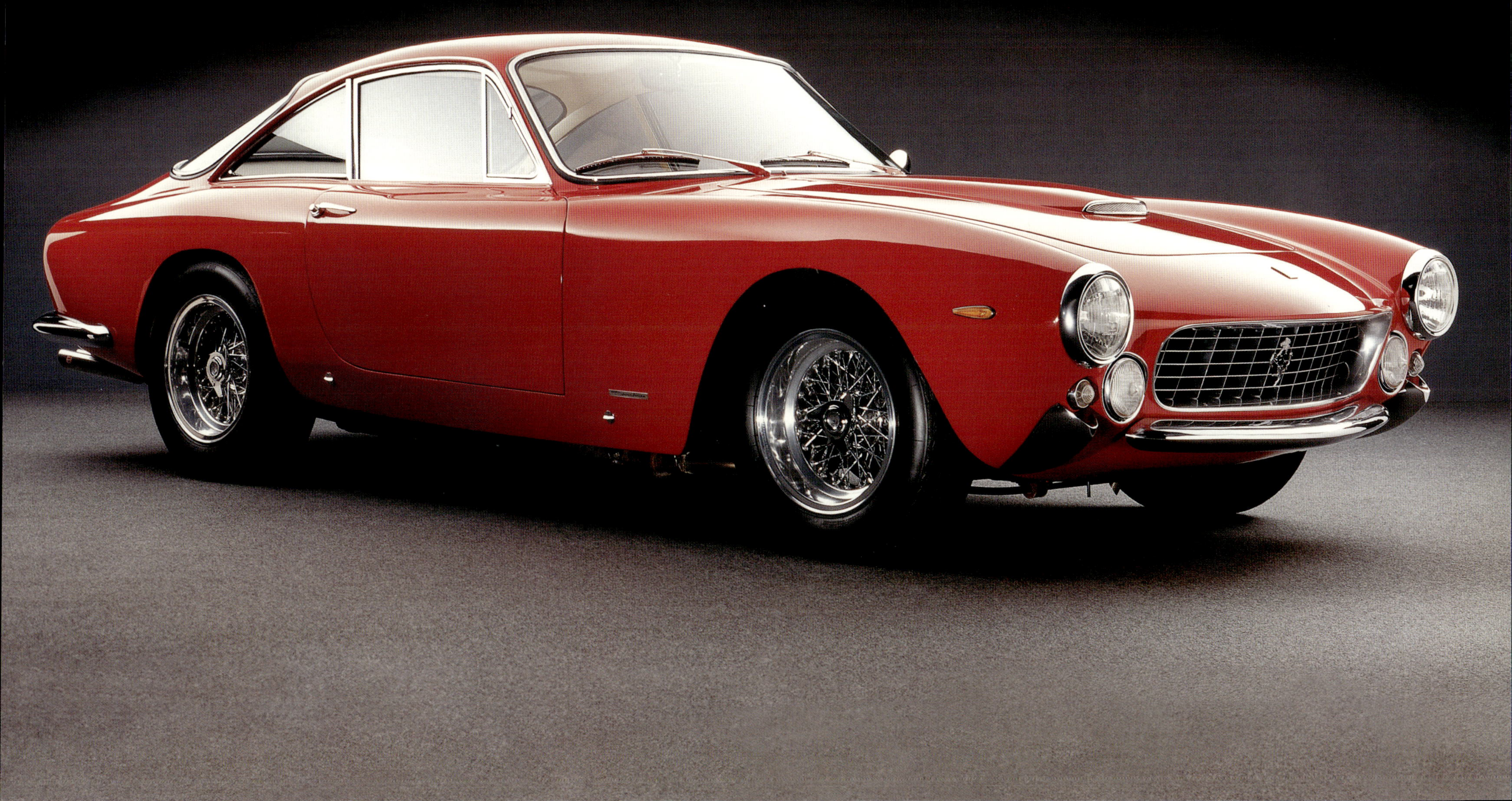

1965 ABARTH 2000OT

Although for ever synonymous with Fiat, Carlo Abarth applied his tuning brilliance to other marques, among the most celebrated of his efforts being those with Simca. Taking as his basis the dowdy 1000 saloon's platform, suspension and steering, Abarth created the first of a long line of Italo-French sports-racers in 1962. With its bespoke 1.3-litre (or 1.6-litre) engine that bore some resemblance to earlier Fiat-based units, the new strain proved the car to beat in numerous racing categories but two years later Simca's new owner, Chrysler, severed the relationship. Unbowed, Abarth pressed on with his all-conquering OT series.

By 1965 the Abarth-Simca had evolved into the Omologato Turismo, retaining the modified 1000 platform upon which hung the engine, suspension and Mario Colucci-styled body, made from glass-fibre by Sibona & Basano of Turin. Debuting in that year's Nürburgring 500-km (310 miles) race, the 1289-cc coupé finished an astonishing third overall. A year later the OT had morphed into the 2000OT, still using the Simca foundations but with revised suspension and a new 1946-cc, four-cylinder engine, designed by Luciano Fochi, that produced 215 bhp at 7600 rpm. The 2000OT was identifiable from its lesser brethren by the addition of a larger Perspex rear engine cover to improve aerodynamics, but the most radical departure was an extended air-scoop atop the roof. First seen on a Fiat 500-based record breaker in 1958, the device was used on the 2000OT to dissipate cockpit heat by sucking air into the cabin, this dramatic addition earning the car the nickname 'Periscopica'.

A debut class win for Luigi Taramazzo in the April 1966 San Remo Trophy opened the door for great success for the marque of the Scorpion. In the firm's twenty-two-year existence, Abarth won a scarcely believable 7400 races and captured countless speed records. Fiat bought the company and rights to the name in 1971, Carlo Abarth returning a year later to his native Vienna, where he died in 1979.

Inside the OT's cramped cabin the dashboard is dominated by the large rev counter, while the pedals are offset towards the car's centreline to counter the intrusive wheel wells.

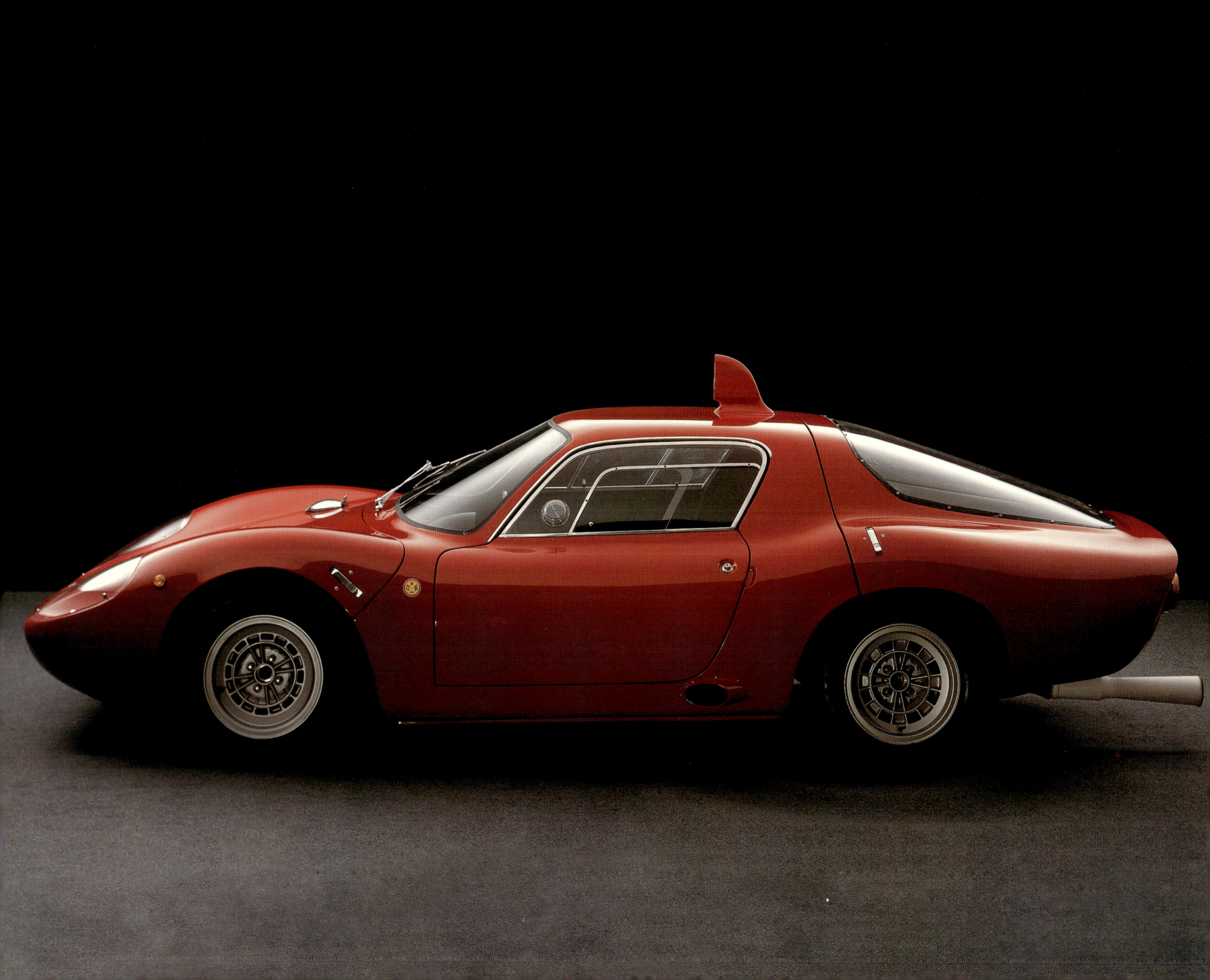

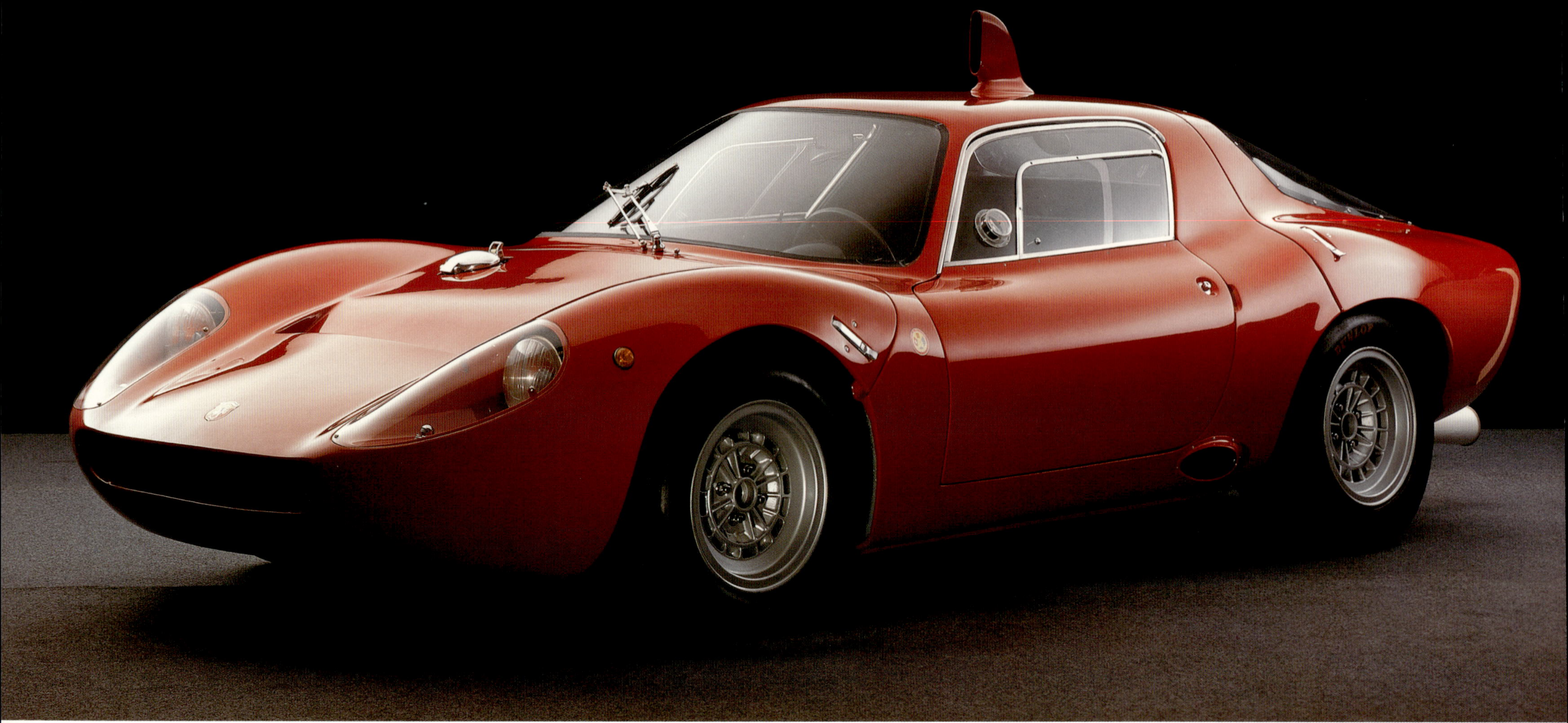

Opposite: The pretty glass-fibre body was an evolution of previous Abarths. A distinctive air scoop mounted on the roof served to dissipate cockpit heat.

Right: Based on a humble Simca platform, the OT was nonetheless largely custom made. The expansive rear glazing area was added over earlier OT variations to aid airflow.

Abarth 2000OT   201

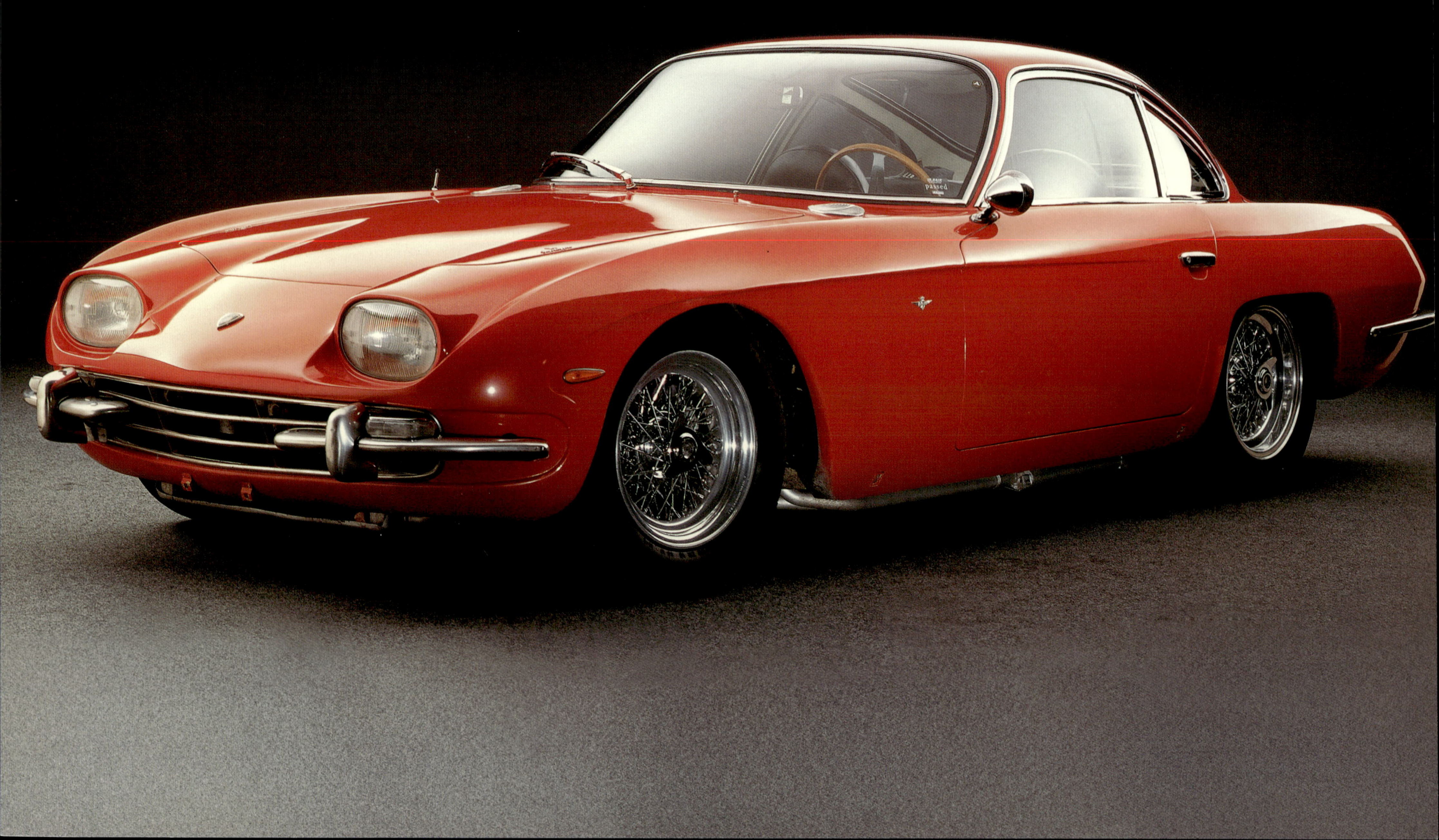

1965 LAMBORGHINI 350GT/400GT

Legend has it that the only reason Ferruccio Lamborghini entered the motor industry was to upstage Ferrari. Having made a fortune building tractors, he apparently decided to invest in a Maranello product, only to be left kicking his heels for hours on end when he visited the factory. With pride dented, he resolved to get his own back by becoming a motor mogul. The truth is probably more mundane: there was more gratification and prestige in having your name on a supercar than on an agricultural vehicle.

Whatever his motivation, Lamborghini realized his vision with élan. After a false dawn with the 350GTV, styled by Franco Scaglione and first displayed at the October 1963 Turin Salon, the initial production model, the 350GT, entered manufacture the following year. Lamborghini lost around £1000 on each car, although this is understandable, given his insistence on not building them down to a price while at the same time undercutting the competition.

Although derived from the earlier GTV, the outline was heavily revised by Carrozzeria Touring, which also built the bodyshell using its patented *Superleggera* method of construction: a framework of small tubes on to which aluminium panels were attached. The tubular semi-spaceframe chassis was designed by Giotto Bizzarrini (and built by Neri & Bonacini), the former Ferrari engineer also producing (with refinements by Gian Paolo Dallara) the 3464-cc, four-cam V12 engine, which was allied with a German five-speed ZF transmission.

The largely steel-bodied 400GT arrived in 1965 with displacement increased to 3929 cc, and was joined a year later by the 2+2, most noticeable among the changes being four headlights (instead of two), a lowered platform and raised roof and, of course, two extra seats. Although unconventionally attractive (or, to some, conventionally unattractive), Lamborghini's first foray into the automotive arena was probably its best, the attention to detail lavished on these wonderful machines raising the bar for its European rivals.

Lamborghini's first offering was a mishmash of seemingly discordant angles and soft curves. Yet the result was captivating, the 350GT, as here, being among the finest GTs of the 1960s.

204

Although the car was much praised for its handling and performance in its day, positive press was not enough to stop Lamborghini losing a fortune on each 350GT made. This was a result of not building it down to a price.

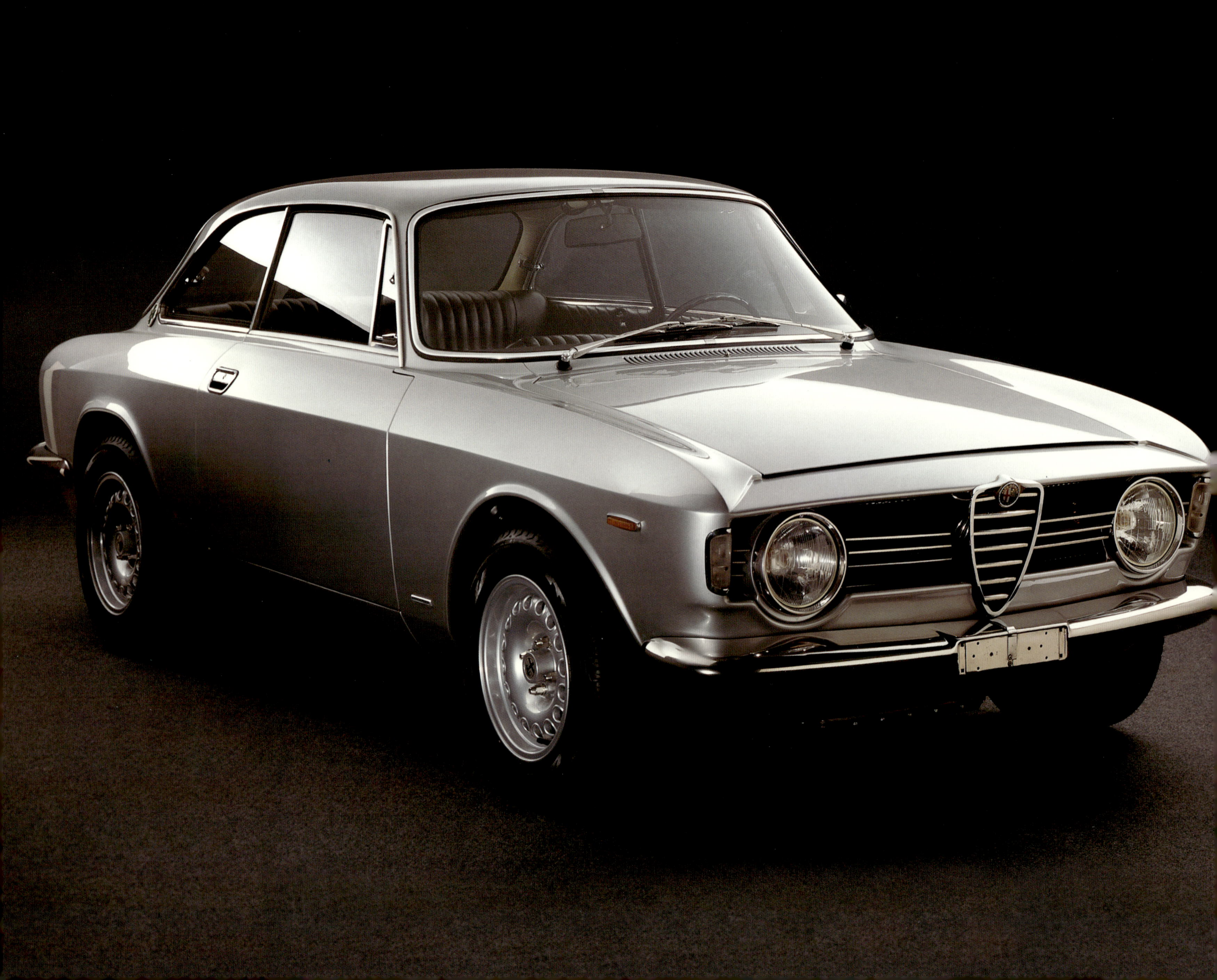

1966 ALFA ROMEO GIULIA SPRINT GT

Presented to the world at the 1963 Frankfurt Motor Show, Alfa Romeo's Giulia GT was a modernist take on the alchemist's dream of turning base metal into gold. In this instance there was a better starting point. The Tipo 105 Giulia saloon had been introduced a year earlier with an all-alloy, twin-cam, four-cylinder engine and five-speed gearbox. Although a literal rendition of the 'three-box' idiom, it handled brilliantly, was deceptively quick and marked a seismic shift in quality and design integrity for its target audience.

Conceived by Carrozzeria Bertone, the Sprint was originally intended as a small-scale coachbuilt variant on the Giulia, but Alfa Romeo's management was so enamoured with the prototype that it became a production model. Styled by Bertone's prodigiously talented twenty-three-year-old *wunderkind* Giorgetto Giugiaro, it was in effect a distillation of his previous efforts. Present were all of the former artist's trademark styling traits, in particular the delicately arced roofline and spindly door pillars that aped his earlier Gordon-Keeble and Alfa Romeo 2600 Sprint, and the sharp creases that ran from front to back along the flanks.

Offered in 1290-cc and 1570-cc configurations, the Sprint was an immediate success, ultimately spawning larger-capacity versions, and remained in production until 1977. But it is the original that impresses most, the finest feature being the point where the leading edge of the bonnet overlapped the top front panel, for some of the styling purity was lost on later editions. Notoriously dispassionate about his creations, the immensely successful Giugiaro remains uncharacteristically pleased with the Sprint GT, latterly claiming that it is among the best of his 150 plus car designs. Ironically, it was several years after the model had been launched that he was in a position to buy one; even then, it was the entry-level 1.3-litre version.

1966 DE TOMASO VALLELUNGA

History has not been kind to the De Tomaso Vallelunga. As the first mid-engined road car – although the French claim this honour for the equally little-known René Bonnet – this achingly pretty little device cast a long shadow, yet it is the myriad copyists who followed in its wake that won the kudos. Yet this is no great surprise, for even when new the Vallelunga languished in a netherworld between vague recognition and outright obscurity.

The car was named after the racing circuit near Rome where Argentinian émigré Alejandro de Tomaso had enjoyed minor racing success, the future industrialist's greatest honour being victory in the Index of Performance at the 1958 Le Mans 24 Hours with co-driver Colin Davis. The Vallelunga, his maiden venture into road-car production in 1963, was made with the sole intention of helping fund his nascent racing team, the De Tomaso marque ultimately reaching Formula One by the dawn of the 1970s.

In line with existing racing-car practice, the Vallelunga featured a backbone chassis with all-wishbone suspension and a 1.6-litre Ford Cortina engine driving through a VW-based Hewland gearbox. Carrozzeria Fissore was contracted to style the car, the first prototype being an open roadster. The Savigliano-based coachbuilder constructed the initial batch of three cars with aluminium bodies but lost the contract to build more to its rival Ghia, which de Tomaso would subsequently acquire before selling it on to Ford.

The only real flaw in the plan was de Tomaso's wavering interest: he was always looking at the next project, finding great success the following decade with the Ford-sponsored Pantera supercar. Just fifty-eight Vallelungas were made to 1965, only one (Lotus twin-cam powered) car being made in right-hand drive. If nothing else, it gained some cachet when exhibited at the Museum of Modern Art in New York as "an example of technical progress and outstanding design".

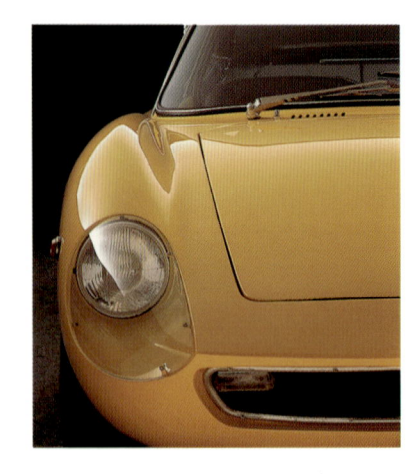

De Tomaso's divine Vallelunga was later adopted as an art exhibit. Sadly, its beauty was not enough to ensure commercial success.

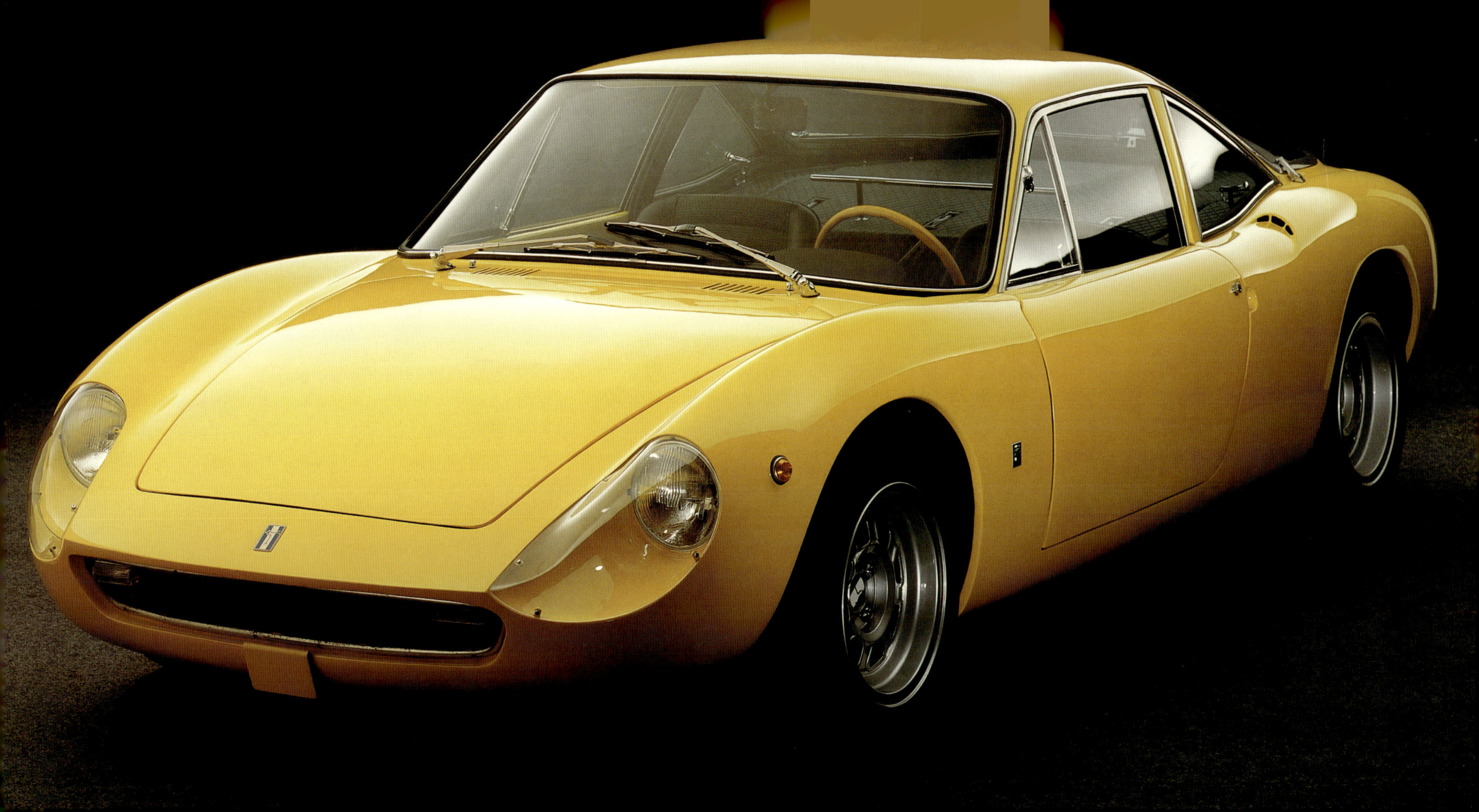

1966 LAMBORGHINI MIURA

Nineteen sixty-six was year zero for the supercar. The term was coined specifically for the Miura and rarely has it been more appropriate. When launched at the 1966 Geneva Salon, Ferruccio Lamborghini's innovative masterpiece immediately rendered all competition redundant. Never mind that it was not fully developed, and some would argue that it never really was; that was not what mattered. The Miura belonged to a different era: the future. When it was displayed in bare-chassis form at the previous year's Turin Salon, few took Lamborghini seriously. It was less than two years since the impudent tractor manufacturer had started making cars and here he was planning to embarrass the establishment. Come the close of the Geneva show, nobody was laughing.

Breathtaking, audacious and brimming with originality, the Miura's sinuous outline, by Carrozzeria Bertone's Marcello Gandini or Giorgetto Giugiaro (both have claimed at least partial authorship), hid the brilliant feat of packaging achieved by Gian Paolo Dallara and Paolo Stanzani. Both wanted the Miura to be as compact as possible and, taking inspiration from the Mini, redesigned the existing Lamborghini engine block in a single unit with the gearbox and final drive, the monstrous V12 being housed transversely behind the two seats within a 2425-mm (97 in.) wheelbase.

Yet such daring came at a cost. When the first P400 Miuras reached their expectant owners in 1967, the shortcomings of the transverse layout soon became all too obvious. Engine and transmission shared oil and a few teeth knocked off the cogs and into the hot, brown liquid swiftly rendered a Miura a very expensive ornament. For the final SV evolution of the model, the V12 and gearbox were separated and the suspension redesigned, which necessitated wider wheels and flared arches to accommodate them. To some this was a retrograde step aesthetically. Even so, the Miura set the template for a what a supercar should look like and it is yet to be bettered.

The Lamborghini marque was barely three years old when it ushered in the Miura. It redefined what was possible in sports-car design and led the way for ever more outrageous machines from Sant' Agata.

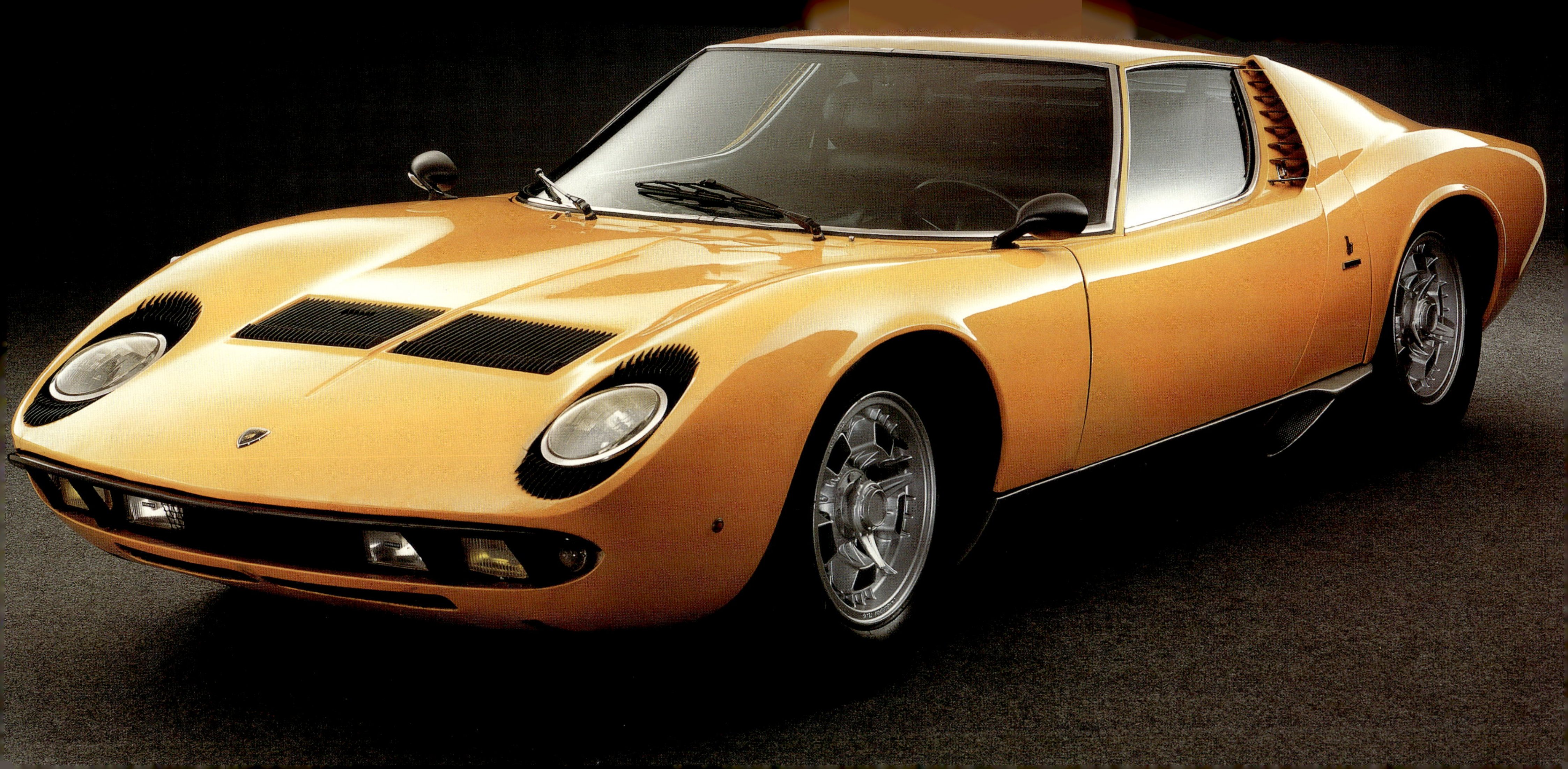

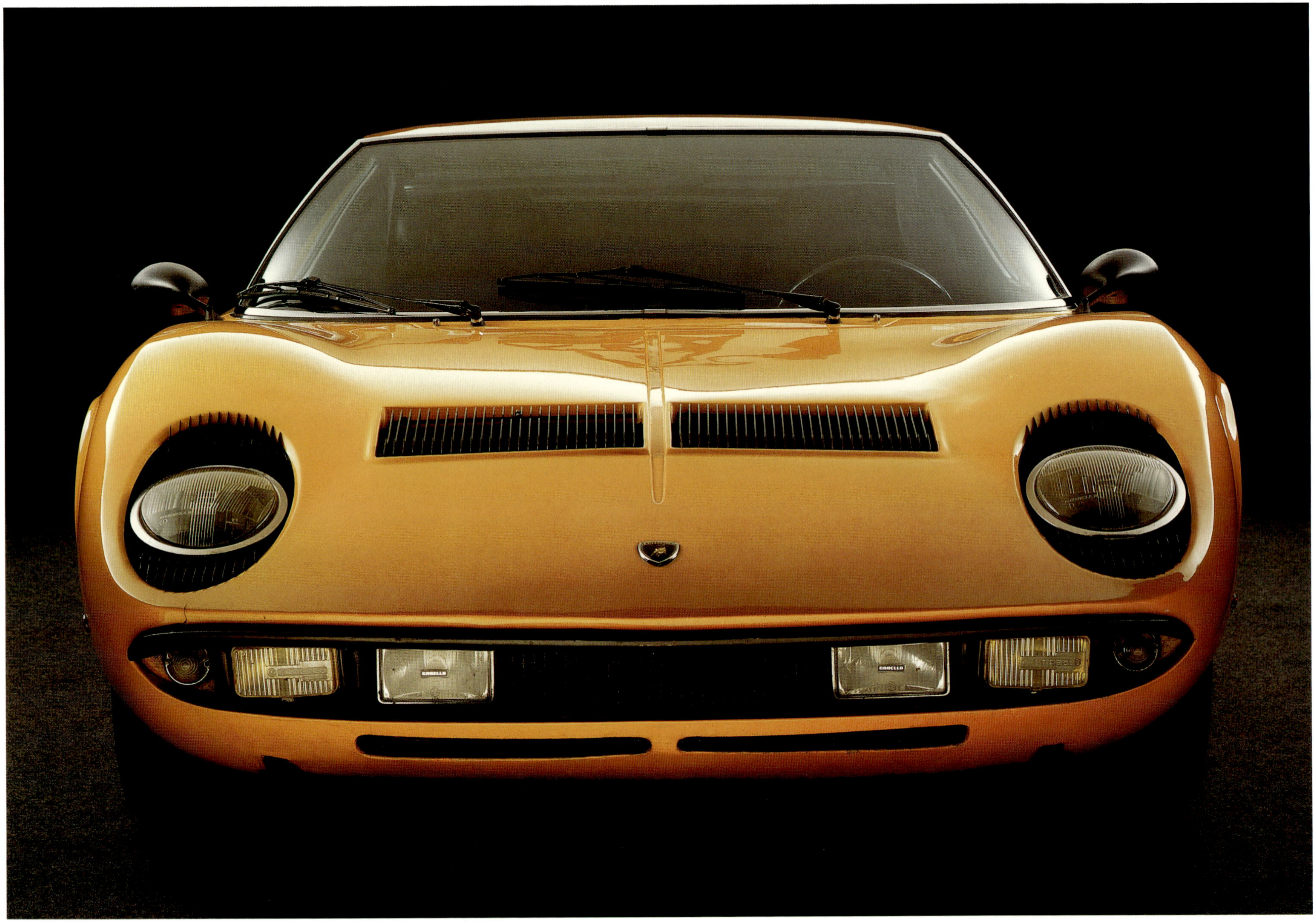

Opposite: The term 'supercar' was invented to describe the Miura, which married technical bravery with incomparable beauty. The outline was attributed to the Bertone design house, although both Marcello Gandini and Giorgetto Giugiaro have claimed authorship.

Above: Ironically, when the idea of the Miura was first mooted, a small-capacity sports car was envisaged, possibly using a British Mini engine.

Lamborghini Miura

The passage of time has done nothing to diminish the sense of drama surrounding the Miura's outlandish outline. In 2006 Lamborghini unveiled a retro take on the theme to tie in with the model's fortieth anniversary.

Lamborghini Miura

1968 FERRARI 330P4

For the cognoscenti, Ferrari's 330P4 is the most beautiful sports-racing car ever made, a final hurrah before aerodynamic developments prompted geometric designs that were slab-sided and low on style. The artisans of Piero Drogo's Carrozzeria Sports Cars hand-formed the P4 by eye and intuition, the bodyshell pitching and diving with sensuous harmony around the ellipsoidal windscreen. Not even numerous air-intake ducts and wingtips could blight the picture.

Built in Spider (open) and Berlinetta (closed) forms, the P4 was Ferrari's retort to the Ford GT40, which had inflicted a humiliating defeat on the *scuderia* at the 1966 Le Mans 24 Hours. Although apparently similar to the outgoing P3, the new car differed greatly. Power came from a mid-mounted 36-valve, 4-litre V12, related in part to a Formula One engine designed by Franco Rocchi that had first appeared at the 1966 Italian Grand Prix. Ferrari claimed a power output of 380 bhp at 10,000 rpm, although most outsiders considered this optimistic. The car's chassis was unusual, comprising a multi-tubular spaceframe stiffened by aluminium panels and a glass-fibre undertray that housed the fuel tanks. The 885-kg (1950 lb) car was claimed by the factory to have a top speed of 319 kph (198 mph), making it marginally slower than the 7-litre Ford challenger. It was, however, far more nimble, and easier on its brakes.

All of this became apparent at the car's 1967 Daytona 24 Hour debut. Ford had entered six GT40 MkIIs, Ferrari two P4s backed up by privateer P3/4s (effectively P3s uprated to P4 specification but with 24-valve engines fed by Weber carburettors rather than fuel injection; also known as the 412P). Against the Florida track's challenging mix of banking and road circuit, the works Ferraris soaked up the punishment as the Fords dropped out one by one. P4s finished first and second with a P3/4 in third place. The sole remaining GT40 ended up seventh, seventy-three laps behind the winner. Ferrari had won back its bragging rights.

Ferrari's retort to Ford's GT40, the P4 was powered by a mid-mounted 4-litre V12 unit that benefited from grand-prix-car technology. The entire rear bodywork hinged forward for superior engine access.

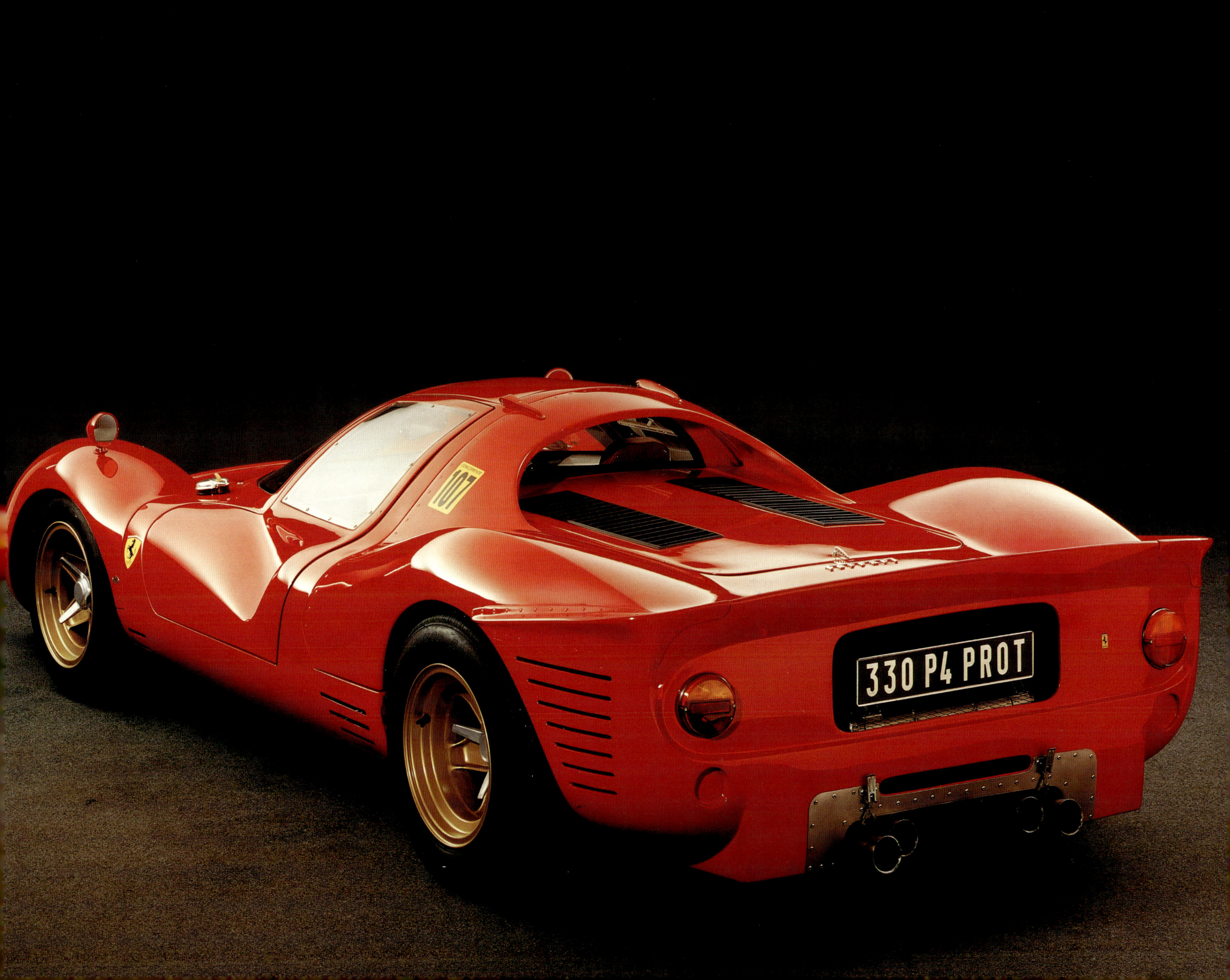
107
330 P4 PROT

Left: The gearshift is mounted to the driver's right. The P4's cabin was claustrophobic: perhaps one reason why an open version was built.

Opposite: The most beautiful racing car ever made? Created without the aid of wind tunnels, the P4's sexy bodywork was crafted from aluminium by hand. It's a work of art.

Ferrari 330P4

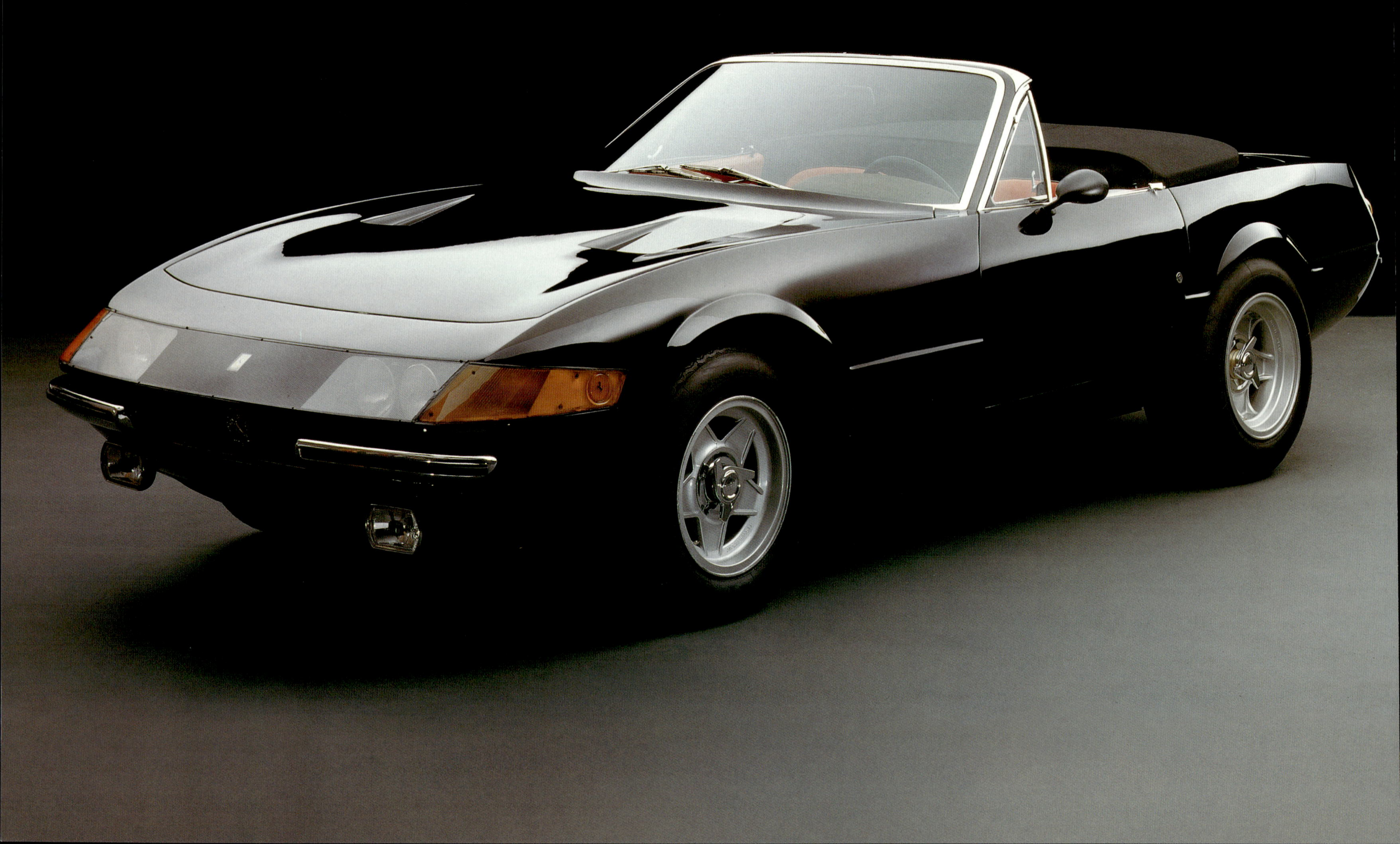

1968 FERRARI 365GTS/4 DAYTONA

In just one week a sleep-deprived Leonardo Fioravanti shaped the Daytona coupé – or, by its less romantic factory designation, 365GTB/4 – which on its debut at the 1968 Geneva Salon immediately rendered the 275GTB forerunner obsolete after barely three years in the Ferrari line-up. The Pininfarina stylist created a masterpiece; seemingly all bonnet with one perfect arc sweeping from its priapic snout to the bobbed tail, the taut roofline curving gently around the shallow side glazing. There was no extraneous clutter, with windscreen wipers hidden beneath a lip at the base of the screen and tiny door handles all but invisible at the base of the windows. Capable of 280 kph (174 mph) and 0–161 kph (0–100 mph) in just 12.6 seconds, the Daytona was officially the fastest car then on sale, eclipsing Lamborghini's Miura.

Always a slightly odd blend of technology and old-school coachbuilding, the Daytona was underpinned by a steel chassis on to which hung the 4390-cc, twin-overhead-cam V12 engine, along with the double-wishbone suspension, with numerous other smaller frames supporting the radiator, unstressed body panels and floor. Unusually, this was a glass-fibre tub that also formed the door sills and the front and rear bulkheads, all bonded together to form one unit. To this, Scaglietti formed the bodies from individual sheets of metal that were shaped over wooden bucks before being welded together.

Of the 1400 or so Daytonas made to 1974, most coveted today are the open GTS/4 Spiders. Just 125 are believed to have been built by Scaglietti, with only seven of these in right-hand drive. With a 100% price premium over the coupé, it is no surprise that many closed cars have undergone surgery. Most of these fake open-tops are identifiable by their flat rear decks, the factory originals featuring a slight tumblehome, or inward curve.

The open GTS/4 version of the Daytona was the rarest of the breed and is nowadays the most coveted. Headlights with Plexiglas covers were later replaced with pop-up lights.

1969 PININFARINA FERRARI 512S

Unencumbered by the usual constraints of designing a car to be viable for production, Pininfarina's take on the Ferrari 512S hinted at the future without giving much thought to the present. It was a concept car. Unveiled to a shocked audience at the 51st Salone Internazionale dell'Automobile in 1969, this radical, wedge-shaped projectile married sports-prototype racing technology with great stylistic flair and was built in close collaboration with the Polytechnic of Turin as "an exploration of new aerodynamic solutions".

Underneath the dart-like outline lay a Ferrari 512S semi-monocoque chassis with a 550-bhp, 4993-cc V12 engine mounted amidships. Apart from the wheel arches, there was scarcely a curve to the entire body. The front, unfettered by a radiator, ensured a low frontal area, the huge, one-piece plastic windscreen sweeping back almost horizontally to the rear engine deck, replete with three rows of lateral cooling louvres: this styling abstraction was later borrowed, if only in part, for the 1984 Ferrari Testarossa. To either side of the glasshouse were long, rectangular slots to carry cooling air to the radiators, although most onlookers at the time doubted that this feature would ever work. Below the upswept rear skirt, the gearbox and four exhaust pipes poked out menacingly, Pininfarina making a point of not hiding the car's competition pedigree.

With the car measuring just 982 mm (39 in.) from top to bottom, and almost twice as wide, practicality was never an issue. The most extreme aspect was the one-piece flip-up canopy in place of conventional doors, which made ingress to the cabin – with its broad, knee-high sills and seats pushed to the centreline – all the more difficult. Although it is doubtful that the sole prototype was ever a runner, the Pininfarina 512S was a bold slice of futurism and its styling undoubtedly laid the groundwork for more 'mainstream' Ferraris of the following decade.

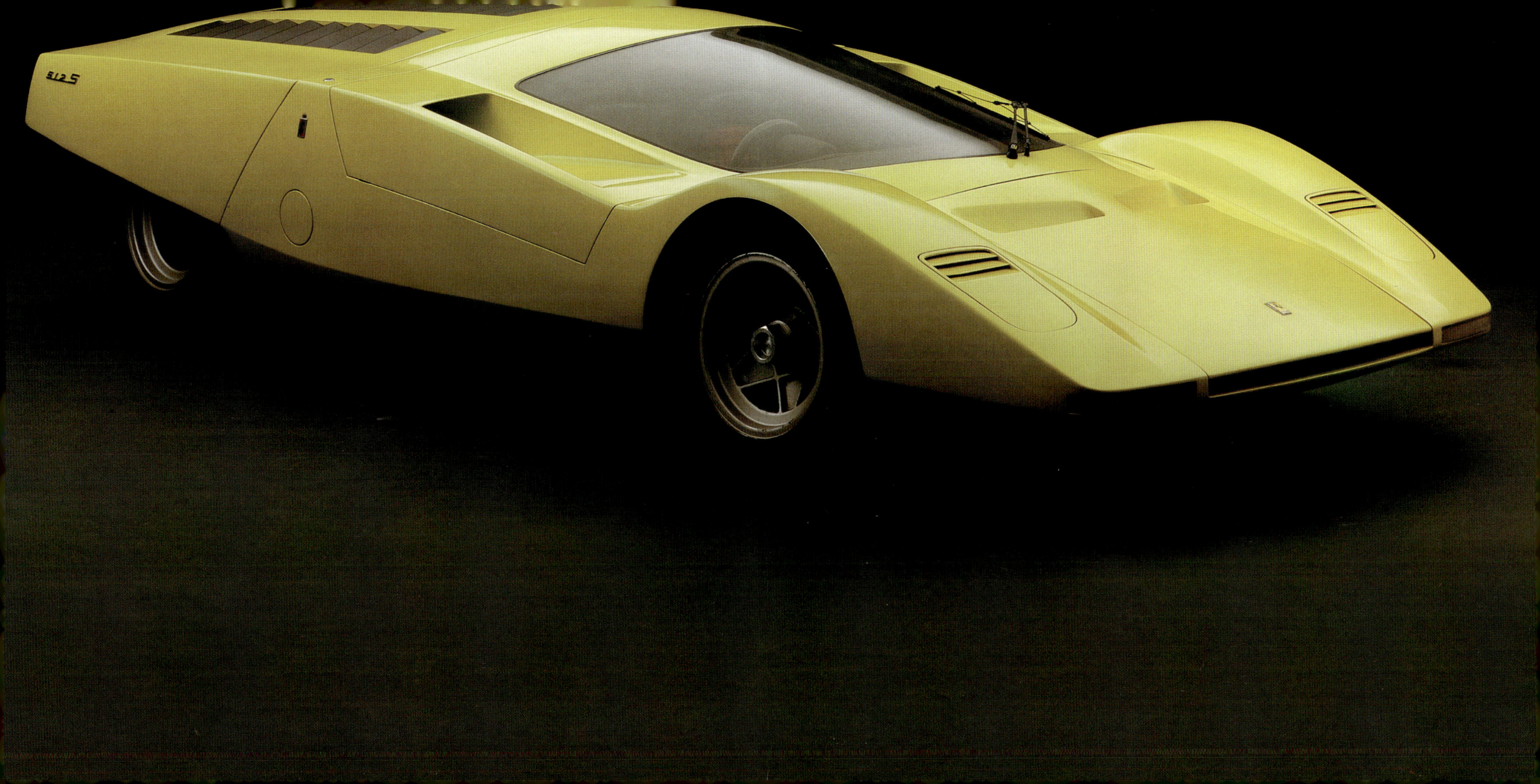

A lift-up canopy allowed access to cockpit, but this system was not the last word in practicality. But then this was a design concept. Several styling trends showcased here filtered down into subsequent production Ferraris.

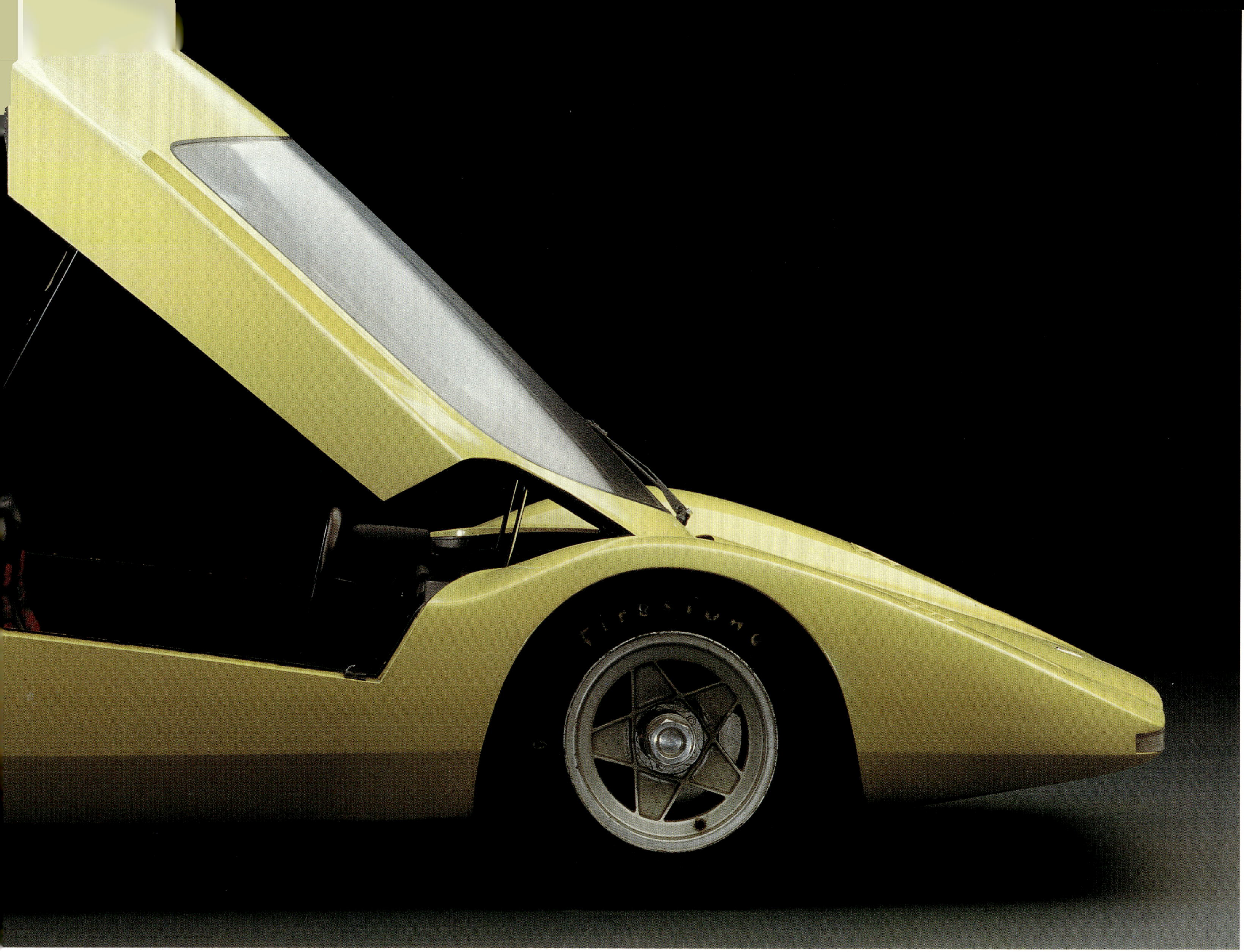

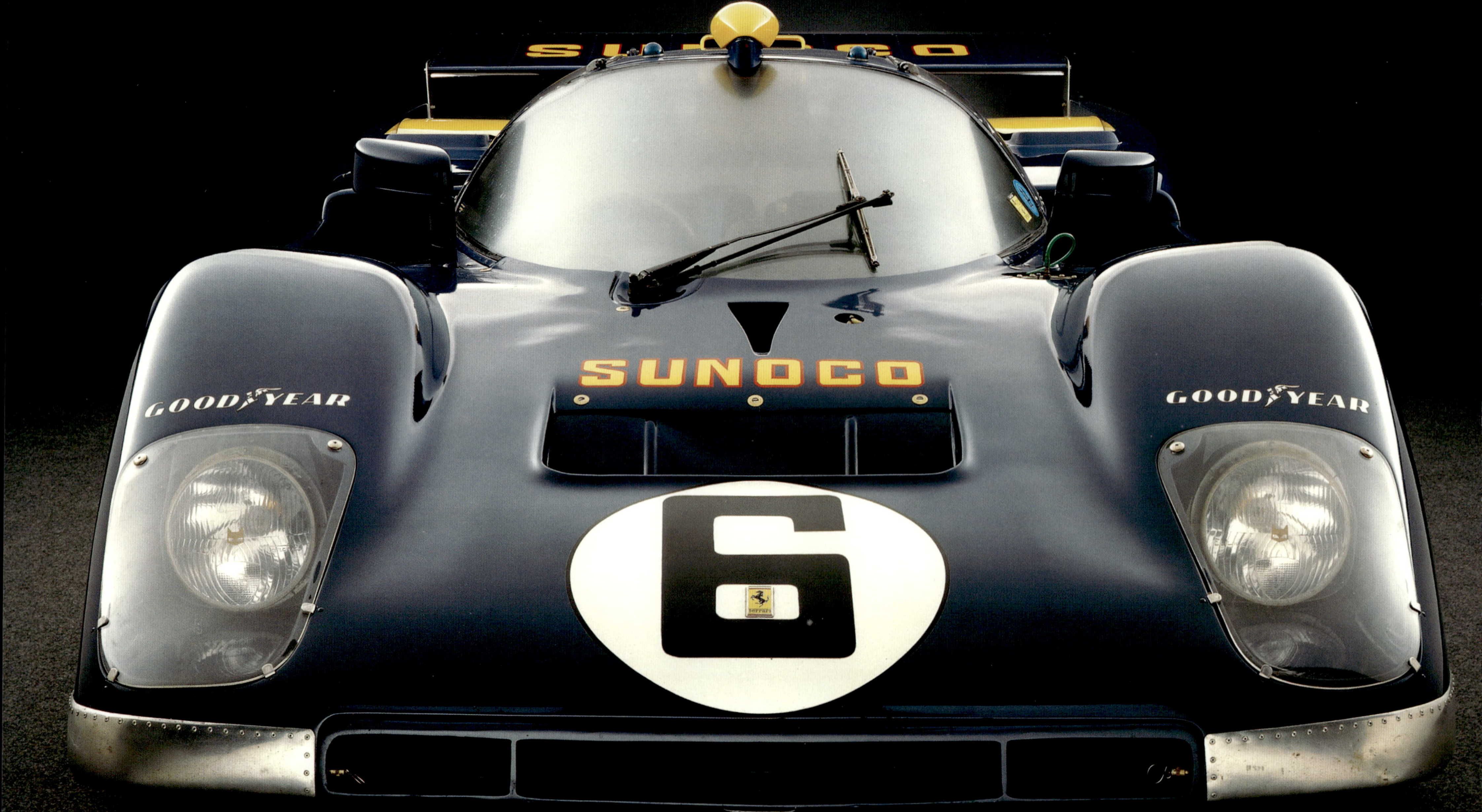
SUNOCO
GOODYEAR
GOODYEAR
6

1970 FERRARI 512M 'SUNOCO'

Mark Donohue called it "the unfair advantage": a means of preparing and developing a racing car to the point that it does most of the work for you. Rather than having to drive around problems and nurse a car to the finish, with a perfectly honed one you would not have to. Together with team principal Roger Penske, Donohue perfected the art, yet, for all their efforts, the 512M 'Sunoco' failed to score a single victory.

It was not for lack of trying. The car started life as a 512S, Ferrari's 1970 challenger to the all-conquering Porsche 917 sports-racer. Driven in a handful of Can-Am races that year by Jim Adams, it was sold at the end of the season to Kirk White, who entrusted its preparation to Penske's équipe for 1971. The Philadelphia team stripped the car to its bare monocoque, making alterations to the suspension and steering geometry, while two Ferrari 5-litre V12 engines were dispatched to Traco, the Los Angeles-based tuner increasing power output to 614 bhp.

Fitted with a new 512M ('M' standing for *modificato*) body and painted in Sunoco's corporate metallic blue and yellow, the car debuted at the Daytona Continental 24 Hours in January 1970, where Donohue and co-driver David Hobbs battled for the lead, only to drop down to an eventual third overall after electrical problems and an accident lost several hours to repairs. It would prove the best result of the year. With the car wearing a new ultra-lightweight body made by Barry Plasti Glass of LA in time for March's Sebring 12 Hours, the duo again led but, after further crashes, fell down the order to an eventual sixth. Donohue retired the car during the Le Mans 24 Hours. At Watkins Glen, where the car was in second place in the final World Championship round for sports cars, a broken steering tie-rod bolt caused it to spear off the road while leading. Entered into the Can-Am race the following day, it failed once more, owing to a broken piston. A sad, if predictable, dénouement.

Mark Donohue sat here. The great American – a winner of the Indy 500 and the Can-Am sports-car title – nonetheless failed to finish a race in first place with this fabulous machine.

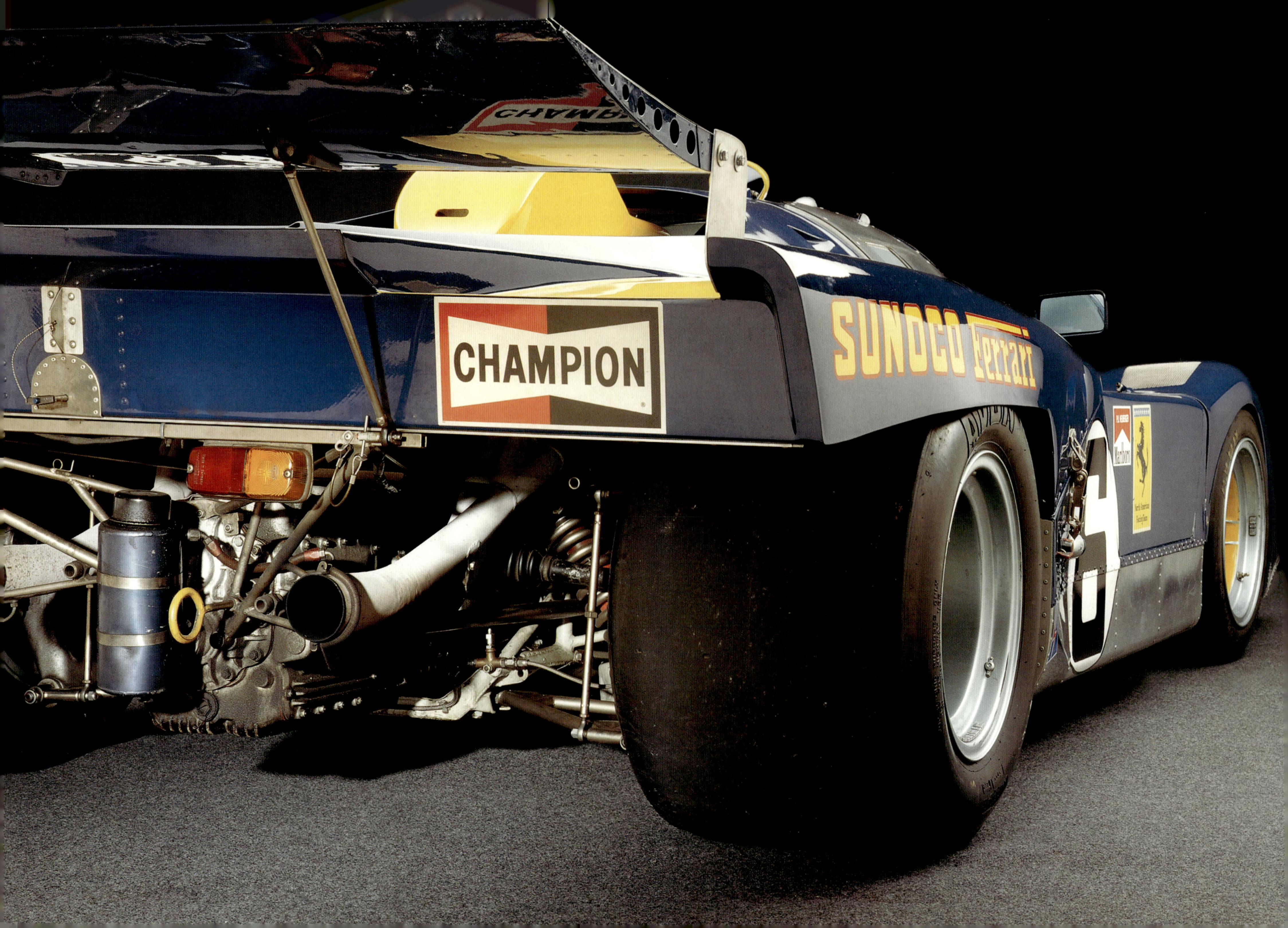
CHAMPION
SUNOCO Ferrari

Opposite: The Penske race team revised the Ferrari's bodywork, crafting its own ultra-lightweight glass-fibre item. Blue and yellow were the corporate colours of sponsor Sunoco.

Above: Ferrari was always popular with customer racing teams but Penske, less than enamoured with the 512M, comprehensively re-engineered the car. However, it was still hobbled short of becoming a winner.

Ferrari 512M 'Sunoco' 229

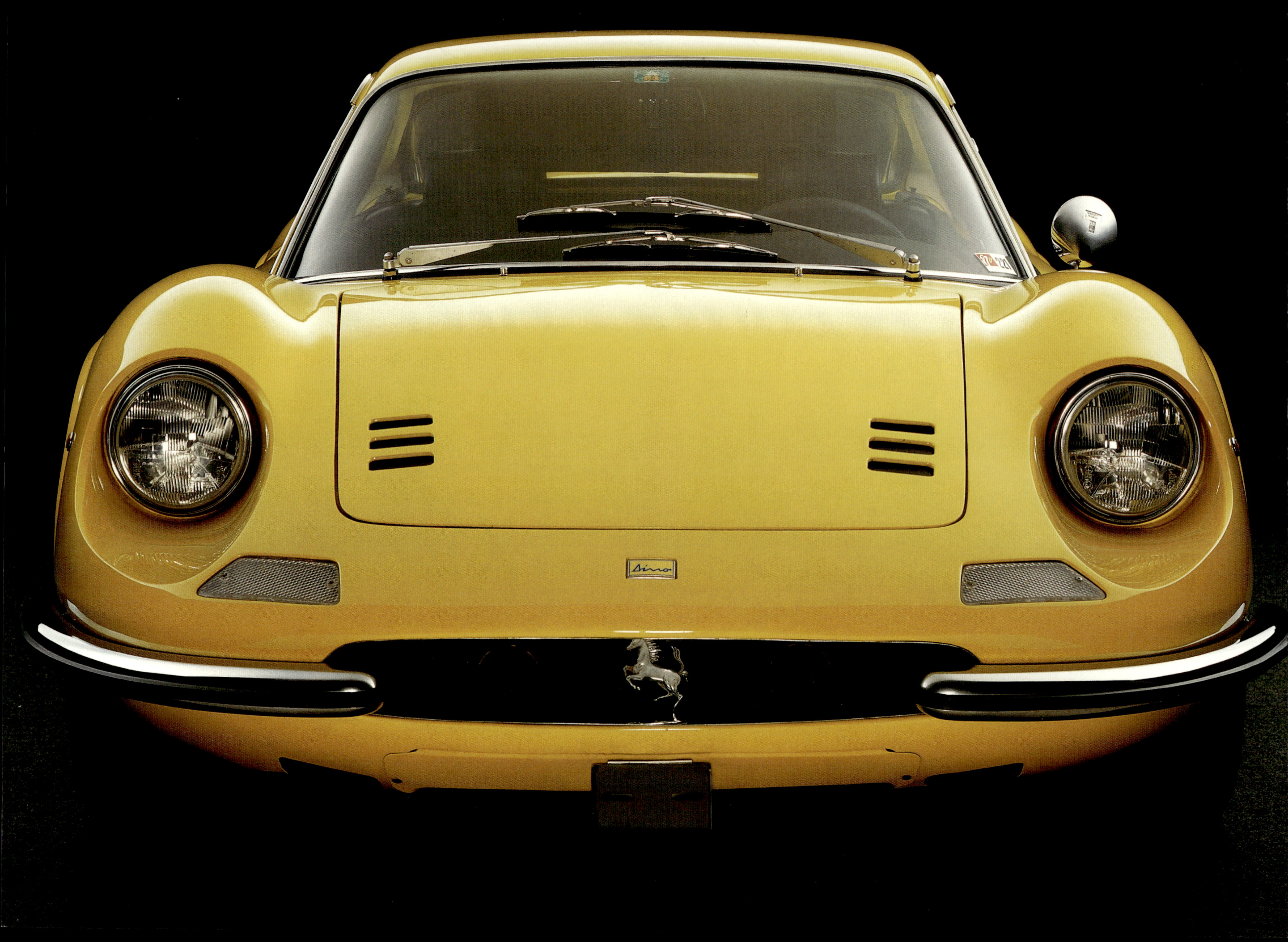

1970 FERRARI DINO 246GT

It is hard to believe now, but the Ferrari cognoscenti were up in arms when the scrumptious Dino was unveiled at the 1967 Turin Salon. It had a V6 engine – in the middle – with a displacement of only 2 litres. And it didn't even bear a prancing-horse badge. But all the complaints that it was not a 'real' Ferrari were dispelled the instant people heard and drove one.

It was a product close to Enzo Ferrari's heart. His only (legitimate) son and heir, Alfredo, or Dino, had died from leukaemia in 1956 at just twenty-four. Keen to honour his memory, and to take the fight to Porsche's 911, Ferrari used the Dino 'baby supercar' to mark the first link with Fiat, which built the engines while also using them in its own model range. Before the decade was over, the Turin giant would buy the majority shareholding in Ferrari.

With its shapely styling by Pininfarina's Aldo Bravarone, and aluminium body crafted by Scaglietti, the Dino 206GT was a work of artistic genius. The all-alloy jewel of an engine, designed by Franco Rocchi, was turned sideways and squeezed behind the occupants. The car was also the first Ferrari to feature rack-and-pinion steering.

Yet production only lasted two years, the much-improved Dino 246GT being ushered in at the 1969 Turin Salon. Marginally longer, taller and heavier (the body was now steel and the engine block cast-iron), this had an enlarged 2418-cc V6 that produced 195 bhp, giving sparkling performance: a top speed of 238 kph (148 mph) and a 0–97 kph (0–60 mph) time of just under seven seconds. Joined in 1972 by the GTS iteration with its removable roof panel, the Dino lasted until May 1974, when it was replaced by the altogether less lovely 308 GT4. A true classic, the Dino still has the power to slacken jaws from a hundred paces. And that's before you hear one at 7000 rpm.

Divine design. The Dino was criticized first time round for not being a 'real' Ferrari. Decades later it is lauded as a styling classic and it will outhandle many cars forty years its junior.

Ferrari Dino Owners Club
Switzerland
Dino gt
CAVALLINO FERRARI CLASSIC III

Opposite: The Dino was intended to be a marque separate from Ferrari and a direct competitor to the Porsche 911. No car left the factory with the prancing-horse symbol.

Above: The sensuous shape of the Dino bore nothing as simple as a straight line. The sculptured side vents were first seen on the Tom Tjaarda-styled Ferrari 365 Spider California.

Ferrari Dino 246GT

A study in symmetry. Aldo Bravarone's outline was a key element of the Dino's success, matched only by its fabulous engine and tenacious handling.

Ferrari Dino 246GT

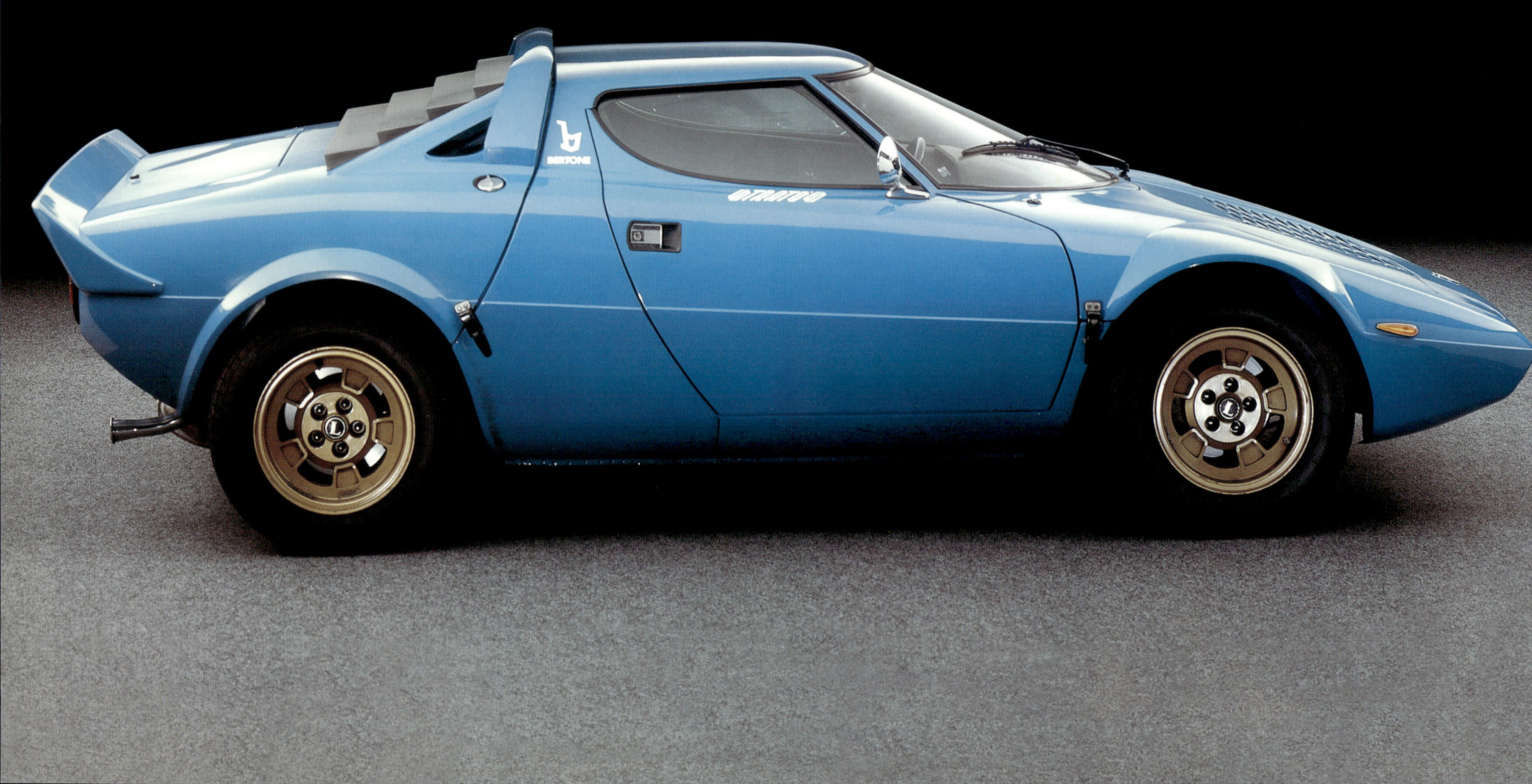
BERTONE

1975 LANCIA STRATOS

With the release of the Stratos, Lancia erased the perceived wisdom that a rally car had to be based on something you would more likely find in a supermarket car park. It was rallying's first 'homologation special', a concept of building a car without the usual requirement to sell replicas to the public. Or at least not very many.

Few who witnessed the unveiling of the original Lancia Zero concept car at the 1970 Turin Salon would have guessed that it would spawn a motor-sport legend. Styled by Bertone's starry-eyed futurist Marcello Gandini, the startling, wedge-shaped outline owed more to science fiction than to production reality.

Yet it triggered a response in Lancia competition manager Cesare Fiorio. Up until now, few had considered building a car purely for rallying. Ford had toyed with a mid-engined machine, the GT70, but dropped the project before it fulfilled its potential. Lancia, by comparison, pressed on with its bold new vision, the definitive Stratos being displayed at the 1972 Turin Salon.

Powered by a Ferrari Dino V6 engine mounted amidships in a chassis designed by Gian Paolo Dallara, the glass-fibre-bodied supercar was given its debut win by Sandro Munari in the April 1973 Firestone Rally in Spain. This was followed by three consecutive victories in the classic Monte Carlo Rally and as many World Rally Championships, and the Stratos would continue winning in private hands until as late as 1982.

As regulations called for 500 cars to be built to satisfy homologation requirements (although this figure was dropped to 400 during the car's lifetime), several road cars were built although not especially well. With panel gaps visible from space and little in the way of soundproofing, the Stratos was extreme and exhilarating. In total, 492 of all types are believed to have been made.

1976 FERRARI 512BB

Despite being for ever overshadowed by the Lamborghini Countach, Ferrari's Berlinetta Boxer was arguably the better car. First shown as a prototype at the 1971 Turin Salon, the original 365BB eschewed contemporary styling gimmicks, instead drawing inspiration from the earlier 512 Modulo and 512S Special Berlinetta show cars. The outline was the work of Pininfarina, or rather its stylist Leonardo Fioravanti, a man responsible for the design of eight Ferraris.

Beneath the striking visage lay a typically Ferrari tubular 'semi-monocoque' frame. In a break with tradition, power came from a new mid-mounted flat-twelve engine, derived in part from the 312B Formula One unit of 1969. Housed longitudinally, this all-alloy gem was extended to 4390 cc and topped off with the Daytona's bore and stroke, rods and pistons. While the engine's 'flat' configuration had the advantage of a low centre of gravity and low height for superior aerodynamics – the crankshaft was about 508 mm (20 in.) off the ground – any notional benefit was negated by the fact that the transaxle sat under an engine offset from the centreline, which produced a tail-biased 40:60 distribution of weight, carried high. So it was a bit tricky on the limit.

Not that Ferrari was finished: the 365 morphed into the 4929-cc 512BB in 1976, the extra displacement from the now dry-sumped engine producing no extra power but 10% more torque. Yet, by the time the BB reached the end of the road in 1984, it had lost its four Weber carburettors and 10 bhp to emission-friendly Bosch K-Jetronic fuel injection, the BBi being more tractable if not quite as fast. According to many, though, it never was especially urgent, tests at the time having made a mockery of Ferrari's seasonally adjusted performance figures: independent reports claimed 262 kph (163 mph) overall against the factory claim of 290 kph (180 mph). Whatever the truth, the BB remains a classic old-school supercar that, while not as uncompromising as its rival the Countach, is not so belligerent either.

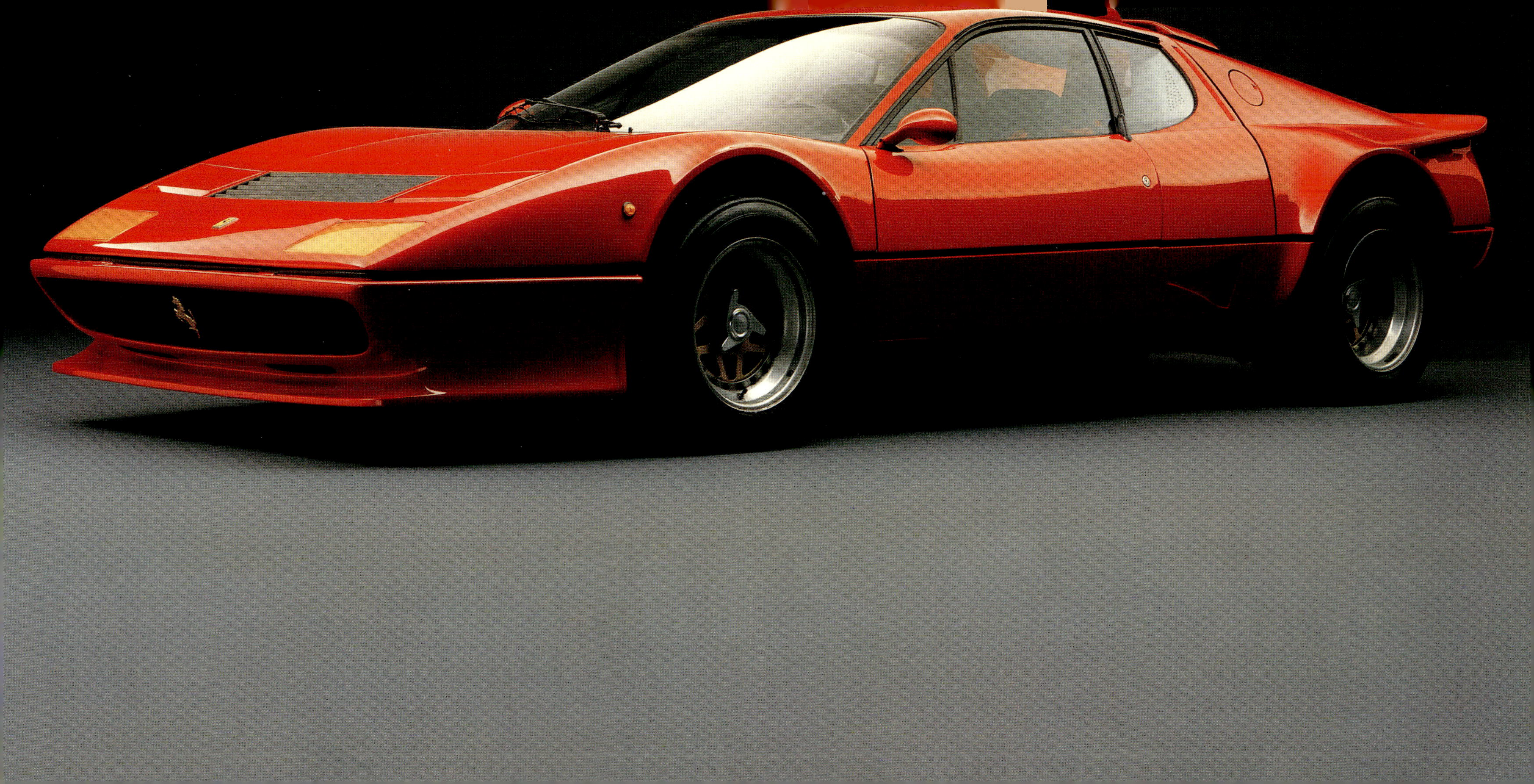

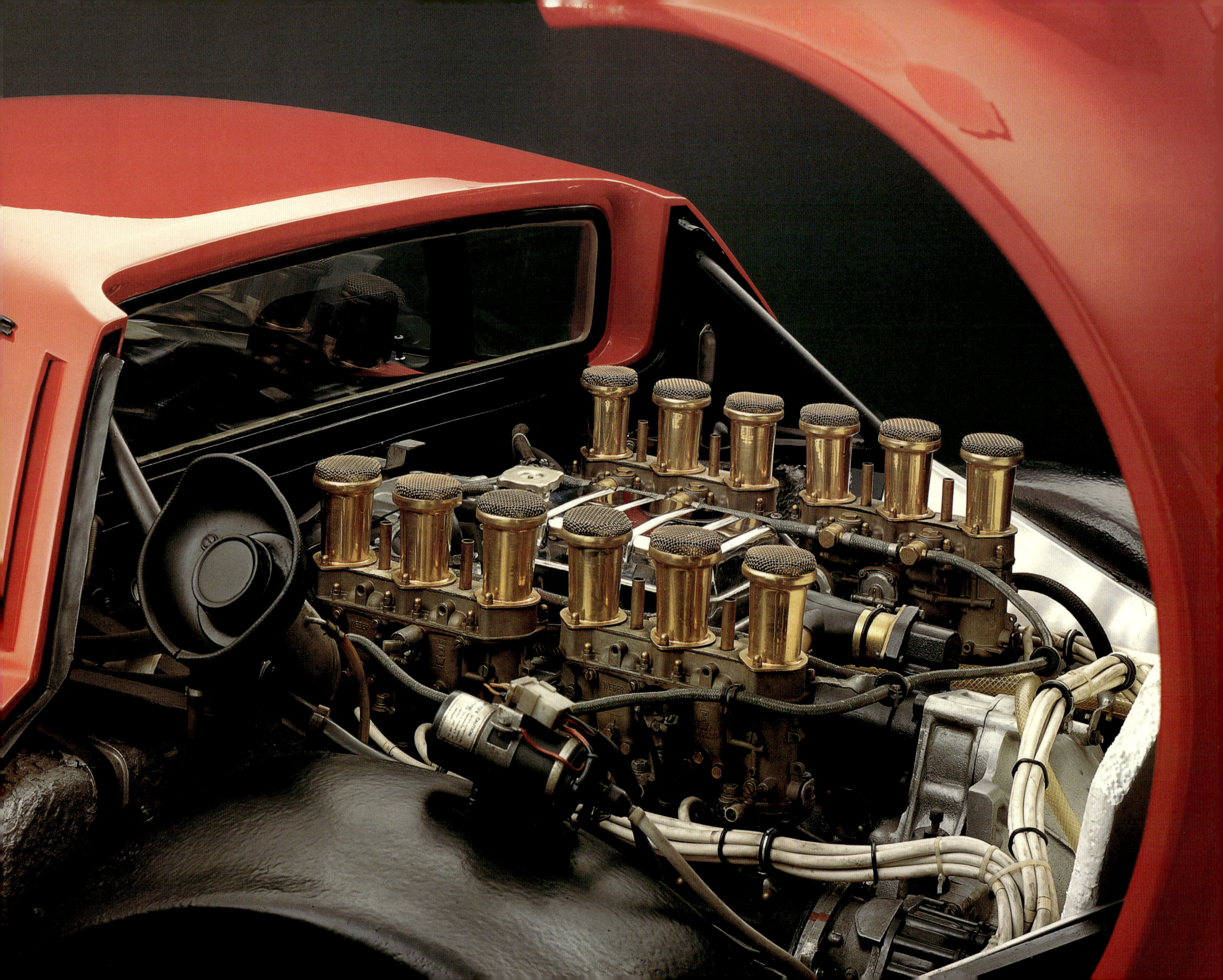

Right: The Leonardo Fioravanti-penned 512BB represented Ferrari's answer to the Lamborghini Countach. Not nearly as outlandish as its rival, the Berlinetta Boxer was an infinitely better car to drive. The rear spoiler here is a non-standard addition.

Opposite and right: The rear bodywork lifts up in its entirety to reveal a grand-prix-car-derived flat-twelve engine. However, because the unit sits on top of the gearbox the car's centre of gravity is high, upsetting the handling.

1984 FERRARI TESTAROSSA

Few cars define a decade quite like the Testarossa. Outlandish in a manner more usually attributable to arch-rival Lamborghini, it came to represent the 1980s to a legion of adolescent males thanks to a prominent role in TV's *Miami Vice*. The Testarossa was simply the landmark supercar of its generation.

Although based on the outgoing 512BB, the 1984 Testarossa was conceived from the outset as a faster, better-handling and more humane breed of supercar; one that you could conceivably spend time actually driving rather than making allowances for. This was achieved, and more.

Typically, Ferrari's favoured styling house, Pininfarina, was responsible for the dramatic outline, the car's most striking characteristic being the heavily stylized engine-cooling vents running backwards from the A-pillar, these multiple vanes inspiring countless copyists. The slatted theme continued to the rear, where a five-bar grille ran the whole width of the tail section, reflecting a decision not to disguise the considerable girth.

Beneath the Testarossa's dramatic skin – steel body, aluminium doors and glass-fibre bumpers – lay a tubular-steel frame aping the 512BB's, home to a 390-bhp, 4942-cc flat-twelve engine fed by Bosch fuel injection: in honour of the 1950s Testa Rossa sports-racing cars, the camshaft covers and intake plenums were painted red. Capable of 0–97 kph (0–60 mph) in 5.2 seconds and with a claimed top speed of 290 kph (180 mph), the Testarossa was not quite as fast as its challenger the Countach QV, but it was infinitely more enjoyable to drive.

Debuting at the 1984 Paris Salon, the 'Red Head' remained in production until early 1992, when it was replaced by the closely related 512TR. During its seven-year production run, 5648 were built, making it one of the most successful of all supercars.

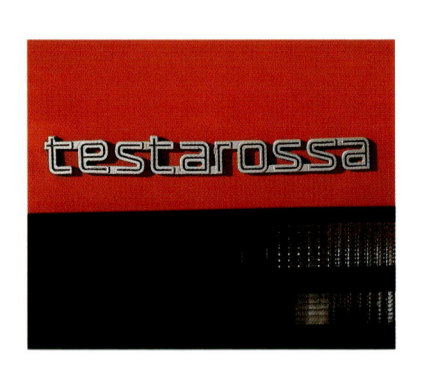

Ferrari revived the Testa Rossa name of the 1950s sports-racing cars, but here it became a one-word contraction. Built to earn back bragging rights from Lamborghini's Countach, this it achieved, and more, thanks to bold styling and product placement on the small screen.

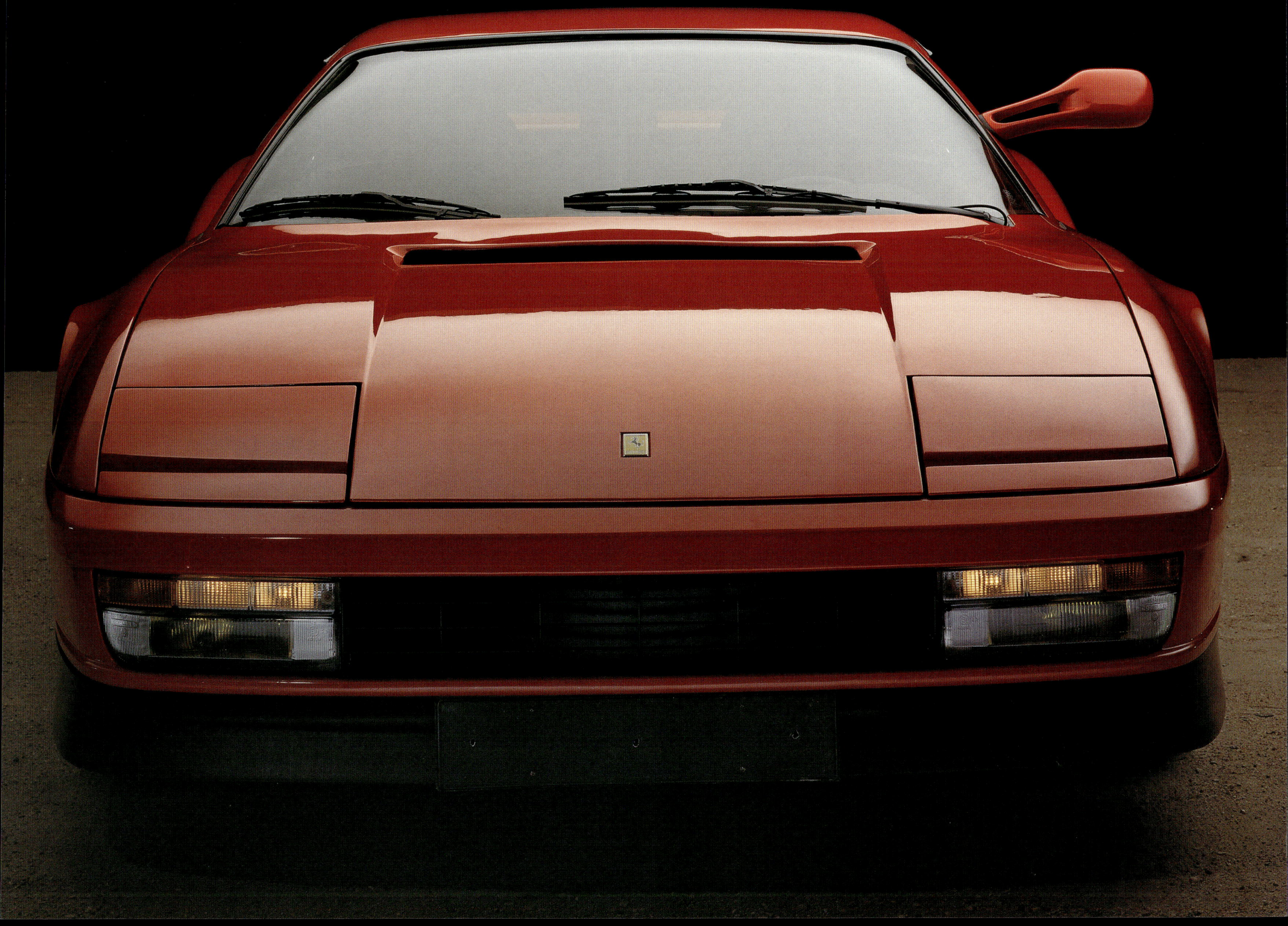

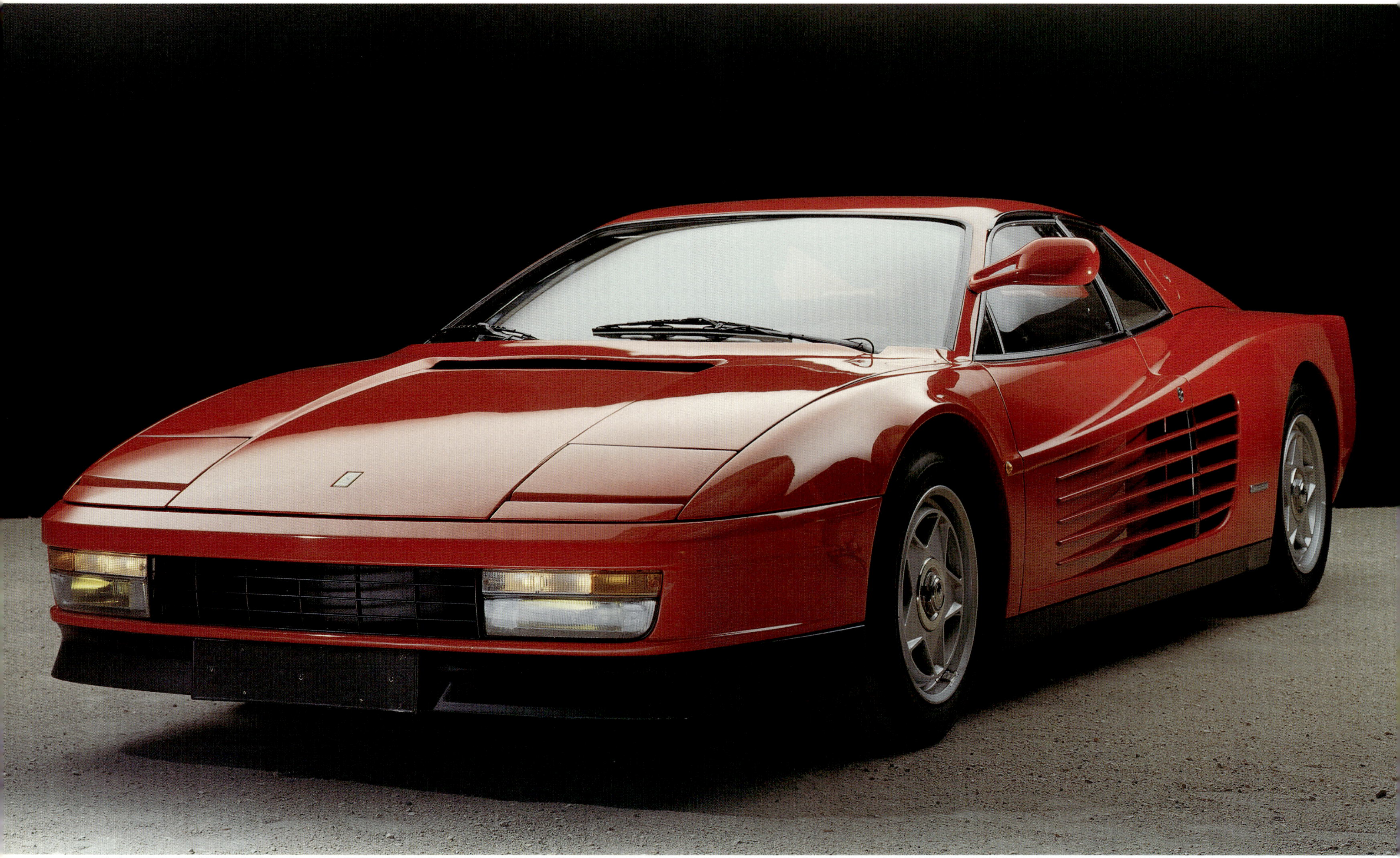

Opposite: Pininfarina and Ferrari have traditionally created elegant, restrained cars, at least by comparison with their arch-rival Lamborghini. The description doesn't fit the Testarossa, however: it redefined supercar extremes thanks to the dramatic air vents on its flanks, which were later mimicked ad nauseam.

Right: A classic Cromadora alloy wheel, another Ferrari supercar constant. The five-spoke pattern was continuously used and updated throughout the 1970s and 1980s.

Ferrari Testarossa

1985 LAMBORGHINI LM002

Patently the goal was not to achieve aesthetic perfection. What the Lamborghini LM002 lacked in architectural grace, it more than made up for in mass, this monstrous device being derived from a military project dubbed the Cheetah. Built at the behest of California's Mobility Technology International in 1977, this Chrysler V8-powered machine underwent brief trials with the US Army, the sole rear-engined prototype being destroyed during these demonstrations. Further American-built variations on the theme subsequently fell foul of patent infringements with the rival FMC Corporation (later responsible for the Hummer) and the plan was scrapped.

Not wanting the project to end there, Lamborghini pressed on with further iterations, but when none of these proved attractive for military purposes concentration switched to a civilian version instead. The LM002 debuted at the 1982 Geneva Salon, although volume production did not get underway until four years later. Featuring a tubular-steel inner structure and aluminium/glass-fibre body, this 4 × 4 monster featured all-round independent suspension with coil springs and telescopic dampers, along with ventilated disc brakes used on the Countach supercar. Featuring the firm's existing 5167-cc V12 engine (now in the front), complete with a sextet of Weber carburettors, this 2700-kg (5720 lb), 4790-mm (186.8 in.) leviathan could reach a scarcely believable 187 kph (116 mph). With leather upholstery and a wooden dashboard completing the ensemble, the LM002 soon found favour, despite an eye-watering price tag of $120,000.

Some 301 of these remarkable machines were made until 1993, including a batch of custom-made estate versions for the Sultan of Brunei. The final production version was introduced at the Detroit Auto Show in 1992, around sixty LM/American editions being built with special badging, upgraded interior trim, nasty chrome bumpers and OZ Racing alloy wheels. At the time of writing, Lamborghini is threatening to return to the 4 × 4 arena with a new LM.

Conceived as a military project, the monstrous LM002 found greater favour as a people carrier for rich Arabs. Its front-mounted V12 was shared with the Countach supercar.

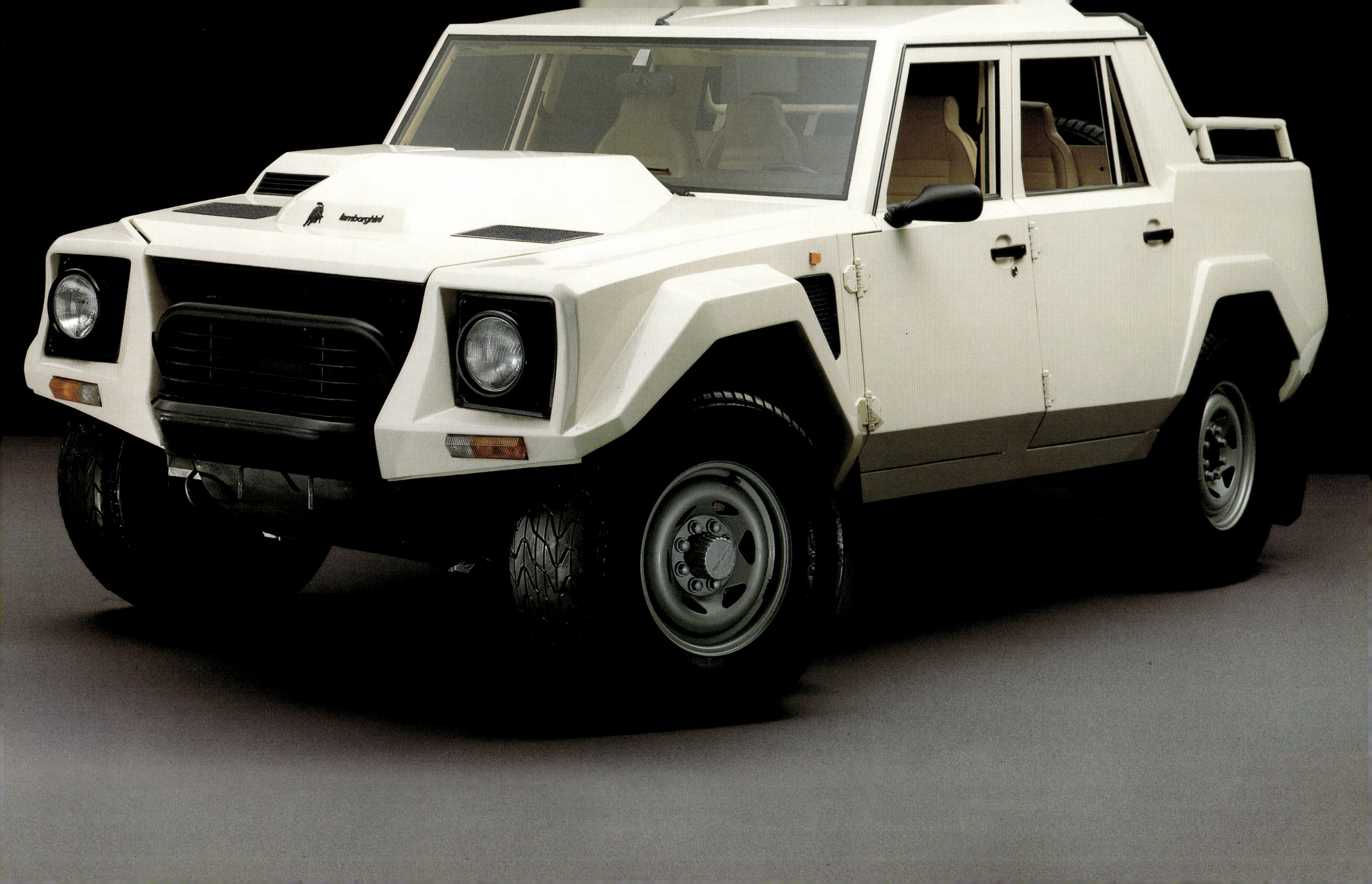
lamborghini

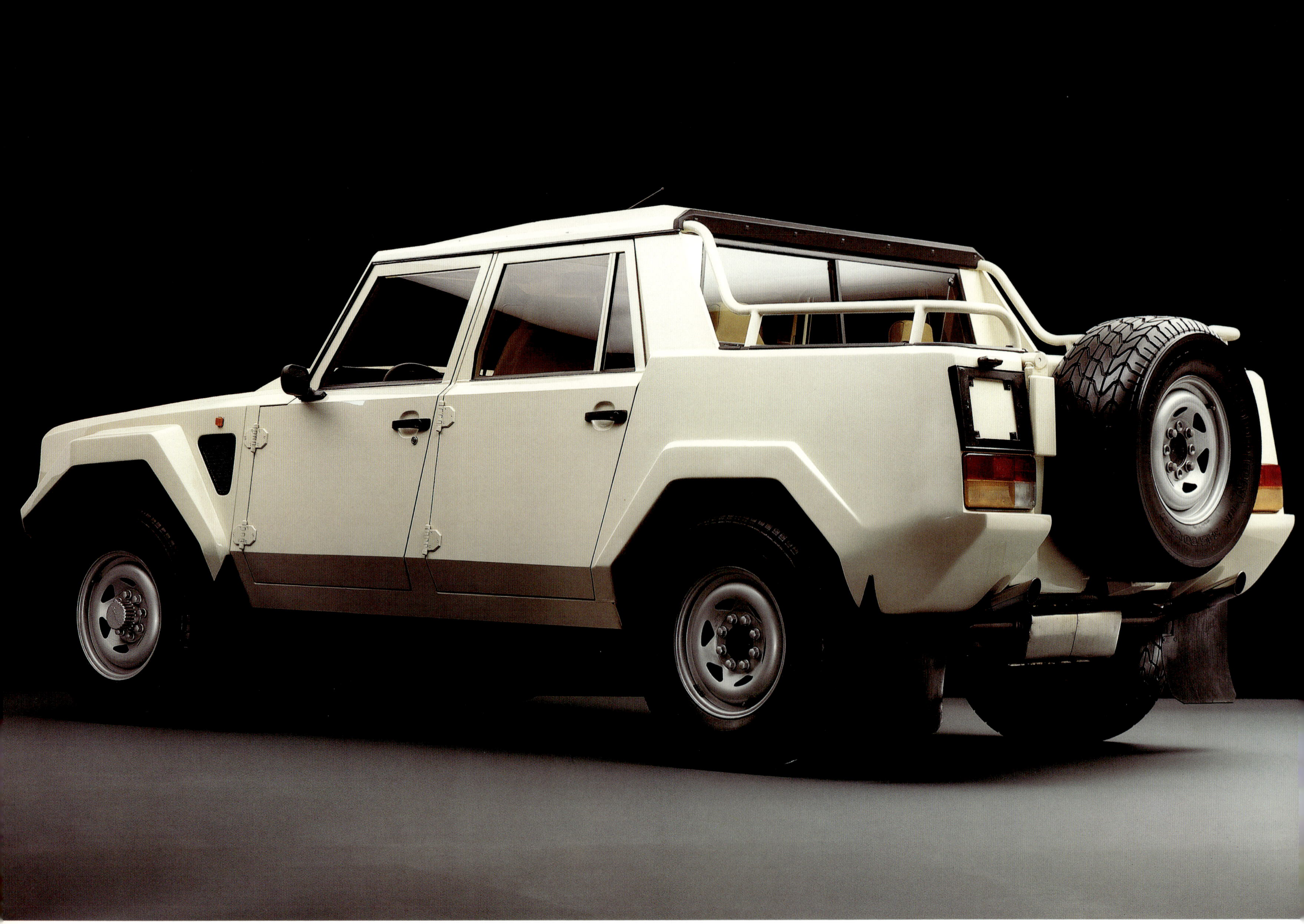

Opposite: Few cars have commanded greater road presence than the LM002. Its ungainly utilitarian looks concealed devastating all-wheel-drive performance. Nor did they hint at its tremendous thirst, although, given that most were sold in the Middle East, this problem was not insurmountable.

Left: For all its functional exterior, the LM's cabin was an oasis of calm with leather trim, air-conditioning and other luxury accoutrements. Thus far it is the only Lamborghini to feature a wooden dashboard, usually the preserve of expensive British saloon cars.

Lamborghini LM002

1987 LAMBORGHINI COUNTACH QV

There is no literal translation, although it is said that *countach* is a Piedmontese expletive indicating a sense of dumbstruck amazement. Indeed it expressed Nuccio Bertone's astonishment when he wandered into his studio and was confronted by 'Project 112'. And the name stuck.

You can understand why. Few cars carry such a sense of occasion and if it appears dramatic now, imagine the reaction to its unveiling at the 1971 Geneva Salon. From the tip of its knife-edge beak through the cab-forward cockpit to its truncated tail, the Countach appeared like no other car, Marcello Gandini's outline becoming an instant icon. The Miura was just a recce; this was the main event.

What lay beneath the startling silhouette truly set the Countach apart from its contemporaries. A multi-tubular spaceframe with an additional tubular structure carried the aluminium body while doubling as a roll-cage. Power came from the classic all-alloy, four-cam V12 engine and, by the time the first LP400 ('Longitudinale Posteriore', with '400' meaning 4-litre) production car appeared in 1974, displacement was 3929 cc.

The template remained largely the same for the better part of two decades, although it was only during the 1980s that the Countach gained real credibility. The 5167-cc, 455-bhp Quattrovalvole of 1985, a reworking by Giulio Alfieri, allowed Lamborghini finally to deliver on the car's potential with an honest top speed of 269 kph (167 mph). The ultimate iteration, introduced in 1988 to mark the twenty-fifth anniversary, was perhaps one variant too far, Horacio Pagani's revised styling papering over the cracks until the Diablo replacement was ready.

Conceived in 1969 when Ferruccio Lamborghini was at the helm, the Countach withstood bankruptcy and serial ownership during the following decade, and outlived its natural lifespan, yet its shadow in supercar lore remains a long one.

A poster wall adornment for thousands of schoolboys during the 1970s and 1980s, the Countach continues to astonish and captivate. An awful car to drive slowly, it's a riot at speed.

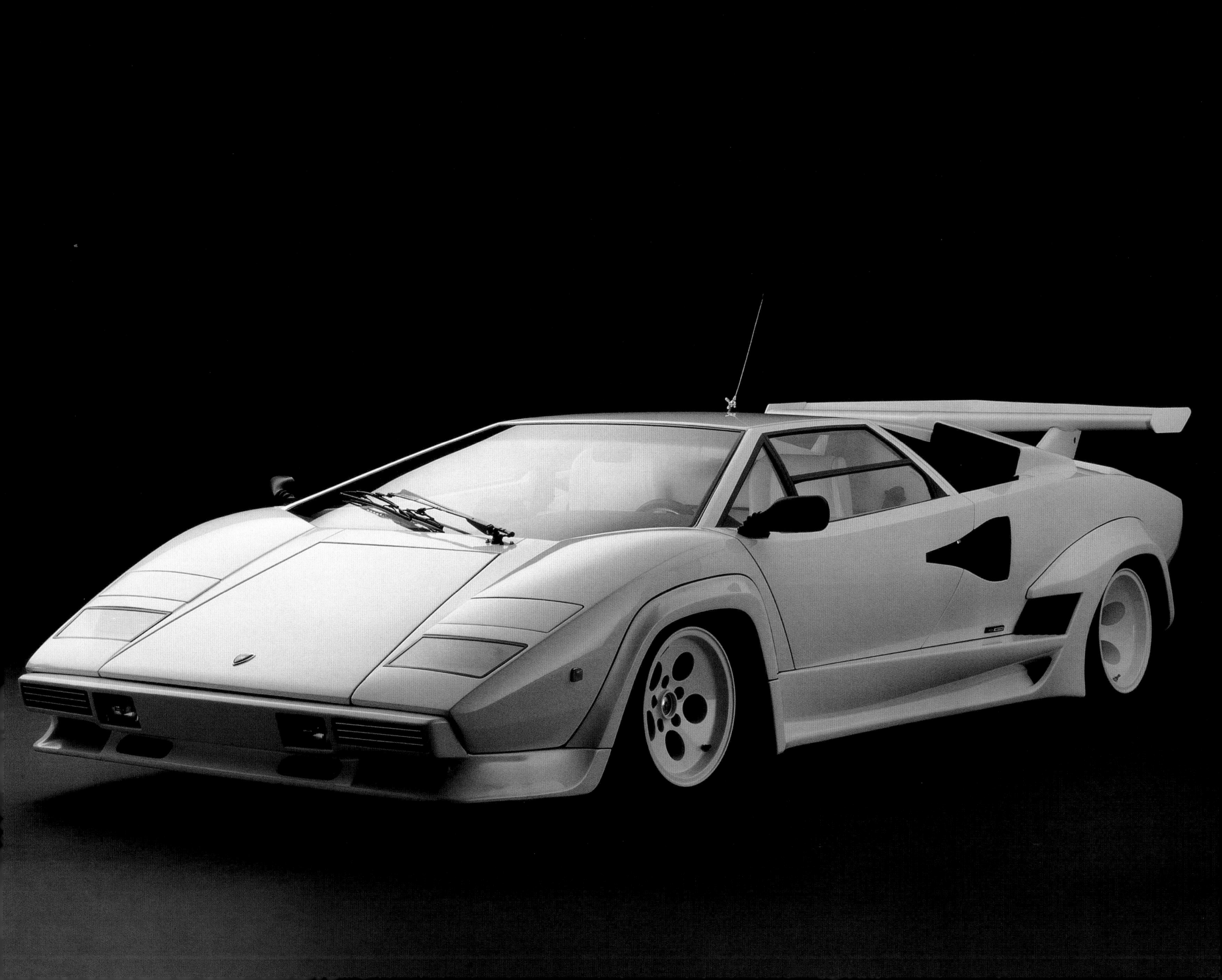

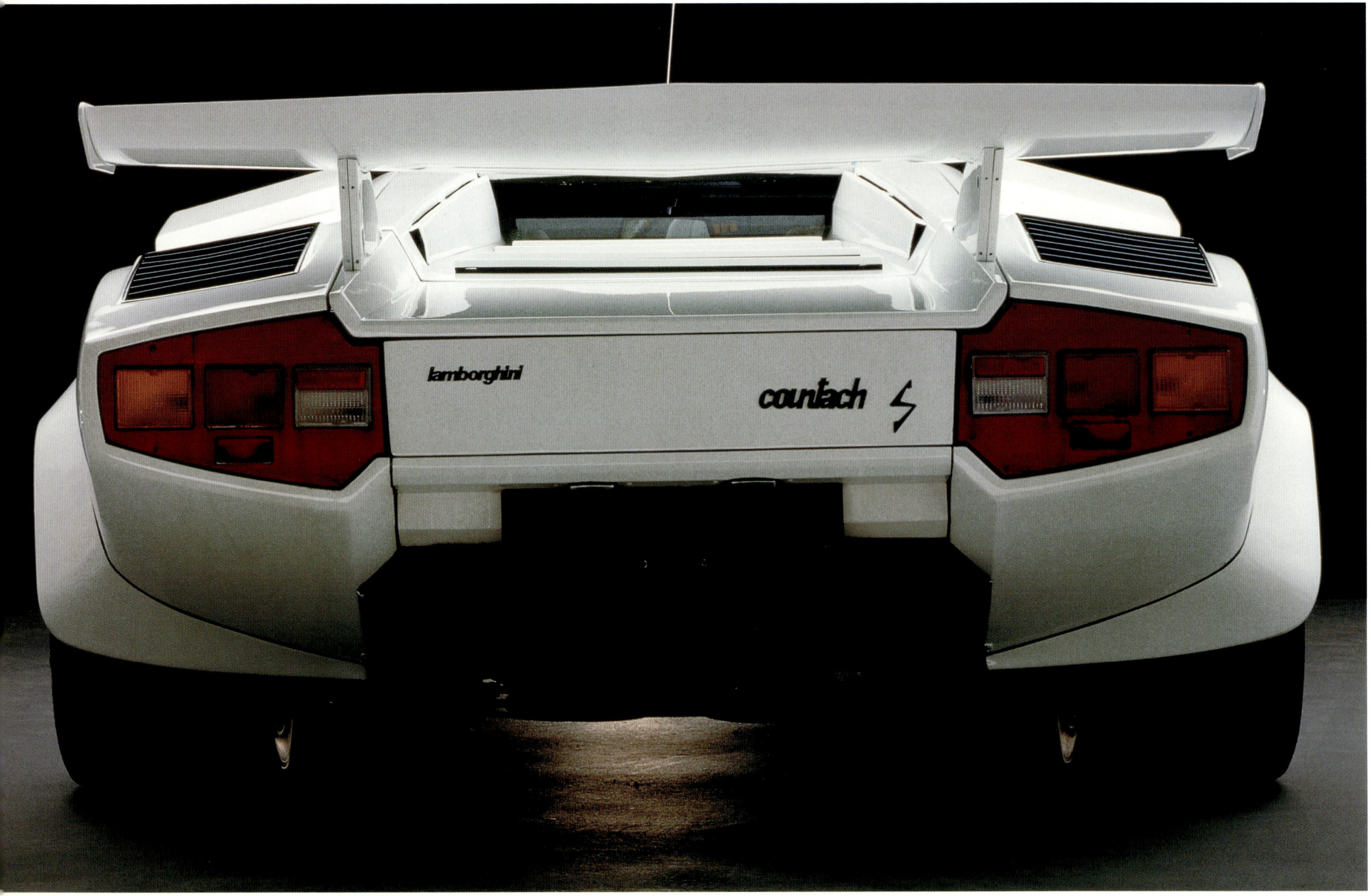
lamborghini
countach S

Opposite: The view most other cars got of the Countach. The rear wing was added on the grounds that it boosted aerodynamic downforce, although in truth it was a styling trick – it actually created drag and slowed the car.

Left: Getting into a Countach required great physical dexterity thanks to the low roofline and wide sills. It was best to put your posterior on the seat and then swing your legs in. It is not comfortable, but then it is a supercar.

Lamborghini Countach QV

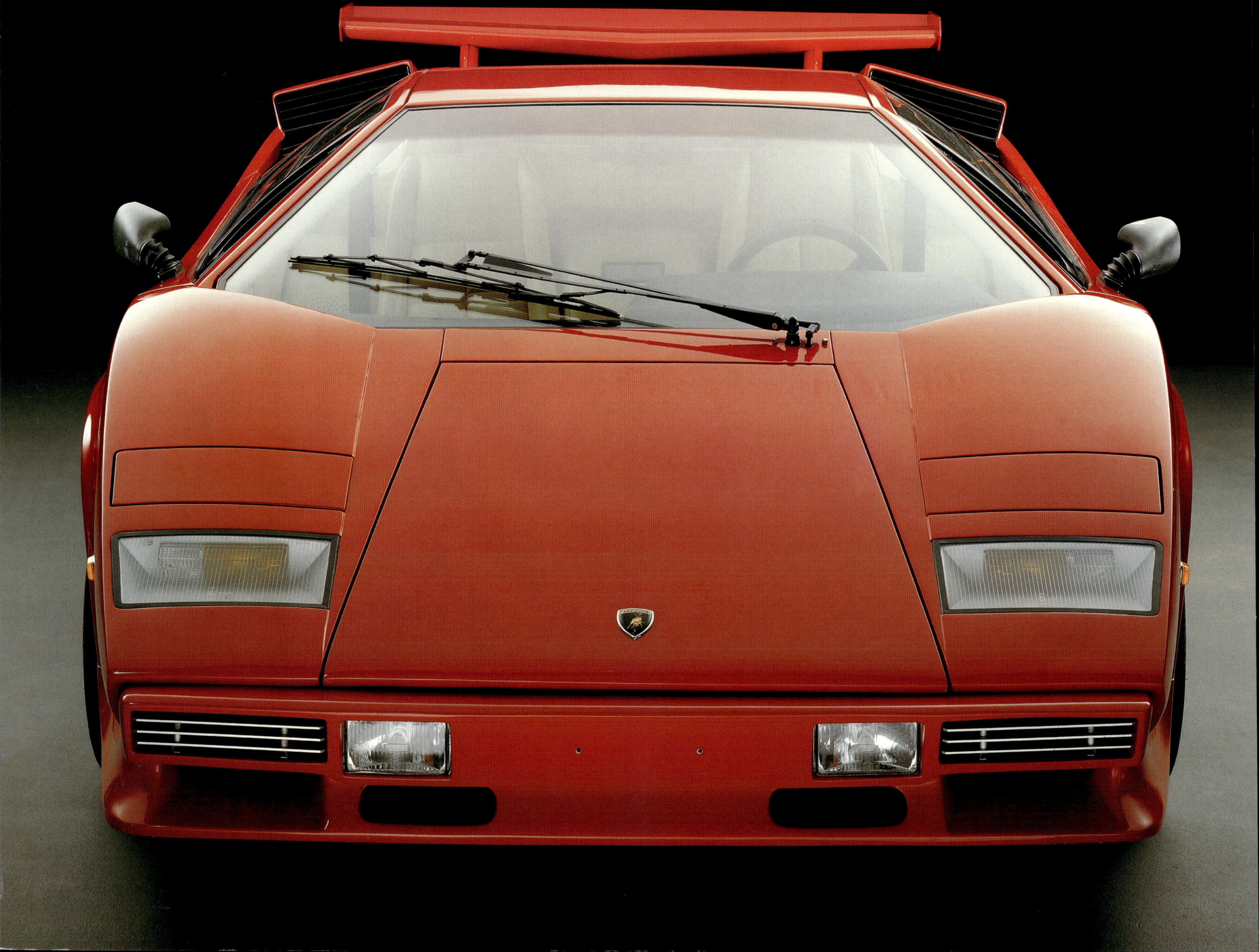

Opposite: To many the spoilers and wheel-arch extensions sullied the Countach's once-pure outline, but later variations on the theme only heightened onlookers' sense of dumbstruck amazement. There was nothing like the Countach — then or now.

Above: It was by no means pretty, but Lamborghini's wondrous wedge-shaped design set the template for ever more outlandish creations. The car outlived its rivals — and its natural lifespan — and was a legend the moment it was born.

1991 BUGATTI EB110GT

Charismatic, entrepreneurial and extraordinarily wealthy, Romano Artioli was the world's foremost Ferrari distributor when he embarked on reviving the Bugatti marque in 1987. Once the benchmark for engineering and aesthetic excellence in both road and racing cars, Bugatti had swiftly declined after its Type 251 grand-prix car flopped in 1956, and ultimately became part of the French state-owned aviation giant SNECMA.

From Artioli's fabulously extravagant factory in Camogalliano, near Modena, emerged a new breed of supercar, the most technologically advanced of its kind. The EB110GT featured a carbon-fibre monocoque chassis with a 3.5-litre, 550-bhp, quad-cam V12 engine mounted amidships. At a time when a car with two turbochargers was considered a rarity, this new strain of Bugatti housed four, power being transmitted via four-wheel drive, to help counter the colossal torque loads. Yet it was the styling that polarized opinion. The outline was the work of Marcello Gandini, although his work was subsequently amended by others, including the factory's architect, Giampaolo Benedini.

Amid much fanfare, the definitive production car was launched at Versailles on 11 September 1991, 110 years after the birth of the marque's founder, Ettore Bugatti, which accounts for the numerical designation. Capable of 344 kph (214 mph) and 0–97 kph (0–60 mph) in 3.4 seconds, the EB110GT was the fastest road-legal car then on sale and, at £281,000 (and more for the 603-bhp Supersport edition), it was among the most exclusive.

The EB110GT was all set to eclipse long-established rivals, but its launch coincided with a worldwide economic depression during which the market for such expensive machines almost evaporated. By the time Bugatti Automobili crashed in September 1995, just 115 cars had been built, including prototypes and racing versions. At the bankruptcy sale two years later, German Jochen Dauer bought a number of partially completed cars and has since built up a further eleven. The marque currently lives on under Volkswagen, whose new 16-cylinder Veyron promises 406 kph (252 mph).

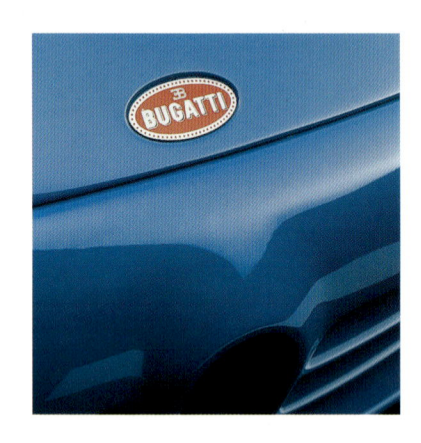

The early 1990s saw a raft of marque revivals, Bugatti's being the most celebrated. Sadly, despite the fact that the EB110 was a technical tour de force, production barely reached triple figures, although the brand lives on under Volkswagen.

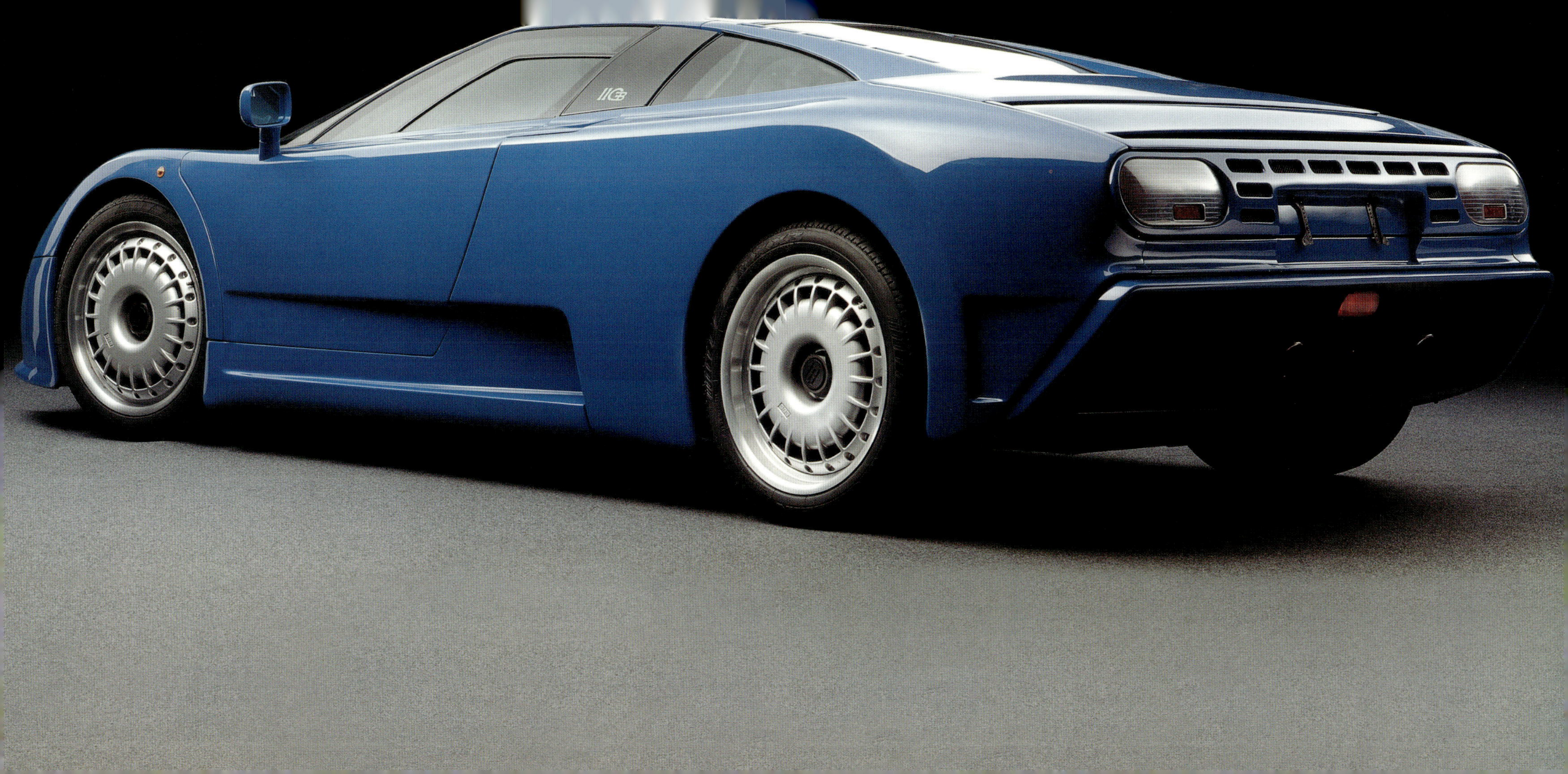

Left: The EB110 was a genuinely usable supercar as opposed to a weekend toy. The cabin was comfortable, had decent ventilation and you didn't have to contort yourself to a neck-cricking angle to see out of it.

Opposite: Marcello Gandini's outline was later reworked by others. When new it was criticized as being less than beautiful, but all these years later it still has a contemporary air.

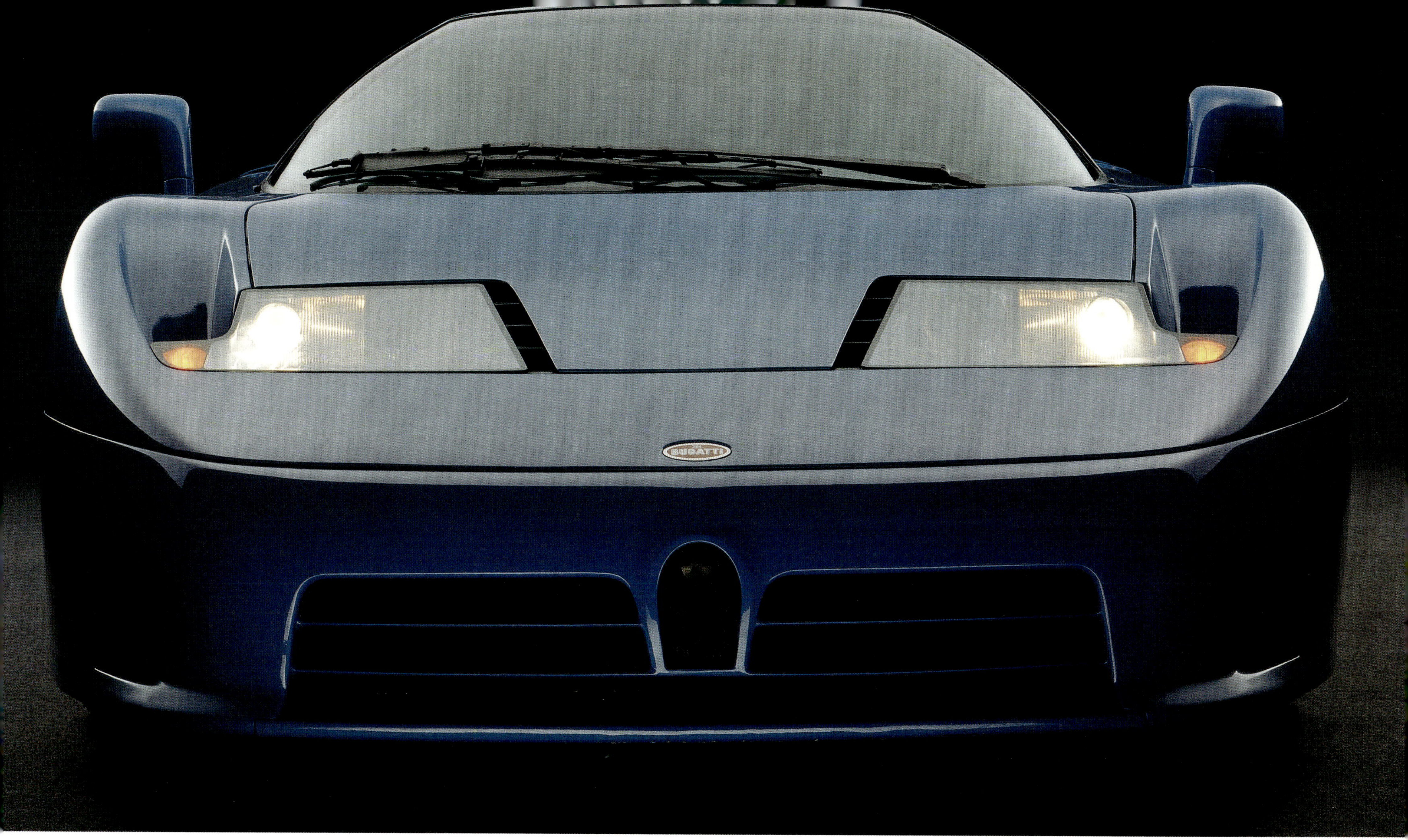

Left: The EB110 didn't make do with just two turbochargers: its 3.5-litre V12 had an astonishing four. This engine was fully bespoke, with power transmitted to the road via four-wheel drive.

Opposite: The use of the Bugatti name and the distinctive horseshoe grille offended many owners of pre-war models. But surely even the original founder of the marque, Ettore Bugatti, would have been impressed by the brave engineering behind the EB110.

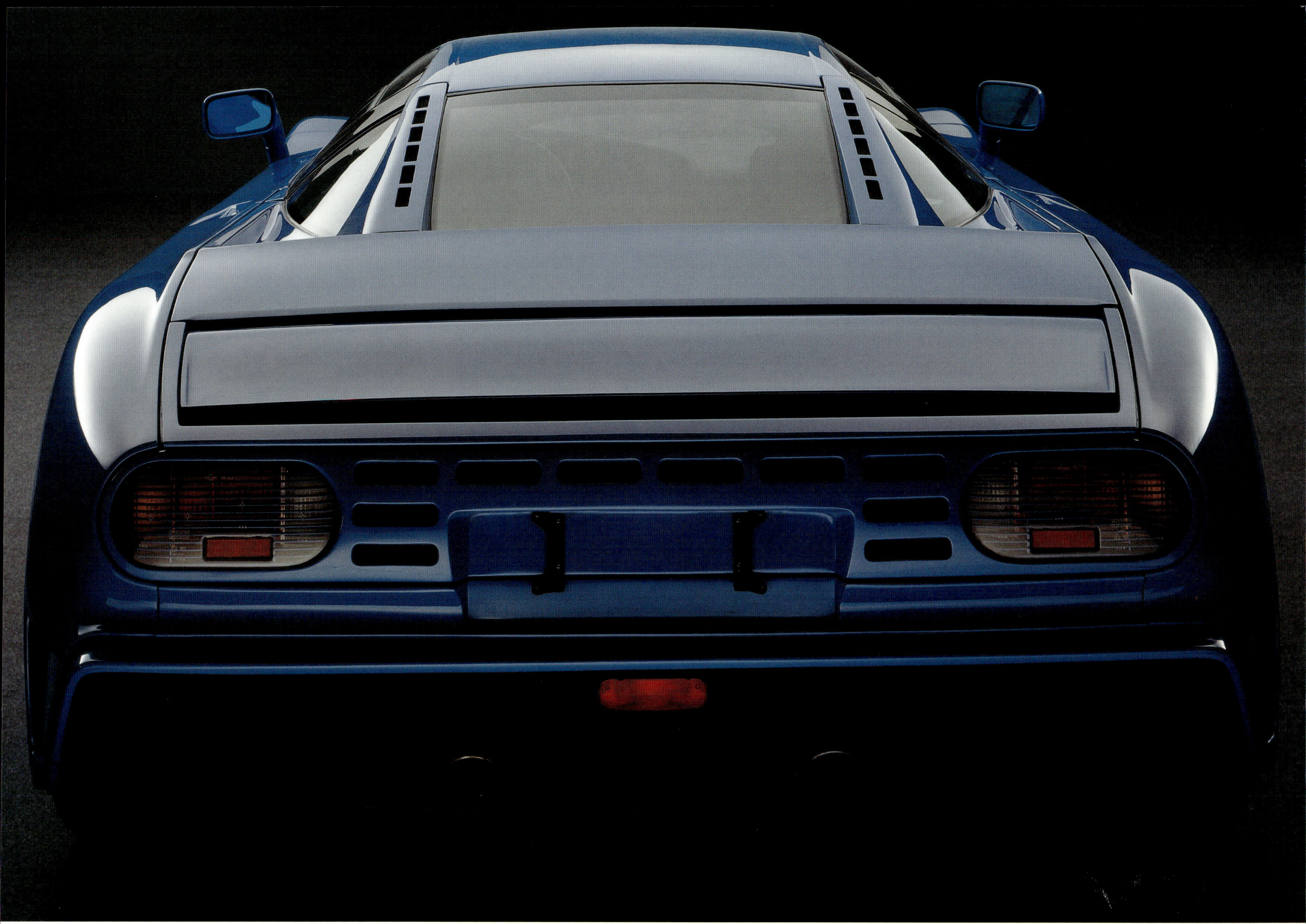

1992 LAMBORGHINI DIABLO

From the tip of its stubby, shovel nose to the outré, scooped rear deck, few supercars define excess like the Lamborghini Diablo. Although it was a fitting replacement for the much-revered and equally reviled Countach, that the car was built at all is remarkable, considering the marque's often precarious financial state. It was under the custodianship of the Mimran family that work first started on the project in 1985, former Ferrari engineer Luigi Maemirolli being charged with developing the car and Marcello Gandini with providing the silhouette. The first example was ready in May 1986 but no funding was available to put it into production. A year later the company was sold to Chrysler, which was less than enamoured with the prototype and requested that Gandini try again. He did, but the Detroit giant was still not satisfied, the definitive form being tweaked and honed in a wind tunnel.

When the car was unveiled to the world's media at Monaco in 1990, it met muted praise. Beneath the dramatic outline the Diablo featured a spaceframe chassis with a mid-mounted all-alloy 5707-cc quad-cam V12 engine, Lamborghini promising a top speed in excess of 306 kph (190 mph). Yet, while the car looked and sounded the part, many journalists expressed reservations about its road manners and handling near the limit.

Some of these criticisms were addressed over the following three years, the four-wheel-drive VT model arriving in 1994. The Diablo continued to lead a charmed life under the auspices of Megatech and, more recently, Audi, with a number of limited-edition models retaining the Diablo's relevance through the 1990s. Most remarkable among these were the rear-wheel-drive, 595-bhp SE30, the stripped-out SV and its SV-R race-only sibling. The model's final manifestation was the post-1999 6-litre variant, identifiable by its fixed headlights (from the Nissan parts bin), the Diablo being finally laid to rest in 2001.

The remarkable Diablo was an effective replacement for the ageing Countach, with bold styling that incorporated its predecessor's upswept 'scissor' doors. Like the Countach, it was styled by Marcello Gandini, although his efforts were lightly reworked by others.

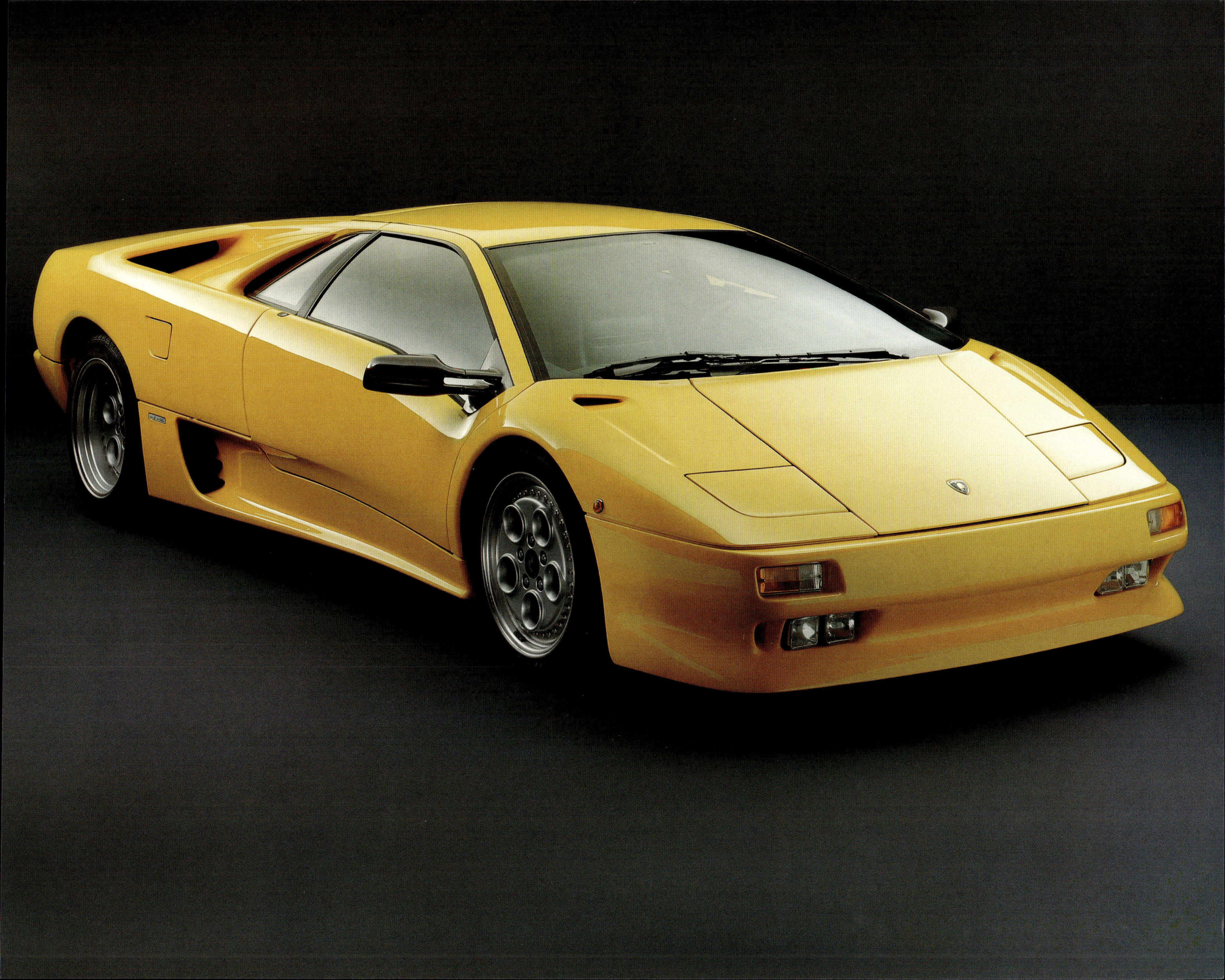

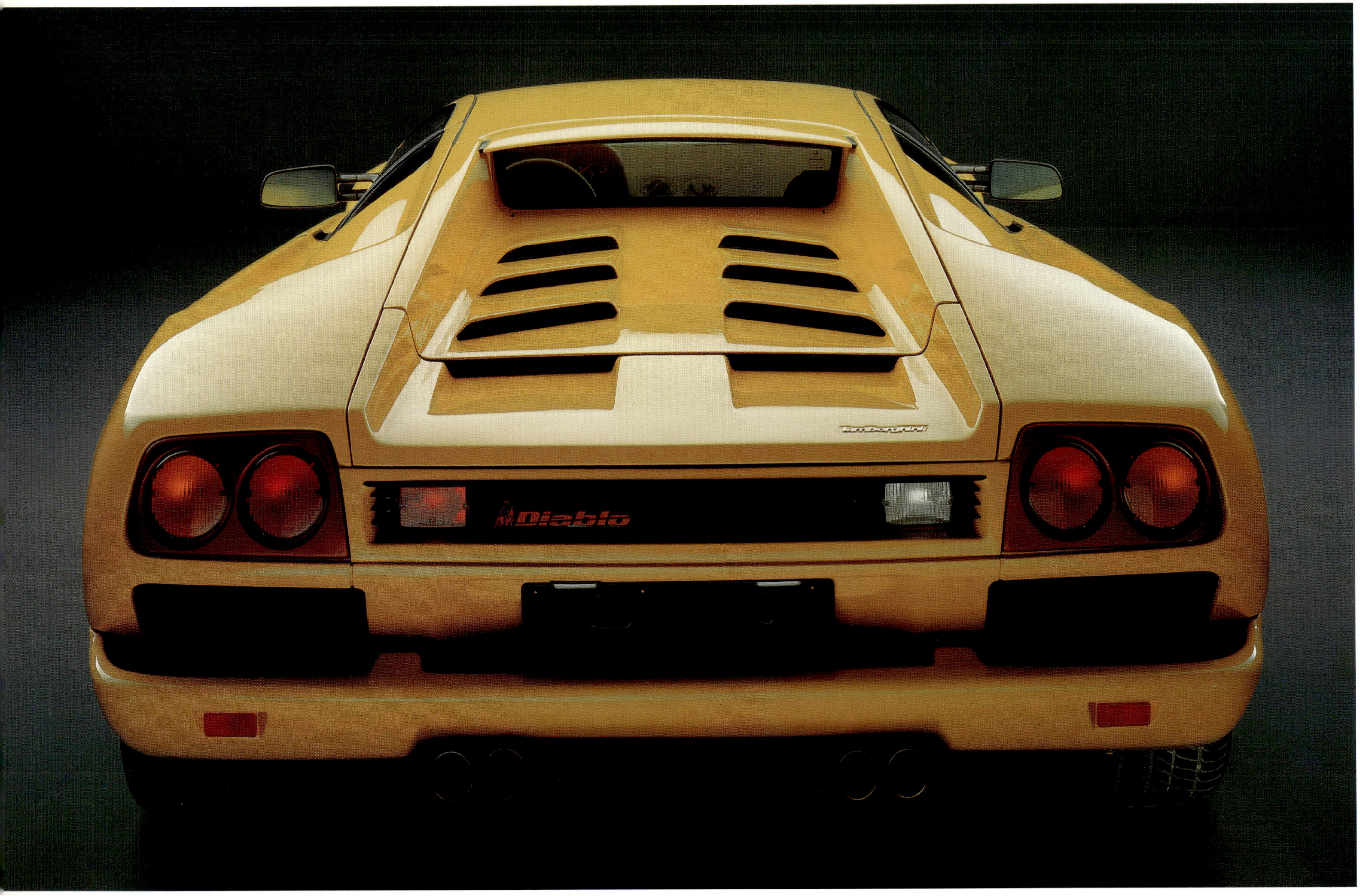
Diablo

Opposite: Longitudinal positioning of the V12 powerplant necessitated lengthy rear bodywork, the Diablo's engine cover being bedecked with air vents to counter the colossal build-up of heat under the bonnet.

Above: The Diablo's cab-forward styling seemed to caricature previous Lamborghinis. It was almost as if every supercar styling cliché was thrown at it and most of them stuck. Somehow the Diablo got away with it.

Lamborghini Diablo

2002 FERRARI ENZO

Arguably the most advanced road car of the modern age, Ferrari's radical Enzo caused a furore when it was unveiled at the 2002 Paris Motor Show. At first glance it didn't appear cohesive. It certainly wasn't beautiful, the tapered outline eschewing design partner Pininfarina's time-honoured purity of line. But here form really did follow function.

The outrageous silhouette was a by-product of packaging and aerodynamic requirements. Borrowing heavily from Ferrari's Formula One experience, the most obvious grand-prix-inspired feature was the raised nose, flanked by a pair of radiators sited ahead of each front wheel. Hot air was directed through ducts to the outer body to prevent under-body airflow upsetting the car's balance. The Enzo's structure consisted of a carbon-fibre monocoque on to which the roof was bonded. Power came from a 650-bhp, 6-litre V12 engine mounted on a cast-alloy subframe with pushrod double-wishbone suspension front and rear. Weighing 1365 kg (3009 lb), the car was slightly heavier than Ferrari's technicians had hoped for, but this remarkable machine could still sprint to 97 kph (60 mph) in just 3.5 seconds, to 210 kph (125 mph) in 9.5 seconds and on to 350 kph (217 mph).

Aside from the leather-clad Sparco racing seats and door inserts, the cabin was stark, with just an expanse of bare carbon-fibre. There were no token concessions to luxury; no air-conditioning or stereo. The steering wheel incorporated multiple function settings governing suspension set-ups and throttle responses, while four-point harnesses came as standard. Perhaps this was just as well, as the Enzo could lap Ferrari's Fiorano test track a scarcely believable 4.5 seconds faster than the previous F50 supercar. Offered in red, black or yellow, all 399 Enzos made to May 2004 were pre-sold at a price of nearly £500,000. An additional car was built later to raise funds for victims of the 2004 tsunami.

Built to celebrate the life of the marque's founder, Enzo Ferrari, this wild supercar received input from Formula One megastar Michael Schumacher during the development stage. All the cars were pre-sold before a single one had been built.

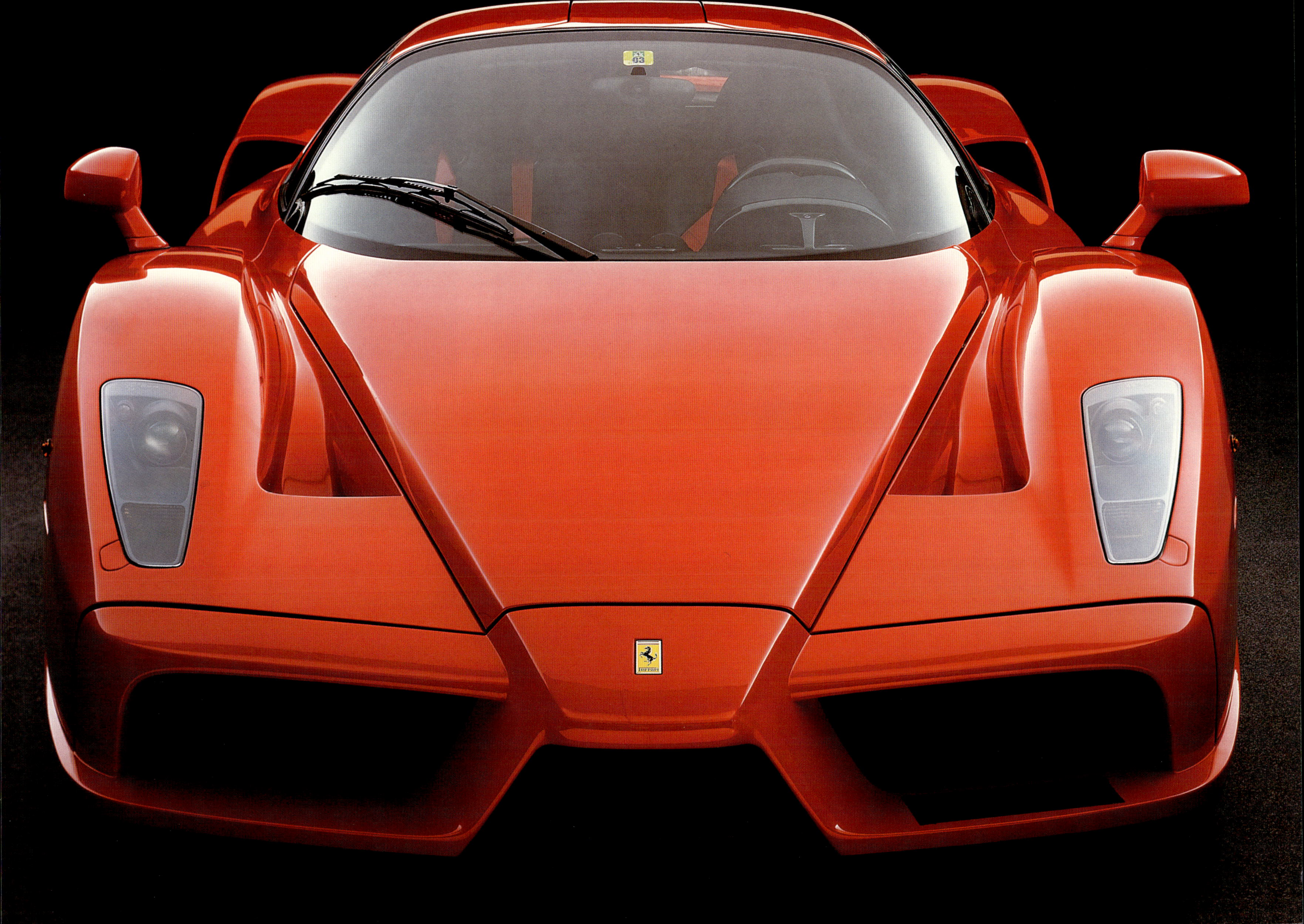

Above: In true Formula One style, the Enzo's steering wheel contains multiple controls that can alter suspension set-ups and throttle responses.

Left: The monstrously powerful 6-litre V12 engine is a work of art and, as such, is visible through the rear glass area.

Opposite: Built by Ferrari for no other reason than that it could, the Enzo threw down the gauntlet to other supercar manufacturers: beat this. So far, nobody has, and the Enzo remains the yardstick.

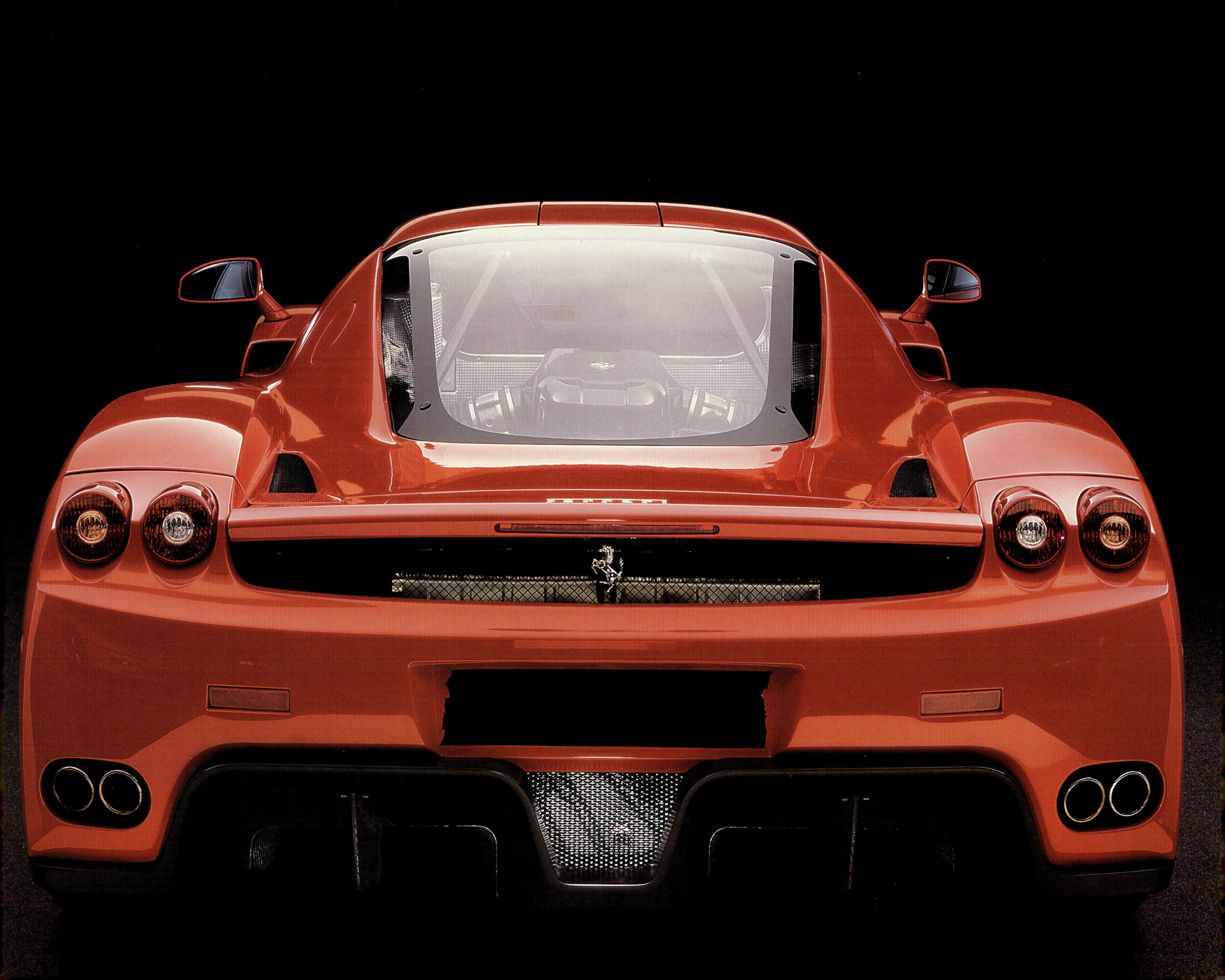

Above and opposite: The Enzo's profile is an artful combination of extreme grace and aggression, the perfect distillation of more than half a century of Ferrari sports cars.

Ferrari Enzo

2004 MASERATI MC12

When is a Ferrari not a Ferrari? When it is a Maserati. A cynical media was highly critical when news leaked in 2003 that Maserati was planning a return to international motor sport with what was effectively a reworked Ferrari Enzo. It was simply a matter of expediency. Maserati did not have the technical or financial clout to develop a new car from scratch, so it borrowed from sister marque Ferrari. The result was the MC12.

From the start the car was intended as a challenger for honours in the classic Le Mans 24 Hours endurance race. As regulations called for twenty-five examples to be built to prove that it was a 'production model', the road- and racing-car production schedules were planned in parallel, although the competition variant appeared first, midway through 2004.

Although the car's mid-mounted 6-litre V12, with four gear-driven crankshafts, produced around 27 bhp less power than in its Ferrari configuration, it is doubtful that many would notice as its overall top speed was verified as 330 kph (205 mph), with the 0–97 kph (0–60 mph) dash taking just 3.8 seconds.

Beneath the dramatic skin, reworked from the Ferrari original by former Mini One stylist Frank Stephenson, lay a carbon-fibre and Nomex monocoque with aluminium subframes front and rear. Inside the road car all the racer reference points were present, with structural carbon-fibre weave mingling with alcantara trim, although the traditional Maserati oval analogue clock looked strangely incongruous. In a nod to the marque's competition history, all road cars had their (carbon-fibre) bodies painted in the blue-and-white livery of the American Camoradi team, which had campaigned Maseratis with success in the late 1950s and early 1960s.

The Le Mans organizers ruled that the MC12 fell outside the spirit of its regulations, so denied it entry in the 2005 event. Nonetheless, the model found considerable success in FIA GT races, taking two wins from four starts in 2004 and performing strongly the following season.

Derived from the Ferrari Enzo, the MC12 caused uproar when news leaked out that it was to participate in GT racing. Although allowed to compete, it was banned from the one event for which it was built: the Le Mans 24 Hours.

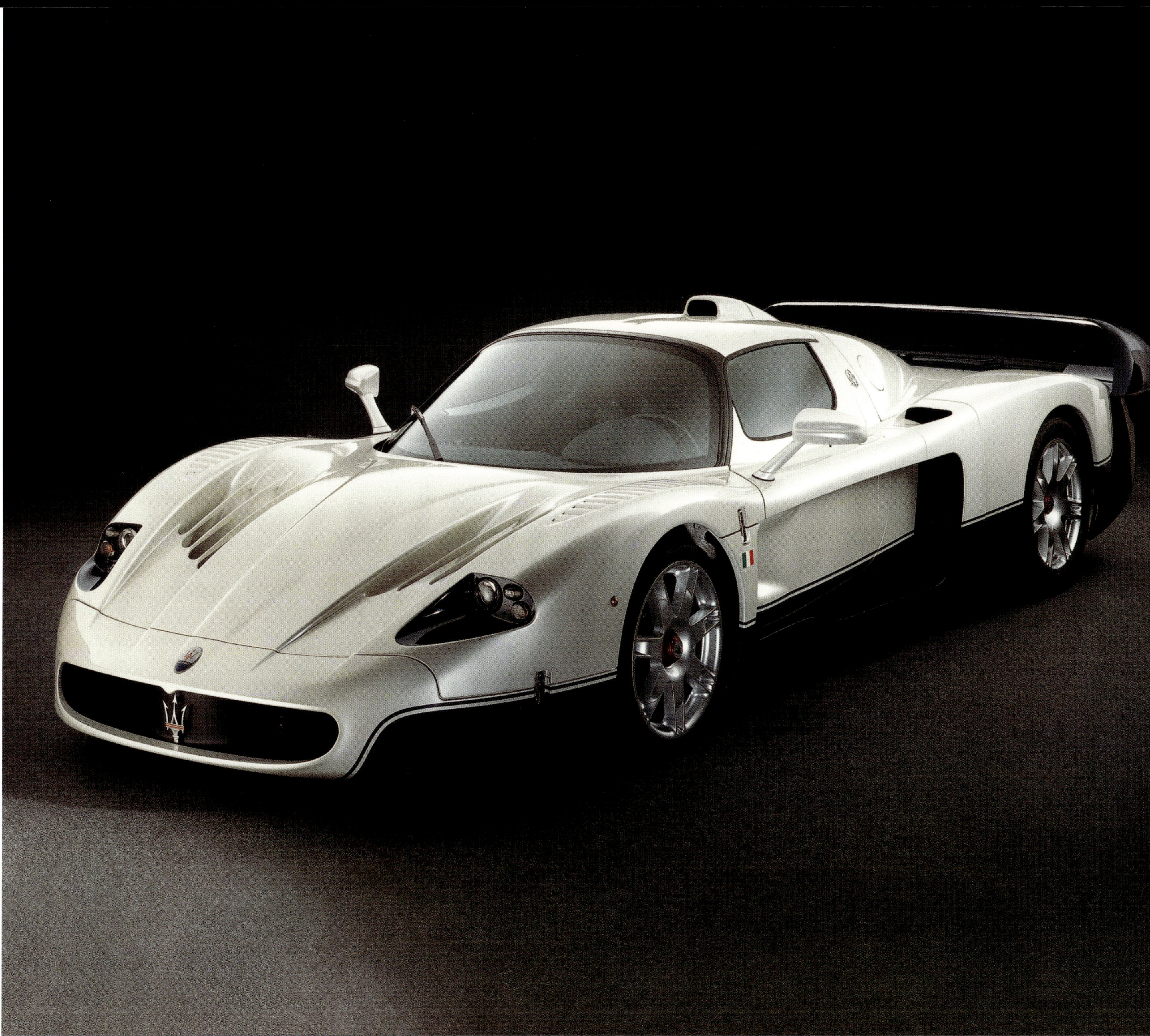

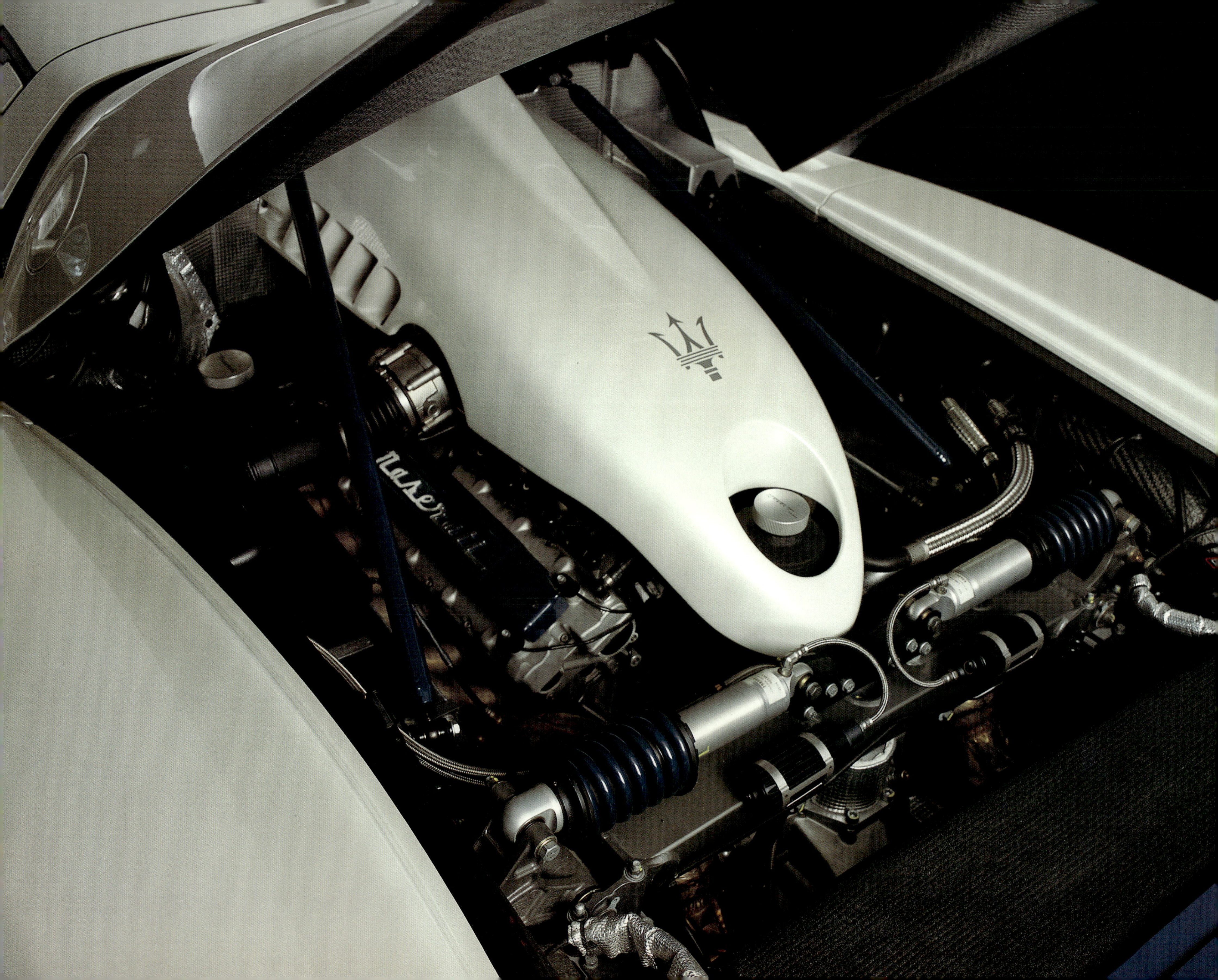

Opposite: The 6-litre V12 produces moderately less power than it did in its original Ferrari application. Even so, the largely carbon-fibre-bodied Maserati can still reach 330 kph (205 mph).

Above: Longer than the Enzo thanks to longer front and rear overhangs, the MC12 was styled by Frank Stephenson, whose background included the altogether more humble Mini One. The blue-and-white colour scheme was a nod to the Camoradi Maserati Birdcage cars of the late 1950s.

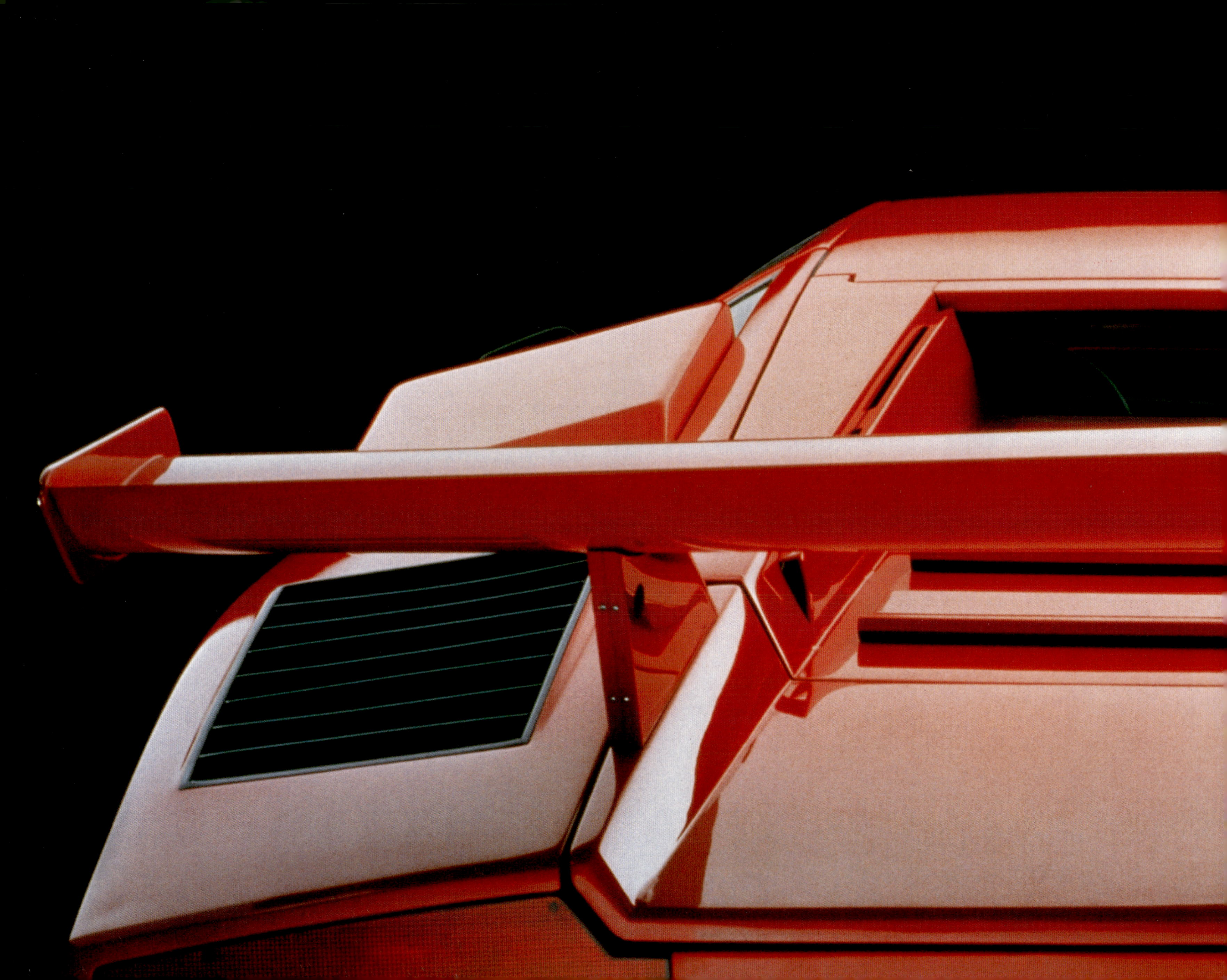

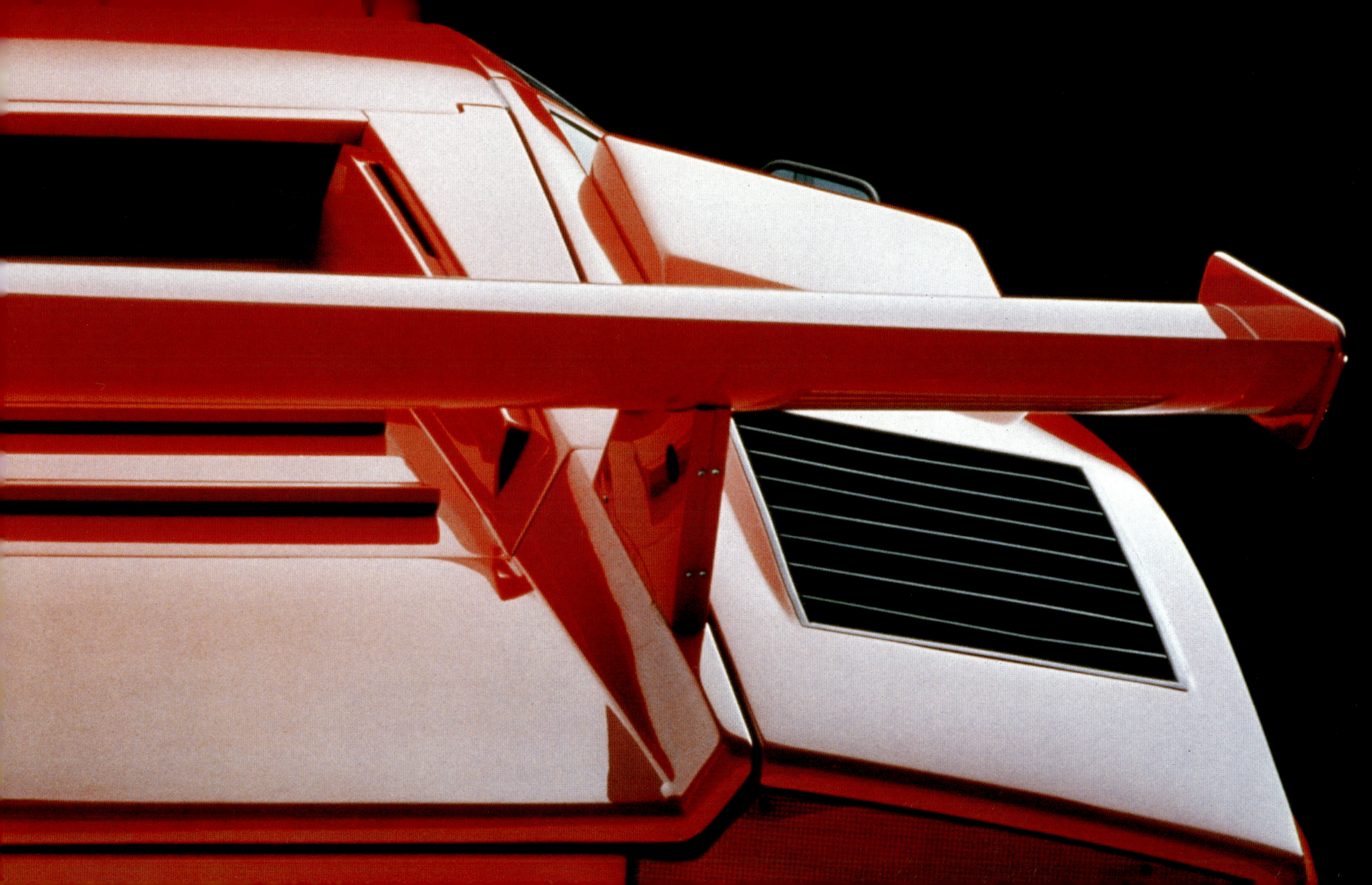

DESIGNER PROFILES

GIULIO ALFIERI
1924–2003

An accountant's son, Alfieri began his rise to prominence by working for Innocenti and Lambretta before joining Maserati in 1953. He swiftly rose to the position of chief engineer and was responsible for turning the 250F into a grand-prix winner while simultaneously designing the Birdcage series of sports-racers. In addition he left his mark on a raft of road-car projects, only to part with the company in 1975 after it was bought by Alejandro de Tomaso. Alfieri arrived at work to discover his desk in the car park, the new owner still bitter that he had blocked a takeover bid the previous decade. He soon bounced back, becoming president of Honda Italy and chief engineer at Lamborghini, where he retained the Countach's relevance with the 48-valve Quattrovalvole model. A personable and likable man, Alfieri later founded a successful electronics firm.

GIOACCHINO COLOMBO
1903–1987

Colombo deserves his place in Ferrari lore for designing the Maranello marque's first V12 engine. Born near Milan, he began his engineering career at Alfa Romeo in 1924, becoming head of the technical department within four years. By 1938 he was chief designer for Enzo Ferrari's Alfa Corse racing team after Vittorio Jano left for Lancia. In 1945 Colombo went to work for Ferrari on his new eponymous marque, only to return to Alfa Romeo, before rejoining Ferrari in 1948 for a three-year stint. Evidently restless, he then went back to Alfa Romeo before working with Maserati in 1952–53. There followed a fruitless three-year diversion at Bugatti, the Type 251 Formula One car spectacularly failing to regain past glories. Subsequently, as a freelancer, Colombo developed engines for Carlo Abarth, designed numerous projects for MV Augusta and conceived an electric car for Zagato.

GIAN PAOLO DALLARA
b. 1933

Arguably Italy's greatest post-war chassis designer, Dallara joined Ferrari in 1959 on graduating from university. He remained there for eighteen months before being headhunted by Maserati. Moving to Lamborghini, he honed the 350GT before finding greater fame for the Miura supercar. He left the Sant' Agata firm in 1968 to join De Tomaso, where he would remain until he formed Dallara Automobili in 1972. After performing research and development roles for a variety of marques – the Lancia Stratos bore his stamp – he moved into producing racing cars under his own name. His Formula Three single-seaters have dominated the category since the early 1990s, while Dallara IRL cars have won the Indianapolis 500 four times. However, success in Formula One eluded Dallara: his designs for the Scuderia Italia team proved also-rans from 1988 to 1992, owing to underfunding.

LEONARDO FIORAVANTI
b. 1938

Although one of the most respected figures in automotive design, Fioravanti is not especially well known to enthusiasts as his efforts for Pininfarina largely went unheralded, the Turin styling house rarely attributing its output to any one person. Born in Milan, Fioravanti took a degree in engineering before joining Pininfarina in 1964, becoming the firm's director of research eight years later. During his time there he would style eight landmark Ferraris, including the Daytona, 365BB, 308GTB and 288GTO, as well as such influential concept cars as the BMC 1800 Aerodinamica. He also oversaw the design of the Ferrari F40 and Cadillac Allante. After brief spells at Ferrari and Alfa Romeo he formed in 1987 (with his two sons Luca and Matteo) the automotive design and architectural consultancy Fioravanti srl. His concept cars are routinely the standouts at the Geneva Salon.

MARCELLO GANDINI
b. 1935

Along with Giorgetto Giugiaro, with whom his early career was linked, Gandini was once one of the world's most influential car stylists. The son of an opera singer, he worked sporadically in the motor industry in the early 1960s before getting his big break by replacing Giugiaro at Bertone in 1965: one of his first roles was to complete the styling of the iconic Lamborghini Miura. He would go on to spearhead wedge design during the following decade, styling the Lamborghini Countach LP400, Maserati Khamsin, Lancia Stratos and Ferrari 308GT4. After forming his own consultancy in 1979, Gandini would continue to be the supercar stylist of choice, penning the Lamborghini Diablo (although his design was altered), short-lived Cizeta Moroder V16T and Bugatti EB110. He also put his talents to humbler products, such as the Citroën BX and assorted Renaults.

GIORGETTO GIUGIARO
b. 1938

By far the most prolific car designer of the past fifty years, Giugiaro initially dreamed of becoming an artist. His career began in 1956 at the Fiat Styling Centre, where he stayed for three years before joining Bertone: wanting money to buy some skis, he produced some renderings for a friend that caught the attention of Nuccio Bertone, who hired him on the spot. Over the next seven years he would style such standouts as the Gordon-Keeble and Alfa Romeo Giulia Sprint, despite the inconvenience of compulsory military service. In 1965 he joined Ghia, creating more timeless classics, including the Maserati Ghibli, before forming his own firm, Italdesign, with Aldo Mantovani in 1968. Since then he has put his name to over 150 designs, embracing the BMW M1 supercar and more prosaic fare such as the Fiat Panda, Volkswagen Gold Mk1 and Daewoo Matiz.

VITTORIO JANO
1891–1965

Deified by Alfa Romeo fans, Milan-born Jano began his career with Fiat, where he would remain for twelve years. After moving to Alfa Romeo in 1923, he produced some of the most successful racing cars of the pre-war era, including the all-conquering P2 single-seater and the 6C series of sports and racing cars that won the Targa Florio and Mille Miglia. Soon after leaving the Milan firm in 1937, he joined Lancia. Over a fifteen-year period he lent his engineering genius to numerous projects, including the highly unusual D50 grand-prix car. When Lancia pulled out of racing in 1955, Ferrari adopted the design and Jano went to Maranello along with it. He would remain with the *scuderia* until 1965, during which time he designed, in part, the V6 Dino engine. After the death of his son Giorgio, he committed suicide in 1965.

GIOVANNI MICHELOTTI
1921–1980

A hugely talented designer, Michelotti began his career at Stabilimenti Farina in 1936. In 1949 he became a freelancer, often working with Pietro Frua and Alfredo Vignale to produce a number of one-off Ferraris and other exotica, along with small-series production cars. He formed his own design consultancy in 1960 and was routinely employed by British marque Triumph, styling several of its TR sports cars as well as the Herald and the 2000 saloons. Hugely prolific, he produced during the 1960s as many as forty individual designs a year, ranging from the BMW 700 to the Alpine A106. He was also one of the first European designers to influence the nascent Japanese motor industry, creating several elegant designs for Hino. In the 1970s his productivity began to decline, although he still found time to style various small-run Ferraris, including a one-off Daytona-based car for actor Steve McQueen. His final flourish was the Reliant Scimitar SS1. Subsequently his son Eduardo took control of the business.

SERGIO SCAGLIETTI
b. 1920

One of the unsung stars of Italy's exotic car market, Scaglietti entered the motor industry aged thirteen, after his father died. He started by repairing and rebodying existing cars before becoming a fully-fledged coachbuilder. In the 1950s his eponymous *carrozzeria* rose to become official body-builder to Ferrari, often transferring Pinin Farina designs into volume products along with clothing the *scuderia*'s racing cars. He would also lend his name to numerous small-run projects during this period, including a batch of custom-bodied Chevrolet Corvettes. Like so many of his generation, Scaglietti crafted cars by eye rather than by relying on models or drawings. Tiring of the political and civil unrest that marked Italy in the 1960s, he sold his business to Fiat at the end of the decade. Ferrari honoured his contribution to its history in 2004 with the launch of its 612 Scaglietti *gran turismo* model.

FRANCO SCAGLIONE
1917–1980

A tragic and troubled soul, Scaglione was once one of the most versatile and brilliant of all car designers, although his hatred of the limelight led him to shun publicity. Born in Florence, he began his design career in 1951, at thirty-four, although his tenure at Pinin Farina lasted just two months. He left for Bertone, styling a custom-bodied MG that ultimately saved the near-bankrupt firm after an order was placed for 200 replicas by American Stanley H. 'Wacky' Arnolt. Over the next twenty years Scaglione would style over fifty individual projects, including the Alfa Romeo Giulietta Sprint and the famous BAT (Berlina Aerodinamica Tecnica) concept cars. In 1959 he abruptly left Bertone to go it alone, his subsequent designs including the Lamborghini 350GTV. He became chief designer of Turin-based Intermeccanica in 1969, his swansong being its Indra coupé. After the firm crashed in 1973, Scaglione disappeared from view. Sadly, an addiction to morphine caused his health to suffer, and he died in obscurity.

GLOSSARY OF MOTORING TERMS AND STYLES

Axle
Shaft carrying the wheels and supporting the body via the road springs. Also refers to non-shaft wheel pairings transversely across the car in independent suspension.

Beam axle
Rigid shaft (not independently sprung) carrying and linking front wheels.

Cam
Eccentric projection, usually elliptical in shape, on a shaft, that moves another component as the shaft revolves.

Camshaft
Shaft that revolves within a housing, incorporating a number of cams, usually to operate valve gear. Can be driven by gears, chains or belts.

Carburettor
Mechanism that mixes petrol with air to atomize it and delivers this mixture to the engine inlet valves. It automatically adjusts mixture strength to suit the engine, road speed and atmospheric conditions.

Coil springs
Suspension mechanism of sprung-steel wire coiled into a helix.

Cubic capacity
Measurement of the total volume of an engine's cylinders swept by each piston in its bore. Engine capacity is measured in cubic centimetres (cc) or litres (l), 1000 cc being 1 litre; or in cubic inches (cu. in.), 1 cu in. being 16.39 cc.

De Dion suspension
Means of reducing unsprung weight by mounting the rear axle's differential and final-drive gear to the chassis or body structure, and connecting the wheels by a separate axle, which is controlled in the centre and sprung at the ends.

Drop arm
Operating lever mounted outside the steering box.

Flat engine
Engine with horizontally opposed cylinders. Also known as a boxer engine.

Independent suspension
Method of attaching a vehicle's wheels so that each has its own independent linkage to the chassis or body. Each wheel is sprung independently so that it can move without affecting any other.

Garagiste
Derogatory term formerly used by the Italian and French motor-racing fraternity to describe constructors of humble origin, particularly British firms such as Cooper and Lotus.

Ladderframe chassis
Chassis in which two spars are laid longitudinally and connected transversely by strengthening and support webs.

Live rear axle
Transverse beam axle connecting both road wheels and housing the differential and final drive.

Monoblock
Engine construction in which crankcase and cylinder block are cast in one piece.

Monocoque
Single-skin car body lacking longitudinal members.

Overhead camshaft
Camshaft(s) mounted above the cylinder head, at the opposite end of the engine to the crankshaft.

Overhead valve
An arrangement of the camshaft in the engine block whereby the valve gear is operated by pushrods situated above the cylinder head.

Perimeter frame
An arrangement of chassis members so that they are outboard or inline with wheels.

Piston
A cylindrical component, with one end closed and the other open, sealed into the engine cylinder with piston rings. Driven down the cylinder bore by the exploding fuel mixture, it bears on the connecting rods, which force the crankshaft to twist.

rpm
Revolutions per minute. Any measure of rotational speed. Usually refers to a crankshaft but can also refer to road wheels.

Running gear
Components that underpin a car, especially engine, suspension and axles.

Semi-elliptical springs
A flat sprung-steel plate, or plates riveted together, forming a semi-ellipse in which the ends are joined to the body or chassis and the centre is joined to the axle. Semi-elliptical springs can be used in pairs as part of a live axle installation, or create an independent suspension by fastening the spring transversely across the car, attaching it to the chassis in the centre and to the suspension at either end. In elliptical springs, one part is joined to the body and one to the axle.

Side-valve engine
Engine block in which inlet exhaust valves are arranged alongside cylinders. Huge volumetric inefficiencies are inherent in this design, so manufacturers produced more efficient, better-breathing overhead-valve and then overhead-cam engines.

Spaceframe
A lightweight rigid framework made from chassis tubes in a geometric pattern to carry all the car's systems and provide a structure on which to hang the bodywork.

Straight-six
Term that describes an engine in which six cylinders are arranged in a straight line. Cylinders may also be arranged in 'straight-eight' or other even-number configurations.

Supercharger
Mechanical air compressor used to charge an engine's cylinders with a greater quantity of petrol-and-air mixture than that inducted naturally.

Superleggera
Italian term for a spaceframe, meaning 'super-light'.

Torsion bar
A sprung-steel bar used as a suspension mechanism in some applications by fastening the bar at one end and connecting it to a lever at the other.

Transaxle
A combined gearbox and final-drive unit positioned at the centreline of a drive axle and used to improve the car's balance or to save space through its compactness.

Turbocharger
A supercharger powered by the expulsion of exhaust gases to compress the inlet charge.

Twin-cam
Term that describes the positioning of more than one camshaft, usually in a cylinder head, so that each camshaft operates directly above the valves it opens. This arrangement allows the engine designer to place the valves in the cylinder head at an optimal angle for best gas flow, so increasing the engine's volumetric efficiency.

Wheelbase
Distance between the longitudinal centrelines of a vehicle's axles.

DIRECTORY OF MUSEUMS AND COLLECTIONS

AUSTRALIA

National Motor Museum
Shannon Street
Birdwood
Adelaide
South Australia 5234
Tel. +61 (0)8 8568 5006
www.history.sa.gov.au/motor/moto.htm

FRANCE

Musée National de l'Automobile
    de Mulhouse
Collection Schlumpf
192 Avenue de Colmar
BP 1096
68051 Mulhouse
Tel. +33 (0)3 89 332333
www.collection-schlumpf.com

GERMANY

Rosso Bianco Collection
Obernauer Strasse 125
D-63743 Aschaffenburg
Tel. +49 (0)6021/21358
www.rosso-bianco.de

ITALY

Museo dell'Automobile
Carlo Biscaretti di Ruffia
Corso Unità d'Italia 40-10126
Turin
Tel. +39 011 677666
www.museoauto.it

Museo dell'Automobile di San Martino
    in Rio
Via Barbieri 12
42018 San Martino in Rio
Tel. +39 0522 636133
www.museodellauto.it

Galleria Ferrari
Via Dino Ferrari 43
41053 Maranello
Tel. +39 0536 943204
www.galleria.ferrari.com

Automobili Lamborghini SpA
Via Modena 12
40019 Sant' Agata
Bolognese
Tel. +39 051 6817611
www.automobililamborghini.com
(factory museum)

Museo Storico Alfa Romeo
Centro Direzionale Alfa Romeo
Viale Alfa Romeo
20020 Arese
Milano
www.museoalfaromeo.com
(by appointment only)

Quattroruote Collection
Via Achille Grandi 5–7
20089 Rozzano
Milano
www.quattroruote.it
(by appointment only)

Pininfarina Collection
Via Nazionale 30
10020 Cambiano
Torino
Tel. +39 011 943811
www.pininfarina.it
(by appointment only)

JAPAN

Motor Car Museum of Japan
40 Ikkanyama
Futatsunashi-cho
Komatsu
Ishikawa
J-923-0345
Tel. +81 (0)761 43 4343

THE NETHERLANDS

Nationaal Automobielmuseum
Steurweg 8
4941 VR Raamsdonksveer
Noord-Brabant
Tel. +31 (0)162 585400
www.louwmancollection.nl

Het Amsterdams Automuseum
Zwanenburgerdijk 281
1161 NL Zwanenburg
Tel. +31 (0)20 4977291
www.amsterdams-automuseum.nl

SWITZERLAND

Fondation Hervé
Z.A. Châble-Croix
CH-1860 Aigle
Tel. +41 (0)24 495 1227
www.fondation-herve.ch

Musée International de
    l'Automobile
Voie-des-Trax 40
Hall 7, Palexpo
CH-1218 Grand Saconnex
Geneva
Tel. +41 (0)22 788 8484

UNITED KINGDOM

National Motor Museum
    Beaulieu
Brockenhurst
Hampshire SO42 7ZN
Tel. +44 (0)1590 612345
www.beaulieu.co.uk

Haynes International Motor
    Museum
Castle Cary Road
Sparkford
Somerset BA22 7LH
Tel. +44 (0)1963 440804
www.haynesmotormuseum.com

USA

National Automobile
    Museum
10 Lake Street South
Reno, NV 89501
Tel. +1 702 333 9300
www.automuseum.org

Imperial Palace Auto
    Collection
Imperial Palace Hotel and
    Casino
3535 Las Vegas Boulevard
    South
Las Vegas, NV 89109
Tel. +1 702 794 3174
www.autocollections.com

Indianapolis Motor Speedway
    Hall of Fame Museum
4790 West 16th Street
Indianapolis, IN 46222
Tel. +1 317 181 8500
www.indianapolismotorspeedway.com

The Petersen Automotive
    Museum
6060 Wilshire Boulevard
Los Angeles, CA 90036
Tel. +1 323 930 2277
www.petersen.org

Directory of Museums and Collections

INDEX

*Main entries for cars and designers are shown in **bold***

A

Abarth 163
  750 **166–67**
  2000OT **198–201**
Abarth, Carlo (Karl) 167, 198
Abbott 69
Adams, Jim 227
Agnelli family 9
Alfa Romeo 7, 11, **12–17**, 22, 62, 99, 102
  6C 14
  6C 1750 **54–57**, 59, 86
  6C 2500 **86–91**
  6C 2500 Villa d'Este **106–11**
  6C 3000 132
  8C 14
  8C 2300 **58–61**
  8C 2900 **78–79**
  24HP Tipo Corsa 13
  159 102
  1750 Super Sport 14
  1900 SSZ 132, **142–43**
  2000 Sportiva **132–35**
  2600 Sprint 207
  C52 Disco Volante 132
  Giulia Sprint GT **206–207**
  Giulia TZ1 **190–91**
  Giulietta Spider prototypes **124–31**
  P2 14
  RL 13, **40–43**
  Tipo 33 191
  Tipo 105 Giulia 207
Alfieri, Giulio 177, 179, 250, **278**
Allemano 18
Ambrosini de Passignano sul Trasimeno 191
Ames, John 38
Artioli, Romano 256
Ascari, Alberto 102
Ascari, Antonio 40
Aston Martin 154
  DB4/5 21, 22
ATS 23
  2500GT 23
Audi 25, 262
Audrey, Gus 177
Austin
  1100/1300 21
  A40 Farina 21
  Cambridge 21
  Westminster 21

Auto-Union 14, 17, 55
Autodelta 191

B

Bandini, Lorenzo 191
Barry Plasti Glass 227
Barzini, Luigi 35
Benedini, Giampaolo 256
Bentley 19
Benz, Karl 7
Bernardi, Enrico 7–8
Bernhard, Prince of The Netherlands 79
Bertone, Carozzeria 11, 18, 21, 124, 126, 132, 207, 210, 237
Bertone, Nuccio 250
Besana, Gabriele 99
Bianchi, Edoardo 8
Bigio, Guido 35
Biondetti, Clemente 79
Birkin, Tim 59
Bizzarrini, Giotto 22–23, 203
BMW M1 supercar 22
Bollée, Léon 12
Boneschi 11, 21, 107
Bonnier, Joakim 143
Borghese, Prince Scipione 35
Bosch 238, 242

Brabham, Jack 22, 154
Bracco, Giovanni 118
Bravarone, Aldo 231, 234
Bricherasio di Cacherano, Emanuele 9
Bristol 174
British Leyland 21
British Motor Corporation 19–21
Bugatti 17, 27, 62
  EB110GT **256–61**
  Type 251 256
Bugatti, Ettore 256, 260
Bühne 69

C

Cadillac 19
Campari, Giuseppe 13
Carol, King of Romania 79
Carrozzerie 11–12, 18, 21
  see also under individual names
Casner, Lloyd 'Lucky' 177
Castagna, Carozzeria 40, 45, 55, 59
Cattaneo, Giustino 45
Cavalli, Carlo 31, 33
Ceirano, Matteo 35

Charles, John 69
Chevrolet 24–25
Chiti, Carlo 22–23
Chizzola brothers 191
Chrysler 17, 18–19, 198, 246, 262
Chrysler-Ghia GS-1 coupé 18
Cisitalia 167
  D46 92
  202 19, **92–97**
Citroën 21, 24
Collins, Peter 154
Colombo, Gioacchino 99, 113, 137, 149, 167, **278**
Colotti, Valerio 149
Colucci, Mario 198
Conrero, Virgilio 191
Cooper 22
Cooper, John and Charles 72
Cortese, Franco 99, 102
Cromadora 245
CSI (Commission Sportive Internationale) 192
Cugnot, Nicolas-Joseph 7

D

Daimler, Gottlieb 7
Dallara, Gian Paolo 203, 210, 237, **278**

Darracq, Alexandre 12–13
Dauer, Jochen 256
Davis, Colin 208
De Dion 7, 8, 132, 149, 177
de Filippis, Luigi 99
de Filippis, Maria Teresa 99
De Tomaso 25–27
   Mangusta 25
   Pantera 27, 208
   Vallelunga **208–209**
De Tomaso, Alejandro 19, 25–27, 208
Dei, Guglielmo 137
Donohue, Mark 227
Drogo, Piero 216
Dunlop brakes 182
Dusio, Piero 92

E

Eldridge, Ernest 38
Ermini 17, 72
Exner, Virgil 18
Eyston, George 38

F

Fangio, Juan Manuel 132, 149, 152, 177
Fantuzzi, Carozzeria 137
Farina 45
Ferrari 7, 10, 18, 22–24, 25, 72, 137, 203
   166 Spider Corsa **98–101**
   212 Export **112–17**
   250 Lusso **196–97**
   250 Testa Rossa **154–61**
   250GT Cabriolet 188
   250GT SWB **182–87**
   250GTO **192–95**
   250MM **118–23**, 140
   275GTB 221
   308 GT4 231
   365 Spider California 233
   365GTS/4 Daytona 23–24, **220–21**
   400 Superamerica Cabriolet **188–89**
   512BB **238–41**, 242
   512M 'Sunoco' **226–29**
   Dino 246GT 196, **230–35**
   Enzo **266–71**, 272
   'Sharknose' 156 22
   Testarossa 27, 222, **242–45**
Ferrari, Enzo 14–16, 22, 23, 40, 99, 101, 231, 266
Fessia, Antonio 72
Fiandri, Carozzeria 137
Fiat 8, 9–10, 24, 27, 198, 231
   8V Démon Rouge **168–69**
   130HP 9, **30–33**
   500 **162–65**
   500 Topolino 10, **72–77**
   600 163, 167
   Mephistopheles **38–39**
   Multipla **162–65**
   Trepiuno 163
   Zero 12-15HP 9
Figoni et Falaschi 11
Fioravanti, Leonardo 21, 24, 221, 238, 241, **279**
Fiorio, Cesare 237
Fissore, Carozzeria 208
Fleetwood Metal Body Company 45
FMC Corporation 246
Fochi, Luciano 198
Ford 24, 25–27, 208
   Cortina 208
   GT40 216
   GT70 237
Ford, Henry 9, 12
Franchini, Nino 13
Fraschini, Vincenzo 8, 45
Frua, Pietro 18, 137, 144

G

Gandini, Marcello 210, 213, 237, 250, 256, 258, 262, **279**
Garavani, Carozzeria 55
Gendebien, Olivier 154
General Motors 19, 24–25
Ghia 18–19, 107
Giacosa, Dante 72, 163
Giannini 163
Giaur 17
Giolito, Roberto 163
Giugiaro, Giorgetto 21–22, 25, 207, 210, 213, **279**
Giuliano, Luigi 118
Guichet, Jean 192
Guizzardi, Ettore 35
Gurney, Dan 177

H

Harriman, George 19
Hewland gearboxes 208
Hill, Phil 22–23, 79, 154
Hitler, Adolf 55
Hobbs, David 227
Hoffman, Max 124
Howe, Earl 59

I

Iacocca, Lee 27
Isotta, Cesare 8, 45
Isotta-Fraschini 11, 13
   Tipo 8A **44–49**
Istituto Ricostruzione Industriale 14
Isuzu 27
Ital Design 21–22
Itala 13, **34–37**

J

Jaguar 182
   E-type 188, 195
   XJ6 21
   XK120 92, 168
Jano, Vittorio 14, 55, 56, 59, 79, 86, **280**

K

Kevill-Davies & March 69

L

Lamborghini 25, 242
   350GT/400GT **202–205**
   Countach QV 27, 238, 241, 242, 246, **250–55**, 262, 276–77

Diablo 27, **262–65**
LM002 **246–49**
Miura 6, 22, 23, 24, **210–15**, 250
Lamborghini, Ferruccio 203, 210, 250
Lampredi, Aurelio 118, 123, 188, 192
Lancia 7, 10
  Aprilia **80–85**
  Artena 69
  Astura **68–71**
  Flaminia Zagato Super Sport **170–75**
  Lambda **50–53**, 69
  Stratos **236–37**
Lancia, Vincenzo 31, 50, 52, 81
Levegh, Pierre 154
Lloyd, Bill 144
Lombardi, Franco 137, 163
Lurani, Count 'Johnny' 196

M
Maemirolli, Luigi 262
Marimon, Onofre 149
Martinengo, Vladimiro 143
Marzotto, Count Umberto 113, 117
Maserati 7, 10, 17, 22, 23, 24, 25, 27, 72
  4CLT **102–105**
  8CM **62–67**
  250F **148–53**
  A6GCS/53 **137–41**
  MC12 **272–75**
  Tipo 61 Birdcage **176–81**
Maserati, Alfieri 62

Maserati brothers 144
Mastroianni, Marcello 170
Megatech 262
Mercedes-Benz 14, 17, 40, 55, 62, 118, 149, 154
Merosi, Giuseppe 13, 14, 40
Michelotti, Giovanni 21, 113, 114, 144, 168, **280**
Mimran family 262
Monterosa 163
Montescani 40
Moretti 17, 163
Moss, Stirling 144, 149, 154, 177, 182
Motto, Carozzeria 99, 100
Munari, Sandro 237
Musso, Luigi 154
Mussolini, Benito 11, 45, 55, 86

N
Nader, Ralph 24–25
Nardi steering wheels 159, 187
Nazzaro, Felice 31
Neri & Bonacini 203
Nissan 262
Nuvolari, Tazio 17, 62, 92

O
Oldsmobile Delta 88 19
OM 11
Orsi family 24, 177
OSCA MT4-2AD coupé **144–47**

P
Pagani, Horacio 250
Palmieri, Pietro 137

Penske, Roger 177, 227, 229
Peterson, Ronnie 168
Peugeot 8, 19
Pininfarina, Carozzeria (Pinin Farina) 11, 18
  Alfa Romeo 6C 2500 86
  Alfa Romeo Giulietta Spider prototypes 124, 130
  Berlinette coupé 118
  and British Motor Corporation 19–21
  Cisitalia 202 92
  Ferrari 250GT SWB 182
  Ferrari 250 Lusso 196
  Ferrari 250MM 140
  Ferrari 365GTS/4 Daytona 221
  Ferrari 400 Superamerica Cabriolet 188
  Ferrari 512BB 238
  Ferrari 512S **222–25**
  Ferrari Dino 246GT 231
  Ferrari Enzo 266
  Ferrari Testarossa 242, 245
  and Lancia 69
  Maserati A6GCS/53 137, 139
Polytechnic of Turin 81, 222
Porsche
  330P4 **216–19**
  911 231, 233
  917 227
Porsche, Dr Ferry 92

R
Rapio, Fabio Luigi 143
Renault 8, 12

Rocchi, Franco 216, 231
Romano, Emilio 79
Romeo, Nicola 13, 14

S
Sala, Cesare 40
Sanesi, Consalvo 143
Savonuzzi, Giovanni 19, 92
Scaglietti, Sergio 24, 154, 156, 182, 184, 188, 196, 221, 231, **280**
Scaglione, Franco 124, 126, 129, 132, 135, 203, **281**
Schumacher, Michael 266
Scuderia Ferrari 15–17
SEFAC 182
Serpollet, Léon 7
Siata 72, 163, 168
Sibona & Basano 198
Simca 198
Sivocci, Ugo 15, 40
Sommer, Raymond 62, 99
Spada, Ercole 170, 173, 191
Sparco 266
Stabilimenti Farina 92, 102, 107
Standard-Triumph 21
Stanguellini 17, 72
Stanzani, Paolo 210
Stephenson, Frank 272, 275
supercars **22–27**

T
Taramazzo, Luigi 198
Taruffi, Piero 62, 102
Thomas, René 38
Tjaarda, Tom 27, 45, 233

Touring, Carozzeria 18, 21, 45, 55, 59, 86, 88, 107, 108, 143, 203
Traco 227
Trevithick, Richard 7
Trujillo, Leonidas Ramadas 19

V
Valentino, Rudolf 45
Vespa scooters 72
Vignale, Alfredo 18, 92, 113, 114, 118, 137, 144, 168
Viotti 11
Volkswagen Veyron 256

W
Wakefield, Peter 102
Walker, Rob 182
Weber carburettors 107, 118, 123, 182, 216, 238, 246
Weinburger 69
Werner, Christian 40
White, Kim 227
Wilkins, Gordon 113

Y
Young, James 55

Z
Zagato, Carozzeria 11, 14, 40, 55, 59, 143, 167, 170, 174, 191
Zagato, Ugo 143
Zanon, Count 168
Zehender, Freddie 62